CONTENTS

PREFACE

When Christopher Columbus took his maiden voyage to the Americas, he knew the earth was not flat. However, he did not know exactly where his journey would lead him. After his amazing experience and discovery, he returned to Spain and became a hero. Many men were enthused and encouraged by his determination to discover new lands and new routes. They too were anxious to overcome the barriers in their way, to break through the small mindedness of people who disbelieved their dreams, and probably most of all, to taste some of the same excitement that comes with discovery. These famous men came to be known as explorers. Amerigo Vespuci, Cortez, Balboa, Jacques Cartier, and Coronado, were just a few of the many who were part of the age of discovery. Merriweather Lewis took his directive from President Thomas Jefferson to map the remainder of the North American continent as they knew it. Even Buzz Aldrin, who went to the moon, finds his way into the category of a pioneer in discovery.

When John Welch discovered a passage of chiasmus on his mission in 1967, he went through some of the same scenarios as Columbus. He was studying the scriptures, but certainly charted new territory in those studies. He was indeed a pioneer. And though he was not the first to identify chiasmus, he certainly was first to get the good news out to the world regarding one of the largest chiastic passages heretofore found, which was in the Book of Mormon.

Over the last 40 years there have been many other explorers who have dived deep into the scriptures, only to find themselves the happy recipient of a large hand full of gems commonly referred to as chiastic passages. There have been lists of criteria that help new travelers along the path to begin to identify these amazing spaces.

Some people have conjectured that chiasmus is only found in sacred writ. Some believe it is a learned skill to write chiastically. But just as Newtonian science has been replaced by quantum physics, belief that chiasmus is a learned skill has been replaced by a myriad of examples impressive enough to diffuse the argument formerly held by those scholars. Since powerful repetitious patterns can be identified in non-scriptural writings, the belief that a specialized training required to write this way has taken a back seat to understanding that a powerful unseen directive causes a person to write chiastically. Chiasm discoveries continue to be made, and more frequently by those considered to be the inquisitive everyday man (or woman).

Chiasmus is mapped out by a few to demonstrate an orderly pattern greater than just a mirror image. It defines a journey. It can be said that it is every man's journey. It is stated by more than one of the authors of this book to convey the Plan of Salvation.

Chiasmus can be identified in the sciences and the arts. It is easily observed in a multitude of places in the human body. It is audible to the most rudimentary music student. How could this be if it is only a Hebraic literary pattern? How can chiasmus be so rampant throughout literature, nature, and the scriptures with those restraints? The only answer would be that it would be a medium that would be in all things, and through all things. It would have to be something that conveys light.

If this is a theory, then it remains to be seen whether you will hold that same belief by the time you have finished the examples contained in this book. Perhaps you will have a paradigm shift of major proportions.

It is up to the reader to prove or disprove the belief that if there is a pattern in all things, that this IS the pattern in all things, for all things testify of Christ. May your journey be an adventure to you, that you will recognize the signs and indicators, and ride the high seas of discovery.

INTRODUCTION

Discoveries in Chiasmus: A Pattern in All Things

The date chiasmus was discovered in the Book of Mormon can be exactly fixed. It was on Wednesday, August 16, 1967. We know this because the young missionary serving in Germany who made the discovery is still with us and will be discussing that event at this Conference today.

John Welch not only made the discovery of chiasmus in the Book of Mormon, but has also excelled in locating and elaborating on this finding. His effort to document the initial finding has been preserved in an article he wrote for the Journal of Book of Mormon Studies, titled *The Discovery of Chiasmus in the Book of Mormon: Forty Years Later*, Vol. 16, Issue 2, pages 74-78.

Of particular delight to me is the role which Brother Welch assigns to revelation in his discovery. As is so often the case with the voice of the Lord, it was early in the morning when a voice awoke Elder Welch with the words: "If it is evidence of Hebrew style in the Bible, it must be evidence of Hebrew style in the Book of Mormon." These words of revelation not only led to the discovery, but they affirm the relationship between the Bible and Book of Mormon as Nephi had promised. (See 2 Ne. 29: 7-14.)

The article is worth reading, and can found on-line through the Maxwell Institute at BYU. It discusses Brother Welch's enthusiastic teaching, using this new discovery as a means to attract converts on his mission. His enthusiasm was met with varying degrees of success by the audiences. However, he persisted in his effort to locate additional chiasms in the Book of Mormon and the discovery of perhaps the best example is worth including here. He wrote: "I particularly remember being on the train when I noticed the chiastic structure of Alma 36—the entire chapter! It was an overwhelmingly exciting moment to watch the length and the detail of that text unfold, which turns out to be one of the very best instances of chiasmus anywhere in world literature. Gazing out of the train window and watching the Bavarian countryside roll by, I was transported by the skill and care of Alma as a writer. Amazed at the power of the chiastic form to focus the reader's attention on the central turning point of Alma's life, I thought how fortunate we are to have the Book of Mormon. I wondered where this train would take me." That chapter is now well known as the premiere example of chiasm in all scripture. Found by a young Elder while serving in Germany, riding a train.

Brother Welch's efforts have also expanded to provide guidance in detecting the presence of chiasmus. He wrote an article for the Journal of Book of Mormon Studies, titled: *Criteria For Identifying and Evaluating the Presence of Chiasmus*, found at Vol. ,Issue 2, Pages 1-14. In the article he suggests there are fifteen criteria which ought to be considered when determining the presence of chiasmus. He will be discussing these later in this conference. This article is also important enough that I recommend you visit the full article on-line through BYU.

The purpose of this conference is to explore the idea of chiasm or other patternism as a phenomenon which occurs both in sacred literature and naturally throughout creation. The most often given reason for the presence of chiasmus in Hebrew tradition is that it developed as an aid to the oral tradition. This theory asserts that it is simpler to memorize passages when the material is organized in a chiasm.

Latter-day Saints are aware, however, that writing began at the time of Adam. "And a book of remembrance was kept, in the which was recorded, in the language of Adam," from the foundation of the world. (Moses 6: 5.) Without a copy of that book we are unable to determine if the original form of chiasmus, or other patterns, were imbedded in sacred writing from the very beginning of time. What we can be certain of, however, is that chiasmus was not an aid to an oral tradition, because the use of written preservation of language was coincident with the time of Adam.

I have written about the potential underlying reason for chiasmus as a lesson for mankind to learn. Christ's admonition to "become as a little child" (Matt. 18: 3) may underlay the reason. In order to go forward we must go back. That is, returning to a child-like time of faith, innocence, and openness to new knowledge is an essential requirement for us to be willing to accept new ideas. We cannot develop without returning to a time when we were willing to develop. For the child, every day is filled with discovery and delight. For the elderly, oftentimes new ideas are threatening. Minds close down, attitudes harden and learning is resisted as we age. To overcome this we must become, as King Benjamin taught: "as a child, **submissive, meek, humble, patient, full of love, willing to submit to all things which the Lord seeth fit to inflict** upon him, even as a child doth submit to his father." (Emphasis added.) This list and its implications are as follows:[1]

"Submissive" denotes acceptance of the Father's will in preference to your own. It does not say you should submit to men. There is nothing about following a man in the concept of "submission." As used here, submission is not just an unanchored term, abstractly applied to anyone or anything. It is submission to God. Christ best exemplified this trait as He defined who He was in His introduction to the Nephites. There He proclaimed that He had "suffered the will of the Father in all things from the beginning." (3 Ne. 11: 11.) He did not submit to the Rabbis, or the scribes and Pharisees. Though He

---

[1] What follows is an excerpt from my book *The Second Comforter: Conversing With The Lord Through the Veil*, © Denver C. Snuffer, Jr., 2006, 2008, Mill Creek Press.

taught their position warranted respect,[1] He did not submit to them in the sense used here. Rather He challenged them and provoked their ire. Ultimately, He so offended them, they had Him killed. And so following "the will in all things from the beginning" does not ever require anyone to submit to the rule or command of a man.

"Meek" is a word Christ used in the Sermon on the Mount, telling us that the meek will inherit the earth. Meekness denotes, among other things, a conscious effort to avoid harming or offending others. It requires an absence of pride or self will. It is not insistent upon being recognized or applauded. It denotes a willingness to suffer without complaint. Others may never recognize the meek, because meekness does not vaunt itself, nor demand notice. They are "satisfied with things they are able to do." There is a great freedom in meekness. It relieves the meek from the burden of seeking their acclaim. It gives them the security of feeling God's approval for their course of living. It is private.

"Humble" is the word we use for a most remarkable trait. If you have children, you see immediately they are by nature more humble than adults. They not only do not have a good working knowledge of practical skills, they are keenly aware of their own ignorance. As a result, children are inquisitive. They search relentlessly for greater understanding, and pester their parents for the "whys" and "hows" and "whens'"of life. As a result, children are willing students and eager to be taught. They not only don't know, they **know they don't know**, and want to be given the chance to learn. They "seek" and "ask" and "knock." Children do by nature just as Christ bids us to do.

In contrast, adulthood is where we find the arrogant and the unwilling. Pride and the refusal to search for knowledge is the typical adult reaction to any new knowledge. Particularly, this hostility is to knowledge that is obtained in a foreign way, which we will discuss further. Nephi wrote a lament typifying the adult mind, stating: "I am left to mourn because of the unbelief, and the wickedness, and the ignorance, and the stiffneckedness of men; for they will not search knowledge, nor understand great knowledge, when it is given unto them in plainness, even as plain as word can be." (2 Ne. 32: 7.) The most eager students are the young. The older the person, the less likely it is they will accept instruction from others with humility. Older people, like the proverbial old dogs, do not willingly accept new "tricks" in their lives. Hence the need for all of us to become as little children again.

The child's patient waiting is not readily apparent. Most children have little impulse control and do not want to wait for anything. "Patience" as used here does not mean what you typically think. Rather it refers to the child's "patience" to grow into adulthood. They are many years ahead to reach adulthood. There is nothing the child can do to change that. Nor do they attempt to do so. Most adults have many years ahead of them before they become fit for the Second Comforter. Just like you cannot rush from childhood into adulthood, but must progress by degrees through the many long months, into many years; so, too, we must progress from a smaller degree to a much larger one. Going back, like going forward, involves effort. Perhaps it takes decades to develop as necessary to receive an audience with Christ. Children persist in waiting, growing and maturing. Their progression into adulthood is gradual. But that process is relentless and marches on through two decades of development and maturity. That is the

---

1 Matt. 23: 1-3: "Then spake Jesus to the multitude, and to his disciples, Saying, The scribes and the Pharisees sit in Moses' seat: All therefore whatsoever they bid you observe, that observe and do; but do not ye after their works: for they say, and do not."

patience spoken of here. You will have to grow, mature and progress gradually by degrees to receive the Second Comforter.

Being "full of love" is what the 13th chapter of 1 Corinthians is all about. Charity is the "pure love of Christ." This childlike attribute comes from a natural disposition to share love which children enjoy by their native status. As we progress into adulthood and experience the disappointments of other's failings, we become less willing to love others. We suspect their motives. We distrust their worthiness to be loved. We guard against their potential for causing us mischief. These are learned fears. Little children are "too trusting" because they find it easier to love than to fear. We all found it easier to love when we were children.

The final quality of being "willing to submit" again reminds us of Christ. His knee bent to the Father in all things. And although every knee will ultimately submit to Him, many of those kneeling at the last day will do so from fear or regret, although most will do so from gratitude. Submitting to Him now, when there is no great persuasion to do so and all of the world may be aligned against His ways, stands as proof you really are willing to submit.

Christ asked: "And why call ye me, Lord, Lord, and do not the things which I say?" (Luke 6: 46.) Calling Him Lord is not enough. Willingness to submit requires a willingness to be inconvenienced.

How does the disciple become "childlike?" How does the adult return to the status of their former, childlike mind?

In the Pulitzer Prize winning book *Godel, Escher, Bach: An Eternal Golden Braid* , there are some interesting glimpses of how some of these things can be be fit together.[2] The Crab is a recurring character in the book. The Crab is speaking about its movement on page 200: "It's in our genes, you know, turning round and round. That reminds me – I've always wondered, 'Which came first – the Crab or the Gene?' That is to say, 'Which came last, the Gene or the Crab?' I'm always turning things round and round you know. It's in our genes, after all. When we walk backwards, we move forwards." (Hofstadter, Douglas R. *Godel, Escher, Bach: An Eternal Golden Braid.* New York: Basic Books, Inc, 1979.) You see, for a crab to walk on dry ground, the weight of its forward arms is so great that they must be drug along the ground. They cannot push them by going forward. Instead, that requires the crab to walk backwards. To go forward, it must walk backwards. Since all things testify of God and His ways, the crab is also a testimony of some truth. It tells us by its movement that to go forward we must go backward.

An illustration on page 201, Figure 43, has this commentary: "Here is a short section of one of the Crab's Genes, turning round and round. When the two DNA strands are unraveled and laid out side by side, they read this way:

....TTTTTTTTTCGAAAAAAAAA...AAAAAAAAAGCTTTTTTTTT.....

---

[2] The whole of the book is a chiasm, although its author refers to his discussion in terms of "loops."

Notice that they are the same, only one goes forwards while the other goes backwards. This is the defining property of the form called 'crab cannon' in music. It is reminiscent of, though a little different from, a palindrome, which is a sentence that reads the same backwards and forwards. In molecular biology, such segments of DNA are called 'palindromes' – a slight misnomer, since 'crab cannon' would be more accurate. Not only is this DNA segment crab-canonical – but moreover its base segment sequence codes for the Dialogue's structure." (*Id.*) Interesting how this forward/backward movement goes right to the level of the crab's DNA. The sequence reminds us of chiasmus.[3] The crab's DNA is a chiasm.

Later, on page 661 of *Godel, Escher, Bach* there is a discussion regarding Bongard[4] problems, also relevant to the child's mind: "I still have a certain faith that Bongard problems depend on a sense of simplicity… our notion of simplicity is universal, for what matters is not any of these individual objects, but the fact that taken together they span a wide space." (*Id.*) When I read this the first time, I performed a test using the Bongard problems. I saw no pattern. They seemed too random to my mind. I showed them to my wife, and they eluded her, too. However, when I showed them to my children, they recognized patterns in the sequences which eluded me. Yet the children reduced the problems to such a basic and simple level, they could see the matching patterns which the adult complex mind could not see. The author was right. Bongard problems do depend upon a sense of simplicity. They are greatly aided by seeing them in a simple way with a simple mind. The child's view is infinitely superior to the adult's in seeing the patterns because children can see things simply.

This leads us back to the ancient word form of chiasmus. As John Welch[5] has written about chiasmus, he has not related it to the question of *why* this form of writing was developed in the first place. Writers, including Welch, have suggested it points to the central theme of the writing and emphasizes the thought found there. While this may be true, viewing it in light of the observations made in *Godel, Escher, Bach* make it useful to look at it more simply. In chiasmus the first of the pattern repeats at the last. What came first is repeated in the end. It is a literary way of depicting "the last shall be first, and the first shall be last."

That same pattern appears in the Menorah. The seven lamps have arms which connect the first to the last.[6] If you were to set the lamp stand out in the same form using "ABC" the pattern would look like: **A-B-C-D-C-B-A.**

---

[3] Chiasmus is an ancient sentence structure in which the pattern reaches a central point, then reverses. The pattern can be summarized by the example: ABCDCBA; where the concept in "A" appears in the first and again in the last sentence. Similarly concept "B" repeats in the second to the first and second to the last sentence, and so on.

[4] Bongard developed a series of tests involving patterns and shapes. The discussion uses Bongard's tests to demonstrate analytical and reasoning issues relevant to the text. They depend upon abstract reasoning, but also require an ability to find the simple patterns within a complex set of problems.

[5] It was John Welch who discovered chiasmus in the Book of Mormon while a missionary in Germany. He has written about the subject, including *Chiasmus in Antiquity.* Edited by John W. Welch. Provo: The Foundation for Ancient Research and Mormon Studies, 1981. One of the longest examples of a chiasm in the Book of Mormon is found in Chapter 36 of Alma. The entire chapter is a lengthy form of this pattern of writing.

[6] See Exo. 25: 32: "And six branches shall come out of the sides of it; three branches of the candlestick out of the one side, and three branches of the candlestick out of the other side."

The arms of the Menorah are also a chiasm. The first is also the last. The pattern is the same from beginning to middle and from middle to end, the one being a mirror image of the other. So we have a Temple article containing, by its form, a symbol which mirrors the ancient word form of chiasmus. The pattern seems to have a meaning.

We have a description of the Urim and Thummim from Lucy Mack Smith. She described it as follows: "[On the morning of September 22, after Joseph had returned from the hill, he placed] the article [the Urim and Thummim] of which he spoke into my hands, and, upon examination, [I] found that it consisted of two smooth three-cornered diamonds set in glass, and the glasses were set in silver bows, which were connected with each other in much the same way as old fashioned spectacles." (Taken from *Eyewitness Accounts of the Restoration* by Milton V. Backman, Jr., p.73. Backman, Milton V., Jr. *Eyewitness Accounts of the Restoration.* Salt Lake City: Deseret Book Company, 1986.)

One of these "two smooth three-cornered" stones pointed upward. The other pointed downward. This pattern of two triangles pointing in opposite directions is what the Star of David is made from. One pointing up, and the other pointing down. It, too, is a kind of chiasm. Progression and regression set in a side-by-side pattern. The Urim and Thummim is a chiasm. The Star of David was modeled on the Urim and Thummim, and is also a chiasm.

In ceremony, we move what was on the left side to the right side. The orientation of clothing changes from the one side to the other, forming a mirror image of progression and regression. As husband and wife kneel between the mirrors of the sealing room, facing each other, the right side of the one matches the left side of the other. As the dialogue at the veil concludes, the one acting as proxy speaks words of blessing vicariously for an ancestor, who in turn blesses descendants including the one acting as proxy. The images and symbols fold over upon each other in a repeating pattern of chiasms. Symbol and meaning merge into patterns intended to suggest to the mind a deeper level of meaning.

What do we make of these symbols? These imbedded messages seem to return to a theme. Whatever other meanings as may be contained in these forms, patterns and types, it necessarily includes the notion that to go forward you must go backward. Perhaps this meaning reigns supreme over all the other symbolic meanings of the pattern.

This pattern also reminds us anew of the Lord's injunction: "Except ye be converted, and become as little children, ye shall not enter into the kingdom of heaven." (Matt. 18: 3.) Returning to the mind of a child is necessary as a precondition, according to Christ's words, for us to be able to enter His kingdom.

What is it about the mind of a child that makes him or her more suited to following Christ? Is it innocence? Certainly a child's mind is more innocent than the adult's. But innocence also accompanies the willingness or even the necessity to imagine things. Children are able to hold out the possibilities for Santa and tooth-fairies and Peter Pan. To a child these things are possible. It requires failures and disappointments to form an adult mind. Those failings and disappointments make the adult mind skeptical, and unbelieving. Things once held in honor by the childish mind become impossible to believe into adulthood.

After a parable about camels and the eye of a needle making salvation seem unlikely, the disciples exclaimed it wasn't possible for such men to be saved. "But Jesus beheld them, and said unto them, With men this is impossible; but with God all things are possible." (Matt. 19: 26.) Men do not believe enough. Children do.

This feature of the child's mind needs to be reclaimed. Hard though it may be, the opening up for yourself of the possibility you, too, may receive these things must come first. You will not receive until after you have been first proven. And you will not be up to the test if you are unwilling to believe it is possible for you to receive these things.

Simplicity marks the child's mind. Things are much clearer to a child than they are to an adult. Craftiness and cunning develop in the maturing adult mind and are alien to the child's mind. Part of the process of developing involves learning people can be mean, cunning and manipulative. Adults can generally recall specific events in their childhood when they felt betrayed for the first time. All of that is a part of the mortal curriculum because we have come here to receive knowledge of good and evil.

Adult cynicism and skepticism, however, ill-serves us as we seek higher things. The Lord was teaching a profound principle in telling us we must become as little children if we wish to enter His kingdom. It is a requirement. We will need to explore this further.

For any of us to go forward we must go back. We must return to what we were in a more innocent time. Because of our individual "Fall" in the "Garden of Eden" of our youth, we need to regain God's presence for our lives. That childlike innocence we all came with, including believing, trusting, wanting, hoping, and accepting, must be found again.

Our minds are more of an impediment than an asset in this struggle. Margaret Barker's comments about the early Christian worldview of evil are relevant here, and a good point to end with. Speaking of the Christians at the time of Christ she writes: "They had a picture of a vast conspiracy of evil actively engaged in a struggle against humankind, working to corrupt and destroy the creation. People needed protection against this onslaught, and help to overcome its effects. They were not hampered by our sophisticated attitudes, which have come to terms with evil forces by saying that they do not exist, or by turning them into a form of late-night entertainment. Our Christian ancestors in the time of Jesus would have recognized this ploy. The devil, they knew, acted through the human mind, where man was most proud and therefore most vulnerable. To convince a thinking man that evil forces did not exist was indeed a triumph." (Barker, Margaret THE LOST PROPHET: The Book of Enoch and its Influence on Christianity. Sheffield: England, 2005, p. 36.)

Perhaps, therefore, chiasmus is another testimony in pattern designed to remind us to remain open, remain humble, teachable, meek and submissive. It may be a reminder that in order to go forward, we must go back and become first as a little child.

Now, this book has been organized to examine different forms of patternism and how they reflect a higher intelligence and God's communication to us. All things testify of Him. We need to develop the eyes to see Him. It may very well be that we all once had that ability and now need to return to what we once were to reclaim that sight. The great chiasm of life itself may be a gift from above. Enjoy what follows, which is offered as the various writers' views and not an official pronouncement by anyone other than those who contribute. It is offered to you as a gift.

DISCOVERING CHIASMUS IN THE WRITINGS OF THE PROPHETS

Greg Carlston

Reading Between the Lines: A Personal Experience

I first learned of chiasmus in the mid 1970's at a fireside given by Jack Welch about his experiences in the original discovery of chiasmus in the Book of Mormon. I was immediately fascinated and during the years since, I have identified and marked many chiastic passages in my own scriptures. Several years ago my wife and I took our family on a trip to the Yucatan Peninsula in Mexico where we toured a number of the Mayan ruins. In the evenings, I would tell my family Book of Mormon stories and during the days, we would visit archeological sites and scramble through the remains of ancient temples and pyramids. One night I told the story of Captain Moroni's defense against Amalickiah, the Nephite traitor, who was inciting the Lamanites to attack the Nephites. Alma 48 describes Moroni making preparations to defend his people by building small forts, throwing up banks of earth to protect his armies, and building walls of stone around their cities. The next day we visited the ruins of Tulum, a small fort located atop a coastal bluff facing the Caribbean Sea. When we arrived, we were excited to see the place was entirely surrounded by banks of earth faced with stone, just as described in Alma 48. It seemed that reading about the Nephite lands was wonderful, but seeing them the next day was even better.

That evening, back in our hotel room, while my family watched videos, I opened the Book of Mormon and again read Alma 48. As I read, I looked at the pencil marks I had previously made on the pages to identify a few chiastic words and phrases that I had noticed some years before. When I read the chapter again, it became apparent that I had missed many of the chiastic repetitions in the chapter. To my great delight, I realized that the entire chapter appeared to be chiastic, from the first word to the last. I have to use the word "electric" to describe how I felt at making this discovery because I hadn't known that chiastic passages could be much longer than a few verses. In this case, just as in Alma 36, the entire chapter is chiasmus. The format of chiasmus is so complex that its existence in the Book of Mormon has been a testimony to me that the Book of Mormon is not just a work of a fourteen year old nineteenth century farm boy. On this occasion, I had a powerful spiritual witness that the evidence *within* the Book of Mormon is so substantial that the external physical evidence of archeological ruins is almost irrelevant. I haven't lost my desire to see more ancient sites, but at that moment, I realized that it's not necessary to travel far and wide looking for "proof of the Book of Mormon" outside of the book itself. That is the significance of the presence of chiastic writing in the Book of Mormon.

A few weeks later, I researched the estimated construction dates for Tulum and found that archeologists think it had been built about 300 years after Captain Moroni's time. So my spiritual experience was validated: The presence of chiasmus in Alma 48 is more reliable evidence than ruins of an uncertain date. The presence of chiasmus throughout the Book of Mormon is but one of its many internal evidences that testify it is what it purports to be: An ancient record of the people to whom the resurrected Christ appeared and ministered.

Why do people find chiasmus so engaging?

Discovering chiasmus is highly enjoyable because it reveals the depth, breadth, and artistry of the writing of the prophets - ancient *and* modern. Chiasmus is about the search for subtle, ingenious literary and spiritual relationships. Looking for chiasmus is like hunting for treasures, not treasures of the world, but treasures of wisdom and increased understanding of our Heavenly Father's work and glory. Chiasmus is intriguing because in searching for it, we learn to see the unseen. Have you have ever wondered what the Savior meant when he said *blessed are those who hunger and thirst after righteousness*? When you first discover chiasmus in the scriptures, you begin to thirst for more knowledge about the Son of all Righteousness and you hunger for a more personal relationship with him. You will pray more and watch television less. As you become better at identifying chiastic writing, you will more fully appreciate the prophets' masterful use of language, a blessing passed down to us through the ages that we might have their testimonies of God's love for each of his children. When we strengthen our ability to see that which is not readily apparent, we recognize the Savior's tender, personal invitation to us to come unto him and to keep his commandments that we might be worthy to have the companionship of his Spirit.

- Top 12 Reasons People Enjoy Studying Chiasmus in the Scriptures (in chiastic order)

  1   To discover sublime principles of salvation and exaltation presented on sacred literary architecture

      3   To gain greater appreciation for literary abilities of the prophets.

        7   To learn a very engaging way to study the scriptures.

          5   To see the beauty, depth, breadth of the scriptures; masterful use of literary metaphor.

            9   To open the eyes of our understanding

              11   To find the words of eternal life in this life and eternal life in the life to come.

              12   To strengthen our relationship with our Heavenly Father and his Son, Jesus Christ.

            10   To see the love of the Lord.

       8 To <u>find order and happiness in a world of chaos and contention</u>.

     6 To <u>find scriptures</u> that will amaze and inspire us.

   4 To <u>get really good</u> at using <u>word</u> processing software.

 2 <u>To find immense personal satisfaction</u> in the process of <u>discovering</u> chiastic writing.

- More chiastic reasons to study chiasmus

  - To avoid being deceived in a world of guile

    A <u>I will give unto you a *pattern* in all things</u>, that ye may not be deceived;

       B <u>Satan is abroad in the land, and he goeth forth deceiving the nations</u>—

       B' And again, <u>he that is overcome and bringeth not forth fruits, even according to this pattern, is not</u>…

    A' <u>Wherefore, by this *pattern* ye shall know the spirits in all cases under the whole heavens.</u> *(D&C 52:14)*

  - To have our eyes opened and our understandings enlightened, that we may be better able to see and understand the things of God.

    A …<u>by the power of the Spirit</u>

      B <u>our eyes were opened</u> , our

        C <u>understandings</u> were

        C' <u>enlightened,</u>

      B' <u>so as to see and understand</u>

    A' <u>the things of God</u> *(D&C 76:12)*

  - To be sanctified from all sin, and enjoy the words of eternal life in this world, and eternal life in the world to come, even immortal glory;

    A …<u>sanctified from all sin</u>

      B that we may have <u>the words</u> of

        C <u>eternal life in</u> this world and

        C' <u>eternal life in</u>

      B' <u>the world</u> to come…

    A' <u>immortal glory</u> *(Moses 6:56)*

The Format: The Short, and the Long, of it.

When you diagram chiasmus, you never know in advance where the center, the turning point ,will be. So when you finally find it, the moment is one of great appreciation for being able to see the prophet's inspired language and the ability to communicate profound spiritual concepts. The following center point reveals that God does indeed speak to man.

K …<u>burn with **fire**</u>…

   L **the LORD our God** <u>hath shewed us his glory…</u>

      M **we have heard** <u>his voice</u>

         N out of the midst of<u>the **fire**…</u>

            O <u>God doth talk with man, and **he liveth**</u>.

            O Now therefore <u>why should **we die**</u>?

         N for<u> this great **fire…**</u>

      M **we hear** <u>the voice of the LORD our God…</u>

   L <u>the voice of **the living God** speaking out</u> of

K <u>the midst of the **fire**</u>, as we *have,* and lived?... (Deuteronomy 5:24-26)

In diagramming more than 150 complete chapters from books throughout all of the Standard Works, I have found that chiasmus - from pairs of single words and short phrases to very long passages - is pervasive throughout <u>all</u> of the Lord's Word. Chiasmus is found in the Book of Moses in his description of Adam. Chiasmus is found in the story of Enoch who lived about 3000 BC, in the biblical writings of Moses around 1450 BC, in over a thousand years of the writings of Book of Mormon prophets, and even in the revelations of the prophets and apostles that live among us today. Being able to recognize and diagram chiastic writing in the Old Testament is crucial to appreciating its presence in modern revelation. Latter-day Saints spend less time in the Old Testament because they don't understand its significance, but if you invest some time with the prophets of the Old Testament, you will gain great treasures of knowledge. Understanding chiasmus in the Bible makes the chiasmus within modern revelations all the more compelling and important.

In addition to spanning individual verses and complete chapters, the following chiastic diagram illustrates that chiasmus can be employed across entire books of scripture as well. This diagram is of the 22 chapters of the book of First Nephi.

THE FIRST BOOK OF NEPHI

A Nephi

 B begins the record of his people—

  C Lehi sees in vision a pillar of fire and—

  C reads from a book of prophecy He praises God,

 B foretells the coming of

A the Messiah, and

A prophesies the destruction of Jerusalem—

 B He is persecuted by the Jews. About 600B.C.

  C Lehi takes his family into the wilderness by the Red Sea— They leave their property

   D Lehi offers a sacrifice to the Lord and

    E teaches his sons to keep the commandments—Laman and Lemuel murmur against their father—

     F Nephi is obedient ... chosen to rule over his brethren. Lehi's sons

      G return to Jerusalem

       H to obtain the plates of brass—Laban refuses to give them up—

        I Nephi exhorts and encourages his brethren—

         J Laban steals their property and attempts to slay them—Laman and Lemuel smite Nephi and are reproved by an angel. Nephi slays Laban at the Lord's command and and then

          K secures the plates of brass by stratagem—

           L Zoram chooses to join Lehi's family

            M in the wilderness.

             N Sariah complains against Lehi *(about the loss of her sons)*— Both rejoice over

              O the return of their sons—They offer sacrifices—

               P The plates of brass contain writings of Moses and the prophets—They identify Lehi as

                Q a descendant of Joseph—

                 R Lehi prophesies concerning his seed and the

                  S preservation of the plates. Nephi writes of the things of God—

                   T His purpose is to persuade men to come unto the God of Abraham and be saved.

                    U Lehi's sons return to Jerusalem and

                     V enlist Ishmael and his household in their cause—

                      W Laman and others rebel—

                       X Nephi exhorts his brethren to have faith in the Lord—

                        Y They bind him with cords and plan his destruction

                         Z He is freed by the power of faith

                          A His brethren ask forgiveness—Lehi and his company offer sacrifice and burnt offerings.

                           B Lehi sees a vision of

                            C the tree of life—He partakes of its fruit and desires his family to do likewise— He sees

                             D a rod of iron, a strait and narrow path, and the mists of darkness that enshroud men—Sariah, Nephi, and Sam partake of the fruit,

                              E Laman and Lemuel refuse.

F   Nephi makes two sets of records; The larger plates deal with secular history; the smaller plates deal with sacred things.

  G   Lehi predicts the Babylonian captivity—He tells of the coming among the Jews of a Messiah, a Savior, a Redeemer—

    H   He tells of the coming of **the one** who should baptize the Lamb of God—Lehi tells of the

      I   death and

        J   resurrection of

          K   the Messiah—He compares

            L   the scattering and gathering of Israel to an olive tree—

              M   Nephi speaks of the Son of God, of the gift of the Holy Ghost, and of

                N   the need for righteousness.

                  O   Nephi sees the Spirit of the Lord and is shown in vision the tree of life He sees the mother of

                    P   the Son of God and learns of the condescension of God—

                      Q   He sees the baptism, ministry, and crucifixion of the Lamb of God—

                      Q   He sees also the call and ministry of the twelve apostles of

                    P   the Lamb.

                  O   Nephi sees in vision: the land of promise; the righteousness, iniquity, and downfall of it's people...; the coming of the Lamb of God among them; how...the twelve apostles shall judge Israel;

                N   the loathsome and filthy state of those who dwindle in unbelief.

              M   Nephi sees in vision: the church of the devil set up among the...; the discovery, colonizing of America; the loss of many plain and precious parts of the Bible; the resultant state of

            L   gentile apostasy; the restoration of the gospel, the coming forth of Latter-day scripture, and the building up of Zion.

          K   An angel tells Nephi of the

        J   blessings and

      I   cursings to fall upon the Gentiles—There are only two churches: the Church of abominable church—

    H   The apostle John shall write concerning the end of the world. Lehi's seed are to receive the gospel from the Gentiles in the latter days—

  G   The gathering of Israel is likened unto an olive tree whose natural branches shall be...

F   Nephi interprets the vision of the tree of life and speaks of the justice of God in dividing the wicked from the righteous.

 E   Lehi's sons marry the daughters of Ishmael—

D   The Liahona guides their course in the wilderness—Messages from the Lord are written on the Liahona from time to ...

 C   Ishmael dies; his family murmur because of afflictions.

B   Nephi is commanded to build a ship—

A   His brethren oppose him—He exhorts them by recounting the history of God's dealings with Israel—

Z   He is filled with the power of God—

Y   His brethren are forbidden to touch him, lest they whither as a dried reed..

X   The ship is finished—The births of

W   Jacob and Joseph are mentioned—

V   The company embarks for the promised land—

U   The sons of Ishmael and their wives join in revelry and rebellion—

T   Nephi is bound, and the ship is driven back by a terrible tempest—

S   Nephi is freed, and by his prayer the storm ceases—

R They arrive in the promised land.

  Q Nephi makes

   P plates of ore and records the history of his people—

    O The God of Israel shall come six hundred years from the time Lehi left Jerusalem—Nephi tells of His sufferings and crucifixion

     N The Jews shall be despised and

      M scattered until the latter days, when

       L they shall return unto the Lord..

        K The Lord reveals his purposes to Israel—

         J They have been chosen in the furnace of affliction and are to go forth from Babylon—Compare Isaiah 48.

        I Messiah shall be a light to the Gentiles and shall

       H free the prisoners—

      G Israel shall be gathered with power in the last days—

     F Kings shall be their nursing fathers—Compare Isaiah 49.

    E Israel shall be scattered upon all the face of the earth—

   D The gentiles shall nurse and nourish Israel with the gospel in the last days—

  C Israel shall be gathered and saved, and

 B the wicked shall burn as stubble—

A The kingdom of the devil shall be destroyed, and Satan shall be bound. About 588–570 B.C.(1 Nephi 1-22 - Chapter headings)

"Centrality within Symmetry" is the essence of chiastic writing.

In the previous chiastic diagram, the central concept is perfectly positioned at the focal point between the two mirrored literary sides that lead to the center theme. Nephi's vision of the life of the Saviour and the ministry of the Twelve could not be in a better place to illustrate how two parallel lists of principles, ideas, concepts, historical narrative , prophecies, comparisons, contrasts and many other words and phrases are used to bring the reader to the main idea of the entire book First Nephi.

Some scholars maintain that the longer a passage is, the less likely it is chiasmus. However, I'm not trying to prove anything "scholarly" other than to illustrate this balanced symmetrical format with the important point presented in the center. Even if it doesn't pass the strictest standards to be called chiasmus, the style is very consistent and used consistently throughout all of the Standard Works. Chiasmus or not, it is more than impressive. Seeing the previous illustration of First Nephi, could anyone believe that Joseph Smith could have produced a work as incredibly complex as illustrated in just over 60 days without having anything he dictated read back to him upon returning from rest or a meal, and without rewriting even a single passage? Of course, we believe that Joseph did not write the Book of Mormon, but translated it through the gift and power of God. This means that it was the prophet-writers of the Book of Mormon who were the ones that crafted a book that is complex beyond anyone's imagination and yet it presents the most pure and significant doctrines of any book ever published in the history of the world.

Here are two other examples of *concepts at the center of a narrative*

A. The beginning, the center, and end of the *Book of Ether*

From the Book of Ether, this selection shows the first verse of the first chapter, the center point of all 15 chapters, and the last verse of chapter 15, the last chapter of Ether.

> A those ancient inhabitants who <u>were **destroyed**</u> (Ether1:1)   - opposite of A'
>
> B <u>the **destruction** of nearly all the people of the kingdom</u> (Ether 9:12) - opposite of B', turning point
>
> B' Omer was <u>**restored** again to the land of his inheritance</u>. (Ether 9:13) - opposite of B, turning point
>
> A' if it so be that <u>I am **saved** in the kingdom of God. Amen.</u> (Ether 15:34) - opposite of A

As the focus of chiasmus in the Book of Mormon is often a major concept (usually related to the Father or the Son), it seems like this passage might not be the center point in this example. But consider this: the entire Book of Mormon is about people who are righteous and obedient contrasted with people bent on destruction and enslavement of their enemies. And the object of the conflict? The wicked seek to dominate the righteous for *the land of their inheritance*. In the end, the entire Jaredite nation - and the Nephites as well - is destroyed by fighting over *the land of their inheritance* - so this theme is exactly the appropriate topical center of the Book of Ether.

B. The beginning, the center, and the end of the Book of Mormon?

The Book of Mormon begins with Nephi, the son of Lehi, bearing testimony of his father's vision (1 Nephi 1:1-20). The book ends with the son of Mormon, Moroni, inviting all to come unto Christ, to be perfected in him, and to partake of the blessings of the covenant of the Father unto the remission of sins (Moroni 10:32-34). What is the center or turning point of the entire Book of Mormon? The Book of Mormon, has 531 pages. That would make the middle of page 266 about half way through the entire book. The topic of this part of the Book of Mormon, (Alma 22:15) is the conversion of King Lamoni's father who asks,

> A "<u>What shall I do</u> that I may have this eternal life...   - *question*
>
> B <u>what shall I do</u>   - *question*
>
>   C <u>that I may be born of God,</u>   - *begin a statement*
>
>   D <u>receive his Spirit,</u>   - *turning point*
>
>   D' <u>that I may be filled with joy,</u>   - *turning point*
>
>   C' <u>that I may not be cast off at the last day</u>? Behold, said he, - *completion of statement*
>
> B' <u>I will give up all that I possess,</u> yea,   - *answer*
>
> A' <u>I will forsake my kingdom,</u> that I may receive this great joy." (Alma 22:15) - *answer*

The above passage could very well qualify as the turning point of the Book of Mormon because it focuses on the king's change of heart. And it is the change of heart that will bring any and all of us to the

Father and the Son. Because of the varied lengths of chapter headings, the chapters themselves and the footnotes, it will take some additional work to determine the precise topical center of the entire Book of Mormon. If the center turns out to be in a different place, I have every confidence that it will be equally inspiring and perfectly appropriate.

In the 1800's the prophet Joseph Smith "told the brethren, that the Book of Mormon was the most correct book of any on earth and the keystone of our religion, and a man would get nearer to God by abiding by its precepts, than by any other book." (JSHC 7 Vol., 4:461) After almost two centuries, The Book of Mormon has stood the test of time. But is it truly "the most correct book of any on the earth?" I think the presence of broad forms of chiastic writing in the Book of Mormon goes a long way toward verifying that claim.

It's been more than 35 years since I was first introduced to the idea of that the Book of Mormon contains chiasmus, the very specific literary style of repetition used by the writers of the Old Testament. I was immediately intrigued then and my interest has not diminished to this day. Though I have continued to study chiasmus extensively, I haven't written any books on it. I don't have a PhD in ancient languages. No degrees in chiastic studies. But I do have two credentials that qualify me to write this article: First, is my intense interest in the subject. Second, I have completed diagrams of many dozens of chiastic passages throughout all of the Standard Works. By diagramming, I don't mean just finding a phrase or two in a chapter here and there and making a notation on the page in my scriptures. I have done that a lot, but what I mean by diagramming is finding and charting chiastic writing from the first word in a chapter to the last. These diagrams can take hours to make. (Alma 32 took five hours to complete - and it was worth every minute of effort because the diagram is an awe-inspiring, beautiful display of the powerful spiritual truths within the chapter.) The point here is that you don't need years of study and a stack of academic credentials to be able to understand and be inspired by chiastic writing. And you can find really inspirational chiastic passages as soon as you begin looking for them.

It's easy to find short passages and highly enjoyable to find long passages of chiastic writing

To get started, go to the Neil A. Maxwell Institute for Religious Scholarship website at http://maxwellinstitute.byu.edu and download a free copy of John W. Welch's article, "Criteria for Identifying and Evaluating the Presence of Chiasmus." Then open your scriptures to any chapter that interests you. Using the article as a guide, look for words and phrases that seem to be purposely repeated in the chapter you've selected. At first, don't worry about finding and labeling every pair of related ideas. The objective is to find the beginning, center, and end of the chiasmus in a chapter and make a basic diagram by labeling the related pairs in the ABC...CBA format of chiasmus. How do you know whether or not a chapter has chiasmus in it? Trust me, every chapter of every book of Christian scripture has chiastic writing in it. That's partly what makes looking for chiasmus so rewarding, you will find it everywhere in the scriptures - and every time you find it a new passage, you'll be delighted - no matter how many times it happens. (Tip: When you are doing your first diagrams, choose short chapters like Ether 5. This will save you a lot of the frustration of using long chapters when you are learning.) Next, go to your scripture software or to the Gospel Library at LDS.org, find the chapter of scriptures that you are working on and print it out. This will be your original worksheet. If you started by marking in your scriptures, at this point, transfer your ABC labels to your worksheet. Just use a pencil because you will need to make a lot of changes during this step. After you have a number of labels attached, go back to your computer, create a document, and then place the labels into the document in their respective locations at the beginning of each word, phrase or concept. Next, place your cursor to the left of each alpha label and then hit the "return" key on your keyboard. When you are finished with this step, you will have one long vertical column of paired relationships. Review what you have so far. See if it makes sense. See if the beginning and end match by being related in some way. Don't assume the major chiastic passage in every chapter starts with the first word in the chapter and ends with the last. (See my examples, especially Ezekiel and 1 Nephi 1.) Determine if the center point makes sense. Editing is much easier in the single column, so make as many adjustments as you can before creating the "final" diagram. When you are relatively satisfied that you are ready to create the diagram, set the default tab distance to .18", set the page orientation to landscape, and then use the tab key to tab your concepts into a chiastic diagram so they match up vertically for comparison.

If you try diagramming a few short chapters, I know you will be inspired to look for more chiastic writing in all of the scriptures. No matter how familiar you are with the scriptures, finding and diagramming chiasmus will build your desire to feast on the Word of the Lord and drink deeply of His Living Water. I can promise you that, if you are willing to invest a little time to look through the lens of chiasmus as you search the scriptures, the eyes of your understanding will be touched and your ability to comprehend our Savior's Gospel will be greatly enhanced.

The Substance of Chiasmus

At night, airports turn on landing lights to form a visual path that directs pilots to where safely land their airplanes. When a chiastic diagram of any size is held up and turned a quarter turn to the left, the diagram forms an image that resembles airport landing lights. The longer the chiasmus, the more it looks like the landing light analogy, but instead of guiding pilots, each chiasm is a literary track that guides readers to a greater understanding of the Gospel of Jesus Christ. In the book of Ether, we see an excellent example of how chiasmus can bring our attention to a specific principle. When the Book of Mormon was published, this short passage resolved a question that has confused theologians for almost two thousand years: How could God be both the Father and the Son? Ether 3 provides the answer:

Ether 3:14-17 (The Lord shows himself to the Brother of Jared. About 2700 BC)

N I show myself unto you. Behold,

　　O I am he who was prepared from the foundation of the world to redeem my people.

　　　　P Behold, I am Jesus Christ.

　　　　　　Q I am the Father and

R   the Son.

R'   In me shall all mankind have life, and that eternally, even they who shall believe on my name; and

Q'   they shall become my sons and my daughters...

P'   Behold, this body, which ye now behold, is the body of my spirit; and man have I created after the body of my spirit; and even as

O'   I appear unto thee to be in the spirit will I appear unto my people in the flesh....

N'   Jesus showed himself unto this man in the spirit... (Ether 3:14-17)

After transforming sixteen stones into luminescent lights to be used on the eight Jaredite boats, the Lord shows himself to the brother of Jared and tells him, in line Q, that he, Jehovah, is the Father. In the mirror-image position of line Q', he explains that he is the Father because those that believe in him shall become his *sons and his daughters*. In line R, the Lord explains that he is also the Son. Then in line R' he explains that he is the Son because in him all mankind shall have life and those who believe in him will have *eternal* life - life with our Father in Heaven. So we see that all of the narrative text of Ether 3 leads us to the central point that our Savior is both the Father and the Son and the way to eternal life.

There are few places in the universe of all the literature that can compare to such inspired thinking so elegantly expressed in so few words as in the central point of Ether 3: Jehovah is the Father of those who submit to him - and he is the Son by virtue of his being sent by his Father to be the means of bringing to pass immortality for all - and life with the Father for those who believe in him. Thus we see that mortal life is purposeful according to the mind of our loving Heavenly Father who gave his Only Begotten Son.

Finding Chiastic Centers and the Principles They Present

In this section, I'm including some selections that are from entire chapters that have been diagrammed to show the chiasmus within them. They are shortened due to space constraints. These examples are only my personal take on chiastic writing. That there are many ways to diagram chiasmus is one of the amazing things about it. It can be seen from many different angles on many different levels. Most people recognize shorter phrases. What I've found are very long passages which illustrate the visual impact of the substance of the Word of God. At first, finding chiasmus seems to be the object of searching for it, but the truth of the matter is that chiasmus is a framework on which the Word is displayed. So what we are doing is learning the structure of an unimaginably complex and beautiful architecture that is a metaphorical easel on which the Doctrines of Salvation and Exaltation are displayed in the most elegant way. However intriguing chiasmus may seem, the ultimate objective is to follow the path it creates to the Savior.

The object of these examples is to show how the text of chiasmus is organized to lead the reader to a specific concept in each passage. The gaps in the alphabetical labels are intentional, to indicate where text has be omitted due to space constraints. Although some text has been omitted, no text has been rearranged.

Genesis 1

With the previous reference to landing lights, it's instructive that "light" is the focus of Genesis 1, the first example of chiasmus and the very first chapter of the Standard Works.

Moses wrote the Book of Genesis about 1400 B.C. He wasn't the first prophet, but where did he learn the art of chiastic writing? Frequently, in the Old Testament, the more important point, usually a reference to the Trinity, is at the beginning and end with subordinate points at the center

E   and God saw that *it was* good…

  I   And God said, Let there be lights in the firmament of the heaven…

    J   let them be for lights in the firmament of the heaven to give light upon the earth and it was so.

      K   And God made two great lights;

      K'   the greater light to rule the day, and the lesser light to rule the night:

    J'   *he made* the stars also.

  I'   And God set them in the firmament of the heaven to give light upon the earth.....

E'   and God saw that *it was* good…. (Genesis 1:16-17)

Isaiah 1

This passage may be one of the most sublime concepts anywhere in all of the scriptures - and it is presented at the chiastic center of the chapter - just where it should be.

    Y   Come now, and let us reason together, saith the LORD:

      Z   though your sins be as scarlet, they shall be as white as snow;

      Z'   though they be red like crimson, they shall be as wool.

    Y'   If ye be willing and obedient…(Isaiah 1:18-19)

Ezekiel 1

The introduction (first 8 lines) includes classic chiasmus - words and phrases given in one order and then given in the reverse order. "Rings" as used here in lines Y and Y' could very well be explained in light of Alma 37:8, "his paths are straight, and his course is one eternal *round.*" The word "eyes" is symbolic of omniscience, all-knowing, and the all-seeing eye.) The Book of Mormon restores the plain and precious truths that have been lost from the Bible due to error or intent. Compare Ezekiel 1 to 1Nephi 1 and Ezekiel will become perfectly clear The phrase "the word of the Lord came expressly unto Ezekiel is a perfectly chiastic with "I heard the voice of one who spoke.

> NOW *it* came to pass in the thirtieth
>
> A year, in the fourth
>
>> B month, in the fifth
>>
>>> C day of the month, as I *was...*
>>>
>>>> D the heavens were opened, and
>>>>
>>>> D' I saw visions of God. In the fifth
>>>
>>> C' day of the
>>
>> B' month, which *was* the fifth
>
> A' year of king Jehoiachin's captivity,
>
> A The word of the LORD came expressly unto Ezekiel the priest, the son of Buzi, in and the hand of the LORD was there upon him. And
>
>> B I looked, and, behold,
>>
>>> C a whirlwind came out of the north, a great cloud, and a fire infolding *itself,* and a
>>>
>>>> Y their rings*
>>>>
>>>>> Z they were so high that
>>>>>
>>>>> Z' they were dreadful; and
>>>>
>>>> Y' their rings were full of eyes round about
>>>
>>> C' This was the appearance of the likeness of the glory of the LORD. And when
>>
>> B' I saw it and I fell upon my face, and
>
> A' I heard a voice of one that spake (Ezekiel 1:1-48)

Deuteronomy 5

This passage, a substantial chiasmus in itself, is found inside of a larger chiasmus that includes most of the text of the whole chapter. Who would have thought that the Ten Commandments were chiastic writing? This example illustrates the depth of knowledge, artistry, and literary skill of holy men of God speaking and writing as they were moved by the Holy Ghost. (2 Peter 1;21) j   <u>Keep the sabbath day to sanctify it</u>, as

k   <u>the LORD thy God hath commanded thee</u>. Six days thou shalt labour, <u>and</u> do all thy work: But <u>the seventh day *is*</u>

<u>the sabbath of</u>

l   <u>the LORD thy God</u>: *in it*

m   <u>thou shalt not do any work</u>,

n   <u>thou</u>, nor thy son, nor thy daughter, nor

o   <u>thy manservant, nor thy maidservant</u>,

p   <u>nor thine</u> ox,

q   <u>nor thine</u> ass,

q   <u>nor any of thy</u> cattle,

p   <u>nor thy</u> stranger that *is* within <u>thy</u> gates; that

o   <u>thy manservant and thy maidservant may rest as well as</u>

n   <u>thou</u>. And remember that

m   <u>thou wast a servant in the land of Egypt</u>, and *that*

l   <u>the LORD thy God brought thee</u> out thence through a mighty hand <u>and</u> by a stretched out arm: therefore

k   <u>the LORD thy God commanded thee</u> to

j   <u>keep the sabbath day</u>. (Deuteronomy 5:12-15)

Psalm 23

Parallel thoughts aren't always the same thoughts or words repeated two different ways (especially in the Bible.) Many times its not repetition of words, but the illustration of a relationship that exists between the paired thoughts such as the opposite words, *leadeth* and *follow* in lines D and D' respectively.

A   <u>THE LORD *is*</u> my shepherd;

B   <u>I shall not</u> want. He maketh

C   <u>me</u> to lie down in green pastures:

D   <u>he leadeth me</u> beside the

E   <u>still waters.</u>

F   <u>He restoreth my soul</u>: **he leadeth me…**

G   <u>I walk through</u> the valley of the shadow of **death**. I will fear no **evil**: for

H   <u>thou *art* with me</u>;

I   <u>thy rod</u> and

I'   <u>thy staff</u>

H'   <u>they</u> comfort <u>me.</u>

G'   <u>Thou preparest a table before me</u> in the presence of **<u>mine enemies:</u>**

F'   <u>thou anointest my head</u> with oil;

E'   <u>My cup runneth over.</u> Surely

D'   <u>goodness and mercy</u> **<u>shall follow</u>**

C'   <u>me</u> all the days of <u>my</u> life: and

B'   <u>I will</u> dwell in the house of

A'   <u>the LORD for ever.</u> (Psalms 23:1-6)

1 Nephi 1

The introductory six lines are very strong chiasmus; The turning point of the larger passage makes a very focused presentation of the preeminence of Jehovah and his 12 apostles; The path up to the turning point illustrates the chiastic stepping stones to the turning point.

A   the <u>first year</u> of the reign of Zedekiah, king of

B   <u>Judah,</u>

C   <u>my father,</u>

C   <u>Lehi,</u> having dwelt at

B   <u>Jerusalem</u> in all his days; and in that

A   <u>same year</u> there came many

A   <u>prophets, prophesying</u> unto the people...

C   <u>Jerusalem</u> must be

D   <u>destroyed</u>...

K   he saw <u>the heavens open,</u> and he thought …

L   <u>his throne,</u> surrounded with numberless…

M   <u>singing and praising</u>

N   <u>their God.</u> …he saw

O   <u>One descending</u> out of the midst of <u>heaven,</u> and…

                           P his luster was above that of the sun at noon-day. And he also saw twelve others following him, and

                           P their brightness did exceed that of the stars in the firmament. And

                       O they came down and went forth upon the face of the earth; and

                   N the first came and stood before my father, and gave unto him a ….

                M such as: Great and marvelous are thy works, O Lord God Almighty!

             L Thy throne is high in

           K the heavens, and

         D the destruction of

       C Jerusalem, behold he went forth among…

   A prophesy and to declare unto them concerning… (1 Nephi 1:1-18)

D&C 52 - Chapter Heading

Even chapter headings can be chiastic.

   A The next conference is designated

     B to be held in Missouri; 3–8, Appointments of

       C certain elders to travel together are made; 9–11,

         D The elders are to teach what the apostles and prophets have written; 12–21,

         D Those enlightened by the Spirit bring forth fruits of praise and wisdom; 22–44,

       C Various elders are appointed to go forth preaching the gospel,

     B while traveling to Missouri for

   A the conference.

D&C 89 - The word of Wisdom

I was surprised to find that the principle of "sparingly" is the center of the Word of Wisdom.

    C This is given for a principle with promise…

     N Yea, flesh also of beasts and of the fowls of the air…

      O I the Lord, have

     P   <u>ordained for the use of man</u> with thanksgiving, nevertheless

        Q   <u>they are to be used sparingly;</u> And it is pleasing unto me that

        Q   <u>they should not be used, only in times of winter, or of cold, or famine.</u> All grain is

     P   <u>ordained for the use of man</u> and of beasts, to be

   O   <u>the staff of life,</u> not only for man but for

 N   <u>the beasts of the field, and the fowls of heaven,</u>

C   And <u>I, the Lord give unto them a promise,</u> that… (D&C 89:12-14)

Moses 6

Chiastic writing was used from the first description of Adam and Eve. Compare to Genesis.

   O   <u>the **generations** of</u>

    P   <u>**Adam**</u>, saying:

      Q   <u>In the **day** that</u>

        R   <u>God created man, in the likeness of God made he him; In the image</u> of

          S   <u>his own body,</u>

            T   <u>male and female,</u>

              U   <u>created</u>

                V   <u>he them,</u>

                  W   <u>and blessed them</u>

                  W   <u>and called their name Adam</u> (Hebrew: living)

                V   <u>they</u> were

              U   <u>created and became</u>

            T   <u>living souls</u> in the land upon the

          S   <u>foot</u>stool of God. And

        R   <u>Adam lived one hundred and thirty years, and begat a son in his own likeness, after his own image.</u>…

      Q   <u>the **days** of</u>

    P   <u>Adam,</u> after he had begotten Seth, were

   O   <u>eight hundred years,</u> and (Moses 6 :8-12)

The 13 Articles of Faith

Joseph Smith wrote important doctrines in a divine format. The principle of revelation is at the center of the Thirteen Articles.

 H We believe in the gift of tongues, prophecy, revelation, visions, healing, interpretation of tongues, and so forth.

  I We believe the Bible to be the word of God as far as it is translated correctly;

  I we also believe the Book of Mormon to be the word of God.

 H We believe all that God has revealed, all that He does now reveal, and we believe that He will yet reveal many great and important things pertaining to the Kingdom of God.

The Family: A Proclamation to the World

Modern prophets and apostles write chiastically. The entire Proclamation is beautiful chiastic writing from beginning to end. What follows is an affirmation of the sanctity of life. No higher value could be shown as the center focus of the Family Proclamation.

 A …the sacred powers of procreation are to be employed only between man and woman, lawfully wedded as

  B husband and wife.

   C We declare the means by which mortal life is created to be divinely appointed.

   C We affirm the sanctity of life and of its importance in God's eternal plan.

  B Husband and wife have

 A a solemn responsibility

Do papers on the presence of chiasmus in try to prove that the this m

Does the Presence of Chiasmus Prove a Piece of Writing is from God?

The purpose of this article has been to introduce you to the wide presence of chiasmus in the inspired word of God. But can this be proved? In this regard, I like what Church historian B.H. Roberts said in 1909:

> [The Holy Ghost] *must ever be the chief source of evidence for the truth of the Book of Mormon. All other evidence is secondary to this, the primary and infallible. No arrangement of evidence, however skillfully ordered; no argument, however adroitly made, can ever take* [the] *place* [of the Holy Ghost].

However he continued:

> *Secondary evidences in support of truth, like secondary causes in natural phenomena, may be of first rate importance, and mighty factors in the achievement of God's purposes. [B. H. Roberts, New Witnesses for God, vol. 2 (Salt Lake City: Deseret News, 1909), pp. viviii]*

Though it may be secondary evidence, chiasmus has a beauty and power in itself. So much so that the study of chiasmus leads us to the inescapable conclusion that the scriptures have more depth and breadth than any of us have imaged. As we humbly supplicate for Divine inspiration, we will come to see there is a distinct pattern in the way the Lord speaks to his children. I believe that chiasmus is part of that pattern.

Chiastic Patterns Lead Us to the Savior

These words may bring this article to a close, but I hope for you this conclusion will be the beginning of an "adventure in scripture land."

So, why study the chiasmus of prophets, ancient and modern? Isn't reading and pondering the scriptures enough? Students of the scriptures use concordances, bible dictionaries, commentaries, guides, and many other supporting resources to help them in their study of the scriptures. We attend classes, Sunday School, firesides, General Conference - all to help us understand more clearly the principles of the Gospel. Serious students of the Gospel know the scriptures will always reward us and the more we put into studying them, the more they will reward us.

Chiasmus is about finding orderliness in a universe of chaos. Chiasmus is about finding balance. Chiasmus is about seeing what others see, but thinking what few others think. Chiasmus is about a lot of things, but the central truth of the matter is that it is a tool that helps us see. When we can see a central concept within a balanced literary presentation, we learn to more fully appreciate things that we might not have noticed before. Finding the center of chiastic writing is a metaphor for finding the center of our selves. When we find our true center, that which should be the central focus of our lives, we will discover that it is, and always will be, our Savior, even Jesus Christ.

A Final Note:

Chiasmus is found in small selections. It is found across complete chapters. Chiastic writing spans multiple chapter selections such as 3 Nephi 11-18, which was found by Elder Jeffrey R. Holland. As shown in this article, Chiasmus spans complete books in the Book of Mormon.

What follows is a diagram that I believe illustrates that the entire Book of Mormon can be shown to be a single chiastic passage. Because the original diagram is many pages long, the diagram uses numbers instead of alphabetical labels and is drastically shortened in order to fit the format of this book.

That the numbers skip is intentional to show how much of the diagram is missing due to the space constraints of a printed publication. The diagram is based on the narrative of Book of Mormon rather than on individual verses of scripture. (Imagine what a diagram of all of the verses of the Book of Mormon would look like - it would be many hundreds of pages long.) The full version of this diagram can be downloaded by going to www.scribd.com/gregcarlston and looking up the article <u>The Full Book of Mormon as Chiasmus - Preface, All Chapters</u>.

DAVIDIC CHIASMUS AND PARALLELISMS

A governing literary structure comprising an intricate, specific, and repeated thematic pattern—widely found.

Scott L. Vanatter and (posthumously) Jared R. Demke

Sacred literature demands the reader carefully engage not only the text itself but great and eternal principles. One simple method of active reading is to utilize the 'look for' method.

After many years of such engagement, my friend Jared Demke began to notice specific repeated themes, usually in a certain order. He noticed, for example, that soon after passages where sacred promises and covenants are described, later in the text one would find beautiful verses on how those same promises are fulfilled.

He also found that when covenants are introduced, within a few verses one would often find verbiage having to do with how we find ourselves living in and dealing with the trials and tribulations and troubles of living in a sometimes hostile world. Then later in the same chapter or book, he noticed that the theme was repeated, where instruction was given on how we might overcome the world. He also detected another related theme having to do with how we should act as one of the Lord's servants here on earth – effectively drawing down the blessings of heaven.

Jared began to document the pattern of these repeated themes – found in almost every Old and New Testament book, the Book of Mormon, and in most other sacred literature. He documented six major elements of parallel repeated themes. Sometimes these themes would be direct parallels, for example, themes ABCDEF, ABCDEF. In other cases the second set of repeated themes would be in reverse order— an inverse parallelism, or as it is known among biblical scholars by the Greek term, chiasmus. The themes would begin ABCDEF, but the second set of parallels would be found in reverse order, FEDCBA.

Altogether, we have documented hundreds of examples and published a couple hundred online.

The very center of these chiastic examples (or the endpoint of a six-element parallelism) would usually be a poignant description of Jesus and how he suffered for us; how dearly he loved us; how we can/should identify with Him; and how—most beautifully—one day we would be one with Him, "encircled about eternally in the arms of his love."

On "Chiasmania"

Chiasmus is not everyone's cup of tea. Either they do not see the value, or they simply find it curious. Or, they perceive that some of us tend to get carried away with it. We, our critics might complain, see chiasmus everywhere. IOW, where it ain't. Theoretically, an overzealous or non-rigorous person can match, relate, compare, or connect practically *any* idea to any *other* idea. This is why specific and careful rules have suggested by Brother Welch. We all ought to seek to ensure our chiastic outlines are grounded in evidence and fact; not wild fancy. Exegesis, not Eisegesis. IOW, we should get our chiastic outlines *out of* the scriptures (where it actually exists), and not *read in into* the scriptures (where it does not exist).

Either way, Jared and I propose there are good and valuable rules whereby one can detect and benefit from what we have termed, Davidic Chiasmus and Parallelisms.

On Parallelisms

As chiasmus is but a subset of parallelisms, we at first considered naming the pattern "Davidic Parallelisms and Chiasmus." But we thought it was pithier to shorten it to "Davidic Chiasmus." So, we started with it that way, and it stuck. Every few years I check the Internet and the pattern is referenced on many websites, both LDS and non-LDS, in some university curriculum, in several thought pieces (both pro and con) -- and even in at least one formal narrowly-focused study by two PhDs attempting to discern through statistical analysis whether Joseph Smith wrote chiastically. They used our outline of an 1838 letter he personally wrote Emma from the Liberty Jail.

This brings up a good point, that chiasmus is but an inverse *parallelism*. I have not counted it, but there are a significant number of excellent examples, including those of Jesus himself, of using straight parallelism, not inverse parallelism. Note the following parallelisms Jesus used.

From Luke 11

A -- 9. And I say unto you, Ask,

B -- and it shall be given you;

C -- seek,

D -- and ye shall find;

E -- knock,

F -- and it shall be opened unto you.

A' -- 10. For every one that asketh

B' -- receiveth;

C' -- and he that seeketh

D' -- findeth;

E' -- and to him that knocketh

F' -- it shall be opened.

From Matthew 25

A -- 35. For I was an hungred, and ye gave me meat:

B -- I was thirsty, and ye gave me drink:

C -- I was a stranger, and ye took me in:

D -- 36. Naked, and ye clothed me:

E -- I was sick, and ye visited me:

F -- I was in prison, and ye came unto me. . . .

A' -- [37] when saw we thee an hungred, and fed thee?

B' -- or thirsty, and gave thee drink?

C' -- 38. When saw we thee a stranger, and took thee in?

D' -- or naked, and clothed thee?

E' -- 39. Or when saw we thee sick ,

F' -- or in prison, and came unto thee?

A -- 42. For I was an hungred, and ye gave me no meat:

B -- I was thirsty, and ye gave me no drink:

C -- 43. I was a stranger, and ye took me not in:

D -- naked, and ye clothed me not:

E -- sick,

F -- and in prison, and ye visited me not.

A' -- [44] when saw we thee an hungred,

B' -- or athirst,

C' -- or a stranger,

D' -- or naked,

E' -- or sick,

F' -- or in prison, and did not minister unto thee?

Preliminary Questions

Now, on Davidic Chiasmus, a few preliminary questions and short answers, along the lines of who, what, where, when, why, etc.

Who speaks or writes using the Davidic Pattern? Prophets and apostles and patriarchs, politicians and presidents, members and non-members, the famous, the infamous and the obscure.

What is Davidic Chiasmus? It is an intricate, specific, and repeated pattern – widely found. It contains six repeated thematic areas (Or, it could actually be thought of a three sets of paired themes); these themes found in a certain order.

Where is Davidic Chiasmus found? We suggest it can be found in scripture, literature, poetry, and music, on practically every continent.

When was it written or spoken? Across the millennia, in ancient and modern times.

Why Davidic Chiasmus? Well, now we are getting into something which is not so easily, or rather, simply explained. More on this later.

The question of "Why" asked another way . . . How important is this? How useful? It can make obscure texts come alive, providing the key to understanding. It can provide a lens to make the most popular and well-understood texts of all time come alive again in our minds and hearts; experientially.

What is Davidic Chiasmus?

Davidic Chiasmus is an intricate, specific complex chiasmus, comprised of five pairs of parallel elements, i.e., macro structures, symmetrically arranged around a central "F" element, i.e., AB-CD-EFE-DC-BA, that has a repeated thematic pattern attached to each element. The chiasmus may be as short as a few verses, it may comprise a whole chapter, a short book, e.g., Book of Joel, or even an entire lengthy book, e.g., Book of Isaiah. This chiasmus is found extensively throughout the four standard works and other divinely inspired writings.

Davidic construction has a holistic set of operational procedures and is marked by a set of formal structural markers which divide the text into six distinct elements. Each element, i.e., AB-CD-EFE-DC-BA, within Davidic Chiasmus takes up its own subject exhibiting a point of beginning and ending. The function of each element is to introduce an overriding theme or topic. When a Davidic Chiasmus comprises more than a few verses, each substructure, within an element, may contain additional chiasmus or parallelisms. Nevertheless, it is the larger themes that impart unity to the text as a whole. The substructures within each element provides cogency to its counterpart verses as a way of amplifying the theme and unlocking hidden messages.

Each prophet/writer's utilization of complementary and contrasting literary devices provides a wonderful tapestry of God's word with synergy beyond the mere written text. If a structure "A", for example, contains a chiasmus a-b-c-b-a, the complementary backside structure "A" can often contain the same (or nearly the same) chiastic pattern a-b-c-b-a. If structure "D" contains an extended alternate parallelistic pattern, i.e., a-b-c-a-b-c, the backside "D" will follow with the same (or nearly the same) pattern. Finally, each corresponding sub pattern (or substructure) is an extension, enhancement and fulfillment of its counterpart, i.e., "a" matches "a", "b" matches "b", etc. The entire fabric of literary discourse, in the words of Ernst Wendland, "encompasses a hierarchy that will correspond in broad outline with its previously determined structural-thematic framework" such that "every distinct formal unit of the text – from the line/colon to the composition as a whole – may be viewed as manifesting a particular function, or functional complex, in relation to its audience then and now." (Discourse Perspectives on Hebrew Poetry in the Scriptures, Ernst R. Wendland, p. 19). The hermeneutical value of the entire scriptural text thus becomes greater than the sum of its individual parts.

The Pattern Outlined

Davidic themes attach themselves to each element as follows (these titles are adopted as symbols or mental shortcuts to explain an otherwise complex semantic outline of the whole):

A -- Word of the Lord

B -- New Things (or the Lord's Covenant)

C -- The World

D -- The Lord's Servant

E -- Preservation

F -- The Suffering Servant

E' -- Salvation

D' -- The Lord's Davidic Servant

C' -- Overcoming the World

B' -- Fulfillment

A' -- Salvation Song

The Davidic Pattern and these macro themes are:

- More orient than occident (though it is found in the West)

- More poetry than prose (though it is found in prose)

- More a painting than a blueprint (though it can be thought of as a blueprint)

- More abstract than mathematical (though there obtains an almost mathematical precision in many intricate/famous and obscure examples)

- More art than science

- More an open system than a closed set of limiting rules

- More gnostic than orthodox

- More experiential than intellectual

Key Words and Themes per Macro Element

The following list contains some of the key words most often associated with each macro element.

A -- Hear this, Hearken, Praise, Name, etc.

B -- Promise(s), Inheritance, New Things, Hidden Things, Things of God, Shall Come to pass, etc.

C -- World, Wicked, Contentions, Apostasy, Satan, Egypt, Babylon, Earth, etc. [feminine]

D -- Servant, Prophet, Moses, Truth, Righteousness, Kingdom, Heaven, etc. [masculine]

E – Preserved, Salvation, Pillars, Gates, Manna, Wine, etc. -- boldly

F -- Suffering, Afflicted, Despised, Rejected, etc. -- nobly

F' – Oneness, Unity, Embrace, Kiss, Throne, Name, Glory, etc. -- nobly

E' – Salvation, Exalted, Preserved, Inheritance, Mercy, etc. – independent

D' -- Servant, Prophet, Truth, Righteousness, Kingdom, Heaven, Eternity, etc. [masculine]

C' -- Overcome, World, Wicked, Cut Off, Contentions; Judgment, Destruction, Earth, etc. [feminine]

B' – Fulfill, Restoration, Deliverance, Covenant(s), Promise(s), Inheritance, etc.

A' -- Hosanna, Name, Amen, Sing, etc.

You might notice, I have grouped the six themes into three pairs. A's and B's are closely related, Words introduce Covenants. C's and D's are related, we live in a World sometimes hostile to Servants seeking to Overcome the World. E's and F's are related. After encountering the World, and becoming true Servants, we approach the Divine (in E, and in a Temple template overlay, often we find the text thematically and symbolically bringing the reader to the veil, where we can embrace the Lord, the Divine (the F structure).

What is the significance of Davidic Chiasmus?

Jared suggested several. *First*, Davidic Chiasmus answers the question, "what is the function of chiasmus?" Unless chiasmus reveals something more than what is already apparent, what is the point of determining its very existence in the first place? The proposition is that this pattern constitutes not only a compilation of random couplets and parallelisms, however magnificent or spiritually penetrating the fragments may be, but a purposeful and sustained composition. The arrangement and ordering of parallelisms indicate the presence of purpose, style and logic; all of which conforms to rules governed by Davidic construction. Jared somewhat boldly suggested that an endeavor to explain Chiasmus without the aid of Davidic logic, is analogous to staging the Shakespearian play Hamlet without the prince, or account for the Civil War without Lincoln, or describe Christianity without Joseph Smith.

Second, any scriptural passage may be interpreted literally, allegorically, morally, or anagogically (mystically). We have presented the Davidic pattern according to several templates, e.g., The Lord's (Davidic) servant, Eschatological (last days) imagery, Temple (endowment) imagery. We also suggest an anagogical reading that does not center in the historical past or historical future, but in the transcendence of time and the eternal. (*I'll have more on this at the end or my presentation.*)

Third, Davidic language and style speaks to the listener by giving every word and every sentence an interpretive purpose. The scriptures thereby derive height, depth and width (or latitude and longitude) and thereby gain their full purpose and meaning.

Fourth, Davidic Chiasmus affords each individual prophet/writer the method of providing a built-in table of contents, lexicon, concordance and commentary to his own text. When these literary techniques are used to communicate a message, the resulting poetic passages direct one's attention towards a larger matrix of definitions that go well beyond the mere rhetorical framework. (Accordingly, there is a whole realm of truth and meaning within the text's deepest structure, i.e., through the employment of macro, micro, inter-micro, and inter-chiastic-analysis.)

Fifth, this manner of writing both hides and reveals; it conceals precious truths from the casual reader, and reveals and enriches the Lord's message that ostensibly does not appear on the surface of the text.

[I would add here a couple thoughts: Joseph Smith suggested that when God speaks to us, he does so in the abstract. This, to me, means more often than not when God speaks to us he is sending us pictures -- spiritual images, if you will -- rather than a mathematical formula. Commenting on his movie Crouching Tiger, Hidden Dragon, Director Ang Lee suggested viewers need not have intimate knowledge of ancient Chinese symbolism to know and appreciate – to 'get' -- Crouching Tiger, Hidden Dragon. They need only engage, and let the images, words – yes, the symbolism – flow. Let it work on you and speak to you. Not that having the ideas of the existence of symbolism is a bad thing. Or an idea of what the symbols suggest. It is just that the form speaks to a person whether they are a beginner -- or an expert. Similarly, I would suggest that chiasmus speaks to the reader or hearer, whether they have an awareness of it or not. In other words, those without specific, concrete intellectual knowledge of the pattern are not without benefit . However, of course, the more awareness, 'so much the advantage' in understanding.]

Sixth, a prophet's particular emphasis on contrasts and opposites, using Davidic construction, is in itself stylistic and a work of beauty. The manner of presenting themes, with all their complexity and attendant implications, thereby constitutes a "Davidic signature" unique to each prophetic writer. A modern commentator wrote, "When Alma takes the time to structure his conversation in such a detailed manner, he is using another tool to convey to the reader his feelings of God's glory. The rhyming and contrasting of ideas sharpens, highlights, gives adoration and glory to God. To dismiss an intentional structure with a 'so what' is the equivalent of saying the Mona Lisa is a nice snapshot, the Sistine Chapel a sexual mural, and Beethoven's Ninth Symphony a pleasant tune . . . God is not only intelligent but also a being of glory and beauty."

Seventh, Davidic construction is emblematic of the special intimacy of the ancient oral medium that was conceived for the purpose of committing thoughts, impressions and pathos to memory. Qualities of rhythm, tempo, cadence inherent in its symmetry produces audible dynamics that give it its visceral, as well as cerebral, appeal and expressive resonance.

Finally, this literary structure, through its specific arrangement of the text, makes known the "plain and precious things" and "many covenants" of the Lord (1 Nephi 13:26, 40) and thereby testifies of Jesus Christ, the restoration and the great and marvelous work in the latter days.

The parable of the Prodigal Son from Luke 15:11-32 is such an example that incorporates all these ideas.

Prodigal Son, Outline

    A – The Younger (v 11, 12a)

     B – Divided His Living, Took His Journey (v 12b, 13a)

      C – Riotous Living – A Mighty Famine — In Want (v 13b, 14)

       D – Sent into the Fields to Feed Swine (v 15)

        E – Husks – He Came to Himself (v 16-20a)

         F – His Father Saw Him, Ran, Kissed Him (v 20b)

        E – I have Sinned (v 21)

         F – The Best Robe (v 22-24)

    A – The Elder (v 25a)

     B – Draws Nigh unto the House (v 25b)

      C – No Want (v 25c)

       D – Brother has Come Home (v 26, 27a)

        E – He was Angry (v 27b, 28a)

         F – His Father Comes Out, Entreats Him (v 28b)

        E – Not Transgressed at Any Time (v 29a)

         F – Thou Art Ever With Me – All that I Have is Thine (v 29b-32)

Why is this structure named "Davidic Chiasmus"?

The divine message of this literary structure is summarized with the name "Davidic."

First, in every dispensation, the Lord has given keys of knowledge, power and revelations to prophets, i.e., messianic servants. All of these prophets serve as a type of Jesus Christ, who was called the Son of David.

Also, the word David means "beloved" and the name gives reverence to Jesus Christ, who is the exemplar Davidic servant.

Finally, the name itself implies that all of God's children have it within themselves the regenerative powers to become like Christ. Joseph Campbell wrote, "The cosmogonic cycle is presented with astonishing consistency in the sacred writings of all the continents, and it gives to the adventure of the hero a new and interesting turn; for now it appears that the perilous journey was a labor not of attainment but of re-attainment, not discovery but re-discovery. The godly powers sought and dangerously won are revealed to have been within the heart of the hero all the time. He is 'the king's son' who has come to know who he is and therewith has entered into the exercise of his proper power – 'God's son,' who has learned to know how much that title means. From this point of view the hero is symbolical of that divine creative and redemptive image which is hidden within us all, only waiting to be known and rendered into life." (The Hero with a Thousand Faces, p. 39).

How mysterious is the Pattern?

The Pattern is not mysterious, at least not in a "Bible Code way." In fact, it is not 'hidden' at all. If anything, it is 'hidden in plain sight.' In my opinion, a child can learn and benefit from recognizing the repeated themes, and recognizing when the template obtains. One does not need a computer to detect it. One need not be an expert in literary analysis, ancient languages, or, with respect, a John Welch, a Hugh Nibley, or a Harold Bloom. One need only look for Promises/Covenants/Fulfillment, problems of living in a sometimes hostile and alternatively beautiful world, or how we can live as a servant of God, or how we can identify with and Come Unto Christ, either through our encountering his sufferings for us, or his desiring to be at One with us.

How does one identify Davidic Chiasmus?

What Ernst R. Wendland wrote about textual criticism and translation can equally apply to identifying the existence of Davidic literature. He wrote, "Once a particular poetic composition has been demarcated, at least provisionally subject to a thorough discourse analysis, it is necessary to examine the quality or physical state of the text itself . . . A helpful way of preparing oneself for this task is to read the poem through several times, aloud and in the original, both to get a feel for the whole and also to note any significant phonological features that occur along the way . . . To some, this sort of translational exercise might seem like a waste of time, since there are so many versions and commentaries available to which one could refer in order to derive an exegetical understanding of a poem's microstructure. That may be true, but the discipline of putting everything together in the process of coming to one's own decisions about what the poet was trying to say – and how – is the best way of getting ready for a comprehensive discourse study. In fact, this is the only means of really familiarizing oneself with the text as an act of communication within a specific literary, theological and sociocultural setting. One needs to experience the poetry firsthand and close-up – sensorially as well as cognitively and emotively – before one attempts to analyze it in terms of its broader structures, themes, and purposes." (Discourse Perspectives on Hebrew Poetry in the Scriptures, Ernst R. Wendland, p. 8 – 10).

After having studied a text per Davidic themes, when the person then hears or reads the text again each of the phrases, ideas and principles presented now speak volumes. Every word or phrase launches a myriad of thoughts and connections – and experiences; intellectual and experiential.

I might mention here, several tools we have described on our website to work through and present the various outlines.

- *Macro analysis*: Where the front side Macro structure is related to its backside counterpart.

- *Micro analysis*: Where internal to a Macro element, phrase by phrase and word by word relations are examined.

- *Inter-micro analysis*: Where the details of a front side and backside element are closely examined.

- *Inter-chiastic analysis*: Where two different texts, for example, the Gettysburg Address and the Declaration of Independence are compared and contrasted. This is analogous to the Syncretic level of reading Mortimer Adler describes in his seminal, How to Read a Book.

Levels of Meaning

When Jared first presented elements of the repeated pattern, I asked many questions. "As important as 'Preservation' is, where are the higher principles and themes, such as love, union, peace, joy, etc.?" At the time, his brief answer was, "I don't know." (It took us ten years to flesh it out.)

While I was a skeptic at first, I soon became convinced of the existence of the repeated themes. Promises and Fulfillment. The World and Overcoming the World. Time after time we would uncover beautiful patterns in the most famous, and the most inconspicuous examples. Some of my favorites are up on the new website. Another great favorite, the King Follett Discourse. I remember the day/night I did the first outline. Late into the night I would roll the repeated themes across my mind, over and over. I was amazed and intrigued that such intricate themes were repeated and interwoven throughout the speech. Others of my favorites include some of the most famous of Jesus' parables, Jefferson's Declaration of Independence, Lincoln's Gettysburg Address, and Martin Luther King, Jr.'s I Have a Dream speech. [See appendix below for some examples.]

Ten years ago I was working for a government contractor. On the wall of my Arlington, Virginia office, I kept a framed outline of Lincoln's Gettysburg Address. One day the company CEO came into my office to chat about some business issue. He glanced up at the wall and asked about the outline. After I briefly explained to him the thematic outline, he thought for a moment, then asked, "Have you thought about Patrick Henry's, Give Me Liberty or Give Me Death speech. Sure enough, that evening when I got home, was another beautiful and poignant example of the Pattern.

Over the years, Jared and I enjoyed sharing with each other new books and ideas. While he was cognizant and appreciative of Joseph Campbell's works, it took him a few years to fully appreciate "gnostic" literature and themes. For almost two decades he would make a twice-a-year business trip to the Northern Virginia where I happened to live with my growing family. He would stay with us for a long weekend twice a year. (Between trips we spoke on the phone for a half an hour to an hour every day.) One trip, he got off the plane and announced that he found and had begun reading a great book, How to Know God (by Deepak Chopra.) I said, "You mean, this one?" as I pulled my own copy off my bookshelf. So, finally, we began discussing in earnest an inner/outer interpretation to the pattern. I had previously also tried to interest Jared in reading some of the original 'gnostic' literature from the Nag Hammadi collection. While it took him a while to fully appreciate 'gnostic' literature, he was still one of the most widely read persons I know.

Historically, there has been cited at least four levels of meaning which can be ascribed to a given text:

- *Literal*: The literal, historical, or plain meaning of a given text or situation

- *Allegorical*: The allegorical, symbolic, or metaphorical meaning

- *Moral*: The moral implications of our understanding of a given text informs our actions

- *Anagogical (or Spiritual)*: The experiential, mystical, anagogical meaning (bespeaking, Oneness, Fullness, gnosis, or in other words, "Knowledge of the Heart.")

A few months before he died in 2006, Jared summarized four to five years of our thoughts and conversations on an "inner" or experiential level of understanding of the Davidic pattern. Note: A couple of years prior to his death, Jared expressed regret that we chose such Old Testament oriented labels for the elements of the pattern -- that the Pattern is now permanently identified with that particular level of understanding. Still, even though I had originally balked at using the Old Testament nomenclature, it was through that lens that Jared first discovered the pattern. And we used the focus of the Davidic Servant motif in our becoming aware of the various hidden-in-plain sight examples of the Pattern.

See below for an introduction to our latest thoughts on the Pattern.

Commentary: The Journey Inward

Any scriptural passage may be interpreted literally, allegorically, morally, or anagogically (mystically). Heretofore, we have interpreted the Davidic pattern according to the first three disciplines. Might we also suggest an anagogical reading that does not center in the historical past or historical future, but in the transcendence of time and the eternal. This includes but is not limited to the paradox found in the following pairs of opposites (placed in a Davidic format):

 a. Material / Spiritual

 b. Outward / Inward

 c. Works / Grace

 d. Kingdom Out There / Kingdom Within

 e. Fear / Desire

 f. Abase / Exalted

 f'. Suffering in Joy / Joy in Suffering

 e'. Death / Resurrection

 d'. Kingdom Later / Kingdom NOW

 c'. Law / Freedom

 b'. Tree of Knowledge / Tree of Life

 a'. Lose / Find

This type of mystical interpretation looks beyond the pairs of opposites. As the poet William Blake notably pointed out: "If the doors of perception were cleansed every thing would appear to man as it is, infinite." Therefore, a whole new set of Davidic titles is also required to get our minds focused on man's inward spiritual state. This fourth level of interpretation should be able to take us to the transcendental center and not simply to another point on the physical circumference.

The Mythological Journey Inward

 A – Innocence
 B -- The Call—An Awakening

 C -- The Journey Inward and Backward (Duality)

 D -- Connected with Light

 E -- Gnosis (Experiential)

 F -- Realization (Mind)

 F' -- At-one-ness (Heart)

E' -- Intimacy (Passion / Compassion / Comfort / Peace)

D' -- Full of Light

C' -- The Journey Outward and Forward (Union)

B' – Bliss—Fully Awakened

A' -- Christ Consciousness ("The Mind of Christ")

The general "gnostic" ideals, principles, and terms attached to this interpretation suggests a chosen divine destiny that is inherent in all mankind, i.e., there is no such thing as a being who is not extraordinary. This providence consists of an "inward" journey of descent (CD), initiation (EFFE), and return (DC). The Davidic formula also suggests a psychological birth (AB) and rebirth to life (BA). This further connotes "that life is not merely a series of meaningless accidents or coincidences, but rather it is a tapestry of events that culminate in an exquisite sublime plan."

A -- Innocence

Our original state of innocence/slumbering: We are unaware, unknowing, and mostly in ignorance of the divinity that is deep within us.

B -- Awakening

Inner feelings of being awakened from a deep sleep: and having a great yearning, and desire to approach and explore. If one has the courage to continue on to the potential of something better, there will be overwhelming incredible and sometimes terrifying experiences that changes one's existing paradigm.

C -- Duality

Inner feelings of being separated, unconnected, fragmented, and alone in the world (error, darkness). Terrifying, dark, chaotic encounters within the psyche. Deep retreat in time and space. The world does not communicate to us and we do not communicate to the world. This "Waste Land" condition (described by T.S. Eliot) constitutes a disassociation of spirit from nature.

D -- Connected

Inner feelings of being reunited, connected, together with those in heaven. A wholeness manifested (truth, light). This healing can only be attained by the light/spirit of: 1) spontaneous compassion, 2) a passion or lust for life, and 3) enduring sublime love. Everything is accomplished by the impulse of one's own true nature; nothing borrowed, nothing counterfeited.

E -- Gnosis

Inner feelings of receiving gnosis, knowing, intuition, love. The opposing gates of fear and desire are boldly passed through.

F -- Realization

Inner feelings of receiving comfort, grace, beauty, and wonder. "Privation and suffering alone open the mind of a man to all that is hidden to others." These centering harmonious feelings are reached through the noble experience of joy in a world of suffering.

F' -- At-one-ness

Receiving the full measure of the stature of Christ (within). The accent is on experience, "an experience of identity with the Godhead." To then be able to nobly speak and do, "The Father and I are one."

E' -- Intimacy

Becoming perfect, fully confident in one's standing/relationship with the lord, comforted in all things. Independent of the feelings others place on you; no malice expressed and no offense taken.

D' -- Fullness

Feelings of being full of light with the power and courage to bestow blessings to fellow men. Gratitude and awe of the Infinite. These new powers are experienced both in control over one's own situation and influence with others. One becomes a creative center of the life/light process.

C' -- Union

Feelings of clarity: Living in the present and seeing the world as it really is: perfect, whole and complete just as they are. Our bodies are at one with this world; both of which constitute an "oasis in the desert of infinite space."

B' -- Fully Awakened

A rebirth to life. All desires and all yearnings are fulfilled. We are re-introduced back into the Garden.

A' -- Christ Consciousness

Fully conscious, fully knowing, fully creative, spontaneous, and living from the center.

Did the writers/speakers Know?

The short answer is that Jared was of the opinion that Joseph Smith knew of the pattern. I am not convinced. I believe that these themes are universal, in perhaps a Jungian Collective Unconscious kind of way. When Jared first presented to me elements of the Pattern, I suggested we consider how we might break down the Pattern into its most basic ideas.

Perhaps something along the lines of:

- Issue introduced (Words)

- Situation/Conditions developed (Promises)

- Problems (World)

- Response to, interaction with problems (Servants)

- Results, both temporary and permanent

- Issue resolved, completed, explained, summarized.

A simple view of these six elements might be:

- Issues

- Options

- Problems

- Solutions

- Results

- Answers

Some years after we published our website, I ran across other interesting outlines containing six steps or stages, such as:

- Jean Piaget's sub-stages of Cognitive Development: 1.) Reflexes, 2.) Habits, 3.) Logic, 4.) Intelligence (Goals), 5.) Discovery of new means (to meet goals), 6.) Insight (or true Creativity)

- Lawrence Kohlberg's Stages of Moral Development: 1.) Obedience/punishment orientation, 2.) Self-interest, 3.) Interpersonal accord and conformity, 4.) Authority and social-order maintaining, 5.) Social contract, 6.) Universal ethical principles [Transcendental Morality]

- Abraham Maslow's levels of Self-Actualization: 1.) Physiological, 2.) Safety, 3.) Love/Belonging, 4.) Esteem, 5.) Self-actualization, 6.) Transcendence (Core-Religious Experience)

- James Fowler's Stages of Faith: 1.) Intuitive-Projective, 2.) Mythic-Literal, 3.) Synthetic-Conventional, 4.) Individuative-Reflective, 5.) Conjunctive, 6.) Universalizing

- Bloom's Taxonomy: 1.) Knowledge 2.) Comprehension 3.) Application 4.) Analysis 5.) Synthesis 6.) Evaluation

- Richard Russell's Reasons to Believe: 1.) Experience: It works for us, 2.) Demonstration: We saw it, 3.) Tradition: We have always done it, 4.) Authority: Someone who ought to know said, 5.) Logic: It just makes sense, 6.) Inspiration: It feels right [See appendix below for a comparative chart.]

Definitional vs. Conforming

We are also aware that some examples we offer are, what we term, "conforming" (meaning, the example at hand does fit the pattern, but perhaps does not establish it) while others are "definitional" (meaning, the example at hand is more overt and where words in the front side closely match words of the backside of an outline.

For example, John Taylor was less creative in his inspiration in writing as per the pattern (in other words, he would often employ a word-for-word matching, e.g., in the front side B structure with its related back side B structure. Other writers/authors were more creative in their inspired approach. In other words, their use of related/repeated themes had the effect of hiding in plain sight the Pattern. But, still it obtains. These more "creative" examples of the Pattern often added more insight, as – again, if it obtains – the related themes would often never be thought to be compared, until and unless the Davidic Pattern offered the repeated themes as a Key.

Either way, as has been stated, the Davidic Pattern -- if it obtains -- provides (for any particular literary structure in question) its own built-in Table of Contents, Glossary, and Commentary. And more.

On Non-LDS Examples of the Pattern

An interesting and not widely-known 1978 Statement of the First Presidency (God's Love for All Mankind, 15 February 1978) has been cited by James E. Faust in the Ensign at least 4-5 times since 1980. The second paragraph reads:

> "The *great religious leaders of the world* such as Mohammed, Confucius, and the Reformers, as well as philosophers including Socrates, Plato, and others, *received a portion of God's light*. Moral truths were *given to them by God* to enlighten whole nations and to bring a higher level of understanding to individuals." (First Presidency Statement: God's Love for All Mankind, 15 February 1978)

I appreciate in this statement the generous, open spirit in acknowledging and approving the "great religious leaders of the world" (of other faiths), "as well as philosophers," who the First Presidency declared "received a portion of God's light." And further, that "Moral truths were given to them by God to enlighten whole nations and to bring a higher level of understanding to individuals."

President Howard W. Hunter's also spoke in October 1991 General Conference ("The Gospel— A Global Faith") quoting Elder Orson F. Whitney:

> "Providence is over all. . . He holds the nations in the hollow of his hand; He is using not only his covenant people, but other peoples as well, to consummate a work, stupendous, magnificent, and altogether too arduous for this little handful of Saints to accomplish by and of themselves....

> "All down the ages men bearing the authority of the Holy Priesthood — patriarchs, prophets, apostles and others, have officiated in the name of the Lord, doing the things that he required of them; and outside the pale of their activities other good and great men, not bearing the Priesthood, but possessing profundity of thought, great wisdom, and a desire to uplift their fellows, have been sent by the Almighty into many nations, to give them, not the fullness of the Gospel, but that portion of truth that they were able to receive and wisely use." (Conference Report, April 1921, p.32-33)

It should come as no surprise then that, if the Davidic Pattern obtains, we should expect to discover it in the writings of both David and Martin Luther King, Jr., both Alma and Abraham Lincoln, both Joseph Smith and Thomas Jefferson.

How is it that all these prophets, whose writings transverse millennia, continent and sociological influences come up with the same literary pattern? Did these prophets know they were conforming to the pattern?

Joseph Campbell's book "The Hero with a Thousand Faces" discusses the three stages of heroic cosmic journeys that are preserved in world mythology; namely, departure, initiation and return and examines in detail the role that the cosmic Hero plays in universal cycles of growth, dissolution, and redemption. He calls this heroic narrative the "mono-myth" and describes it in the following manner:

"The mythological hero, setting forth from his common day hut or castle, is lured, carried away, or else voluntarily proceeds to the threshold of adventure. There he encounters a shadow presence that guards the passage. The hero may defeat or conciliate this power and go alive into the kingdom of the dark (brother-battle, dragon-battle, offering, charm), or be slain by the opponent and descend in death (dismemberment, crucifixion). Beyond the threshold, then, the hero journeys through a world of unfamiliar yet strangely intimate forces, some of which severely threaten him (tests), some which give magical aid (helpers). When he arrives at the nadir of the mythological round, he undergoes a supreme ordeal and gains his reward. The triumph may be represented as the hero's sexual union with the goddess-mother of the world (sacred marriage), his recognition by the father-creator (father atonement), his own divinization (apotheosis) or again – if the powers have remained unfriendly to him – his theft of the boon he came to gain (bride-theft, fire-theft): intrinsically it is an expansion of consciousness and therewith of being (illumination, transfiguration, freedom). The final work is that of the return. If the powers have blessed the hero, he now sets forth under their protection (emissary); if not, he flees and is pursued (transformation flight, obstacle flight). At the return threshold the transcendental powers must remain behind; the hero re-emerges from the kingdom of dread (return, resurrection). The boon that he brings restores the world (elixir). (The Hero with a Thousand Faces, p. 245-246). "

In the preface of this book, Campbell wrote the following about letting the power of the symbols.

"The old teachers knew what they were saying. Once we have learned to read again their symbolic language, it requires no more than the talent of an anthologist to let their teaching be heard. But first, we must learn the grammar of the symbols . . . [and] let the symbols speak for themselves. The parallels will be immediately apparent; and these will develop a vast and amazingly constant statement of the basic truths by which man has lived throughout the millenniums of his residence on this planet." (The Hero with a Thousand Faces, p. vii-viii)

The same thing could be said concerning Davidic literature. Campbell wrote that this heroic narrative may be thought of "the secret opening through which the inexhaustible energies of the cosmos pour into human cultural manifestation." (p. 3)

Why Davidic Chiasmus?

In the 1984 masterpiece motion picture "Amadeus," the accomplished composer Antonio Salieri surreptitiously receives a folder of musical scores written in draft form by Wolfgang Amadeus Mozart. He thumbs through these manuscripts and finds to his utter amazement that none of the scores contains a single error or correction. As he peruses each flawless page, rich and vibrant chords of music expand all around him; tears immediately swell up in his eyes. Overcome with emotions by the rather apparent "gift from God" that rested within Mozart, Salieri lets the pages flutter to the floor. If these very same sonatas, concertos and symphonies were introduced in their original form to the untrained, would order be manifested? Yet, if the eye could but understand the notes, timing, rhythm, melody, and harmonious blends of the written score with precision, would they resonate rich luxuriant chords within one's soul, stir our deepest passions, and embrace our very being, as they did Salieri? . . .

This Davidic literary pattern is introduced as the governing structure that binds and incorporates all other poetic and rhetorical devices within prophetico-Messianic literature. This structure testifies of God's preeminent Son, Jesus Christ, his wholeness, completeness and perfection as the Davidic Servant. This pattern further testifies of the "last days" and the hope of redemption for the humble followers who will ultimately inherit the Kingdom of God. Finally, it serves as a model of the story of Adam in his fallen state and his journey back home and thus marks all such conforming scriptural text as "ritual literature."

We will never really understand the paradoxical essence of the scriptures until we understand how the original prophetic writers shaped it. Until then, these scriptures will remain largely beyond us. But once we learn the pattern of God's words, and the laws and principles by which they are governed, we begin to approach the scriptures with renewed reverence and respect. We then will begin to know for ourselves, and "not then be dependent on man for knowledge of God; nor will there be any room for speculation" (TPJS p. 11-12). Only then, we will be able to sing the song of salvation with the heavenly choirs.

APPENDIX: EXAMPLES

When we began the process of systematizing, labeling, and describing the pattern online, I was excited to check all the most famous dreams, visions, speeches, discourses, poems, songs, hymns, passages, prayers, and standalone chapters, such as John 17. In this I have not been disappointed. The center F structure of the Great Intercessory Prayer, from John 17: 11-12:

Summary outline of John 17

A1 — Give Eternal Life

 B — That They Might Know Thee

A2 — Glory, Before the World Was

A3 — I have Manifested Thy Name (Thine They Were)

 C — Given unto Them the Words

  D — Thou didst Send Me

  E — I Come to Thee (I Am No More In The World)

   F — *Keep through Thine Own Name*

F — <u>They May Be One</u>, As We Are

F' — *I Kept Them In Thy Name*

E' — <u>Now Come I to Thee</u> (I Speak In The World)

C' — Given Them Thy Word (Sanctify Them Through Thy Truth)

D' — <u>Thou Has Sent Me</u> (Sanctified Through The Truth)

A1' — <u>May Be One</u>, <u>One In Us</u>, Even <u>As We Are One</u>, <u>Perfect In One</u> (Love)

A2' — Glory, Before The Foundation of The World (Lovedst Me)

B' — I Have Known Thee

A3' — I Have <u>Declared Thy Name</u> (Love in Them, I in Them)

The 23rd Psalm

A. 1. <u>The LORD</u> is *my shepherd*;
B. I shall <u>not want</u>.

  C. 2. He *maketh me to lie down* in <u>green pastures</u>: he *leadeth me beside* the <u>still waters</u>.
  D. 3. He <u>restoreth my soul</u>:

    E. he *leadeth me* in <u>the paths of righteousness</u>
    F. for <u>his name's sake</u>.

    E'. 4. Yea, though *I walk through* <u>the valley of the shadow of death</u>, I will fear no evil:
    F'. for <u>thou art with me</u>; *thy rod and thy staff* they comfort me.

  D'. 5. Thou <u>preparest a table</u> before me
  C. in the *presence of* <u>mine enemies</u>:

B'. thou <u>anointest</u> *my head with oil*; *my cup* <u>runneth over</u>.
A'. 6. Surely *goodness and mercy* shall follow me <u>all the days of my life</u>: [for time]
A'. and *I will dwell in the house* of <u>the LORD for ever</u>. [for eternity]

Psalm 82

a. 1. God *standeth* in <u>the congregation of the mighty</u>;
a. he <u>judgeth among the gods</u>.
b. 2. How long will ye *judge unjustly*,
b. and *accept the persons of the wicked*? Selah.

  d/c. 3. <u>Defend</u> the *poor and fatherless*:
  d/c. <u>do justice</u> to the *afflicted and needy*.

d/c. 4. <u>Deliver</u> the *poor and needy*:
d/c. <u>rid</u> them out of the *hand of the wicked*.

e. 5. They <u>know not</u>, *neither will they understand*;
e. <u>they walk on</u> *in darkness*: all the foundations of the earth are out of course.

f. 6. I have said, <u>Ye are gods</u>;
f. and *all of you* are <u>children of the most High</u>.

c/d. 7 But *ye shall die* <u>like men</u>,
c/d. *and fall* <u>like one of the princes</u>.

a. 8. Arise, O God, <u>judge</u> *the earth*:
b. for <u>thou shalt inherit</u> *all nations*.

The Beatitudes (Mt 5)

"Blessed are . . . "

B. the <u>poor in spirit</u>
A. they <u>that mourn</u>

C. the <u>meek</u>
D. they which do <u>hunger and thirst</u> after righteousness

E. the <u>merciful</u>
F. the <u>pure in heart</u>
E. the <u>peacemakers</u>

D. they which are <u>persecuted</u> *for righteousness' sake*
C. ye, when men shall <u>revile</u> you . . . *for my sake*.

A. <u>Rejoice</u>, and be exceeding glad:*
B. [the <u>rich</u> in spirit]

"For . . . "

B. *theirs is the kingdom of heaven.*
A. *they shall be comforted.*

C. *they shall inherit the earth.*
D. *they shall be filled.*

E. *they shall obtain mercy.*
  F. *they shall see God.*
E. *they shall be called the children of God.*

  D. *theirs is the kingdom of heaven.*
  C. [*ye shall inherit the earth*]

A. [*you will be a comfort to others*]
  B. *great is your reward* in heaven

The Lord's Prayer (Mt 6)

A. 9. Our Father which art in heaven, Hallowed be <u>thy name</u>.
B. 10. <u>Thy kingdom come</u>.

  C. Thy will be done <u>in earth,</u>
    D. as it is <u>in heaven</u>.

    E. 11. <u>Give us</u> this day *our daily bread.*
      F. [Ellipsis*]
    E'. 12. And <u>forgive us</u> our debts,
      F'. <u>as we forgive</u> *our debtors*.

  D'. 13. And <u>lead us</u> not into temptation,
  C'. but <u>deliver us from evil</u>:

B'. For <u>thine is the kingdom</u>, and the power, and glory, forever,
A'. <u>Amen</u>.

Overlay of Davidic Themes for the six elements of E/F of Luke 11

Scripture phrase	Davidic Theme
a. <u>Ask</u>	. . . for the Word
b. It shall be *given* you	. . . the Promise
c. <u>Seek</u>	. . . to Overcome the World
d. Ye shall *find*	. . . the Lord's Servant
e. <u>Knock</u>	. . . to receive the Lord's Presence
f. It shall be *opened*	. . . God's Glory
a. For everyone that <u>Asketh</u>	. . . sings the Song of Salvation
b. *Receiveth*	. . . fulfillment of the Promises
c. <u>Seeketh</u>	. . . Overcomes the World

d. *Findeth*	. . . the Lord's Servant
e. Knocketh	. . . obtains Salvation
f. It shall be *opened*	. . . the everlasting arms of the Lord

Moroni 10, Summary outline

A — Read, Remember, Ponder

B — Ask God, He will Manifest the Truth ←

  C1 — Deny Not the Power of God

  C2 — Deny Not the Gifts of God

  D – The Word of Knowledge

    E — All these Gifts Come by the Spirit of Christ

    F1 — Remember, Every Good Gift Cometh of Christ

    F2 — Remember, He is the Same, Yesterday, Today, and Forever

    E' — All these Gifts of which I have Spoken, are Spiritual

    F1' — There must be Faith, Hope, Charity

    F2' — Ye Can Do All Things which are Expedient unto Me

  C' — Because of Unbelief

  D' — That Which I have Written is True

B1' — Come unto Christ, and Lay Hold Upon Every Good Gift ←

B2' — Come Unto Christ, and Be Perfected in Him ←

A' — Brought Forth Triumphant

D&C 4

a. 1. Now behold,

b. a marvelous work is *about to come forth* among the children of men.

c1. 2. Therefore, O ye that embark in the service of God, *see that ye*

c2. serve him with all your heart, might, mind and strength,

c3. *that ye may stand blameless before God* at the last day.

d1. 3. Therefore, if ye have *desires to serve* God

d2. ye are called to the work;

e. 4. For behold the field is white already to harvest;

  f. and lo, he that *thrusteth* in his sickle

  f. with his might,

  f'. the same *layeth up* in store

e'. that he perisheth not, but bringeth salvation to his soul;

d1′. 5. And *faith, hope, charity and love, with an eye single* to the glory of God,
d2′. qualify him for the work.

c1′. 6. *Remember*
c2′. faith, virtue, knowledge, temperance, patience, brotherly kindness, godliness, charity, humility, diligence.
c3′. [Ellipsis]

b'. 7. Ask, and *ye shall receive*; knock, and *it shall be opened* unto you.
a'. Amen.

By the way, My Missionary Commission? Chiastic.

Sacramental Prayers

Line-by-line comparison

Bread [B]
Water [W]

a. B: O God, the Eternal Father, we ask thee in the name of thy Son, Jesus Christ,
  W: O God, the Eternal Father, we ask thee in the name of thy Son, Jesus Christ,

b. B: to bless and sanctify this bread
  W: to bless and sanctify this wine

c. B: to the souls of all those who partake of it,
  W: to the souls of all those who drink of it,

d. B: that they may eat in remembrance of the body of thy Son,
  W: that they may do it in remembrance of the blood of thy Son, which was shed for them;

e. B: and witness unto thee,
  W: that they may witness unto thee,

f. B: O God, the Eternal Father,
  W: O God, the Eternal Father,

e'. B: that they are willing to take upon them
  W: [Ellipsis]

f'. B: the name of thy son,
  W: [Ellipsis]

d'. B: and always remember him
  W: that they do always remember him,

c'. B: and keep his commandments which he has given them,
    W: [Ellipsis]

b'. B: that they may <u>always</u> have his Spirit to be with them.
    W: that they may have his Spirit to be with them.

a'. B: Amen.
    W: Amen.

A. <u>O God, the Eternal Father</u>, we ask thee in <u>the name of thy Son</u>, Jesus Christ,
B. to <u>bless and sanctify</u> this *bread*

  C. to <u>the souls</u> of all those who *partake* of it,
  D. that they may <u>eat in remembrance</u> of the <u>body</u> of thy Son,

    E. and *witness* unto thee,
    F. <u>O God, the Eternal Father,</u>
    E'. that they are *willing* to take upon them
    F'. <u>the name of thy son,</u>

  D'. *and* <u>always remember</u> him
  C'. and keep <u>his commandments</u> which he has given them,

B'. that they may *always* <u>have his Spirit</u> to be with them.
A'. <u>Amen.</u>

Principle of Ellipsis . . .

The Standard of Truth

      DHC Vol. 4, page 540, Preface to The Articles of Faith

a. . . . the <u>Standard of Truth</u> has been *erected*;
b. no unhallowed hand can stop <u>the work</u> from *progressing*;

  c1. <u>persecutions</u> *may rage,*
  c2. <u>mobs</u> *may combine,*
  c3. <u>armies</u> *may assemble,*
  c4. <u>calumny</u> *may defame,*
  d. but the <u>truth of God</u> *will go forth*

   e. boldly,
   f. nobly,
   e. and independent,

  d. till <u>it</u> *has* [ellipsis]
  c1. *penetrated* <u>every continent,</u>
  c2. *visited* <u>every clime,</u>
  c3. *swept* <u>every country,</u>
  c4. and *sounded* in <u>every ear,</u>

b. till <u>the purposes of God</u> shall be *accomplished,*
  a. and the <u>Great Jehovah</u> shall say the *work is done.*

The King Follett Discourse

A — <u>God Himself was Once as We are Now</u>
 B — <u>You have got to Learn How to Be Gods Yourselves</u>

  C — <u>You must Begin at the Bottom</u>
   D — <u>The Head God called together the Gods in Grand Council</u>

    E — <u>Element, no Beginning, no End</u>
    F — <u>Man, Self-Existent</u>
    E' — <u>Spirits, no Beginning, no End</u>

   D' — <u>The Greatest Responsibility in this world . . . is to Seek after our Dead</u>
  C' — <u>A Man is his own Tormenter and his own Condemner</u>

 B' — <u>Your Expectations and Hopes are Far Above what Man can Conceive</u>
A' — <u>God dwells in Everlasting Burnings</u>

The night before giving the speech, Joseph advised his brother-in-law that he (Joseph) would give an address the next day which would answer once and for all whether he was a prophet. Still a prophet. IOW, an indication that Joseph knew what would be his subject and content for the following day. I wonder how and how much he planned these marvelous things.

The Living Christ

A — The Birth of Jesus Christ — Matchless Life
B1 — Creator of the Earth
B2 – Follow His Example — Purpose, Potential for Sons and Daughters of God

C/D — Sacrament — All Who Would Ever Live Upon the Earth

C/D — Human History — Only Begotten In the Flesh — Redeemer of the World

    E — He Rose From The Grave — Appeared to Joseph Smith

    F — The Living Christ — "I Am"

    E' — "He Lives! For We Saw Him"

  C/D' — Priesthood and Church Restored Upon the Earth

B1' — He Will Someday Return to Earth

B2' — According to Our Works and the Desires of Our Hearts

A' — The Living Christ — Matchless Gift

    Brought to our attention by my future son-in-law, Scott M. Motley.

The Family

A — The Family is Central to the Creator's Plan

B1 — A Divine Nature and Destiny

B2 — Gender is Essential to Our Eternal Identity and Purpose

  C — Obtain Physical Body & Gain Earthly Experience

  D — Family Relationships Perpetuated Beyond the Grave

    E1 — Sacred Ordinances and Covenants

    E2 – Sacred Powers of Procreation

    F — The Sanctity of Life

    E2' — Sacred Duty

    E1' – The Discharge of these Obligations

  D' — Fathers Preside, Provide; Mothers Nurture as Equal Partners

  C' — Disability, Death, or other Circumstances

B2' – Covenants — Fulfill Family Responsibilities

B1' — Disintegration of the Family

A' — The Family is the Fundamental Unit of Society

Profile of a Prophet by Hugh B. Brown

A — Take the Witness Stand (To Give some Reasons for the Hope I Have)

B — Prepare a Brief on Mormonism (This Great Judge, One of the Most Intellectual)

  C — An Examination for Discovery ("Can you tell me why he doesn't speak?" He does.)

  D — Profile of a Prophet

E — John on the Isle of Patmos, 'The Testimony of Jesus is the Spirit of Prophecy.' (Joseph — Bringing Convincing Evidences)

   F — Translating the Book of Mormon, The Ministry of Christ (Persecute and put to Death)

  E' — Paul, in Athens, "He, whom ye ignorantly worship, declare I unto you." (Joseph – 'I say to you that I saw him, and I talked with him.')

   D' — "He will yet Reveal many Great and Important Things"

  C' — A Challenge to Research and Check

  B' — The Reaction of this Judge, an Intelligent Man ("Do you Appreciate the Import of What you Say?")

A' — Two or Three Reasons Why, I say, I Do Know

Bruce R. McConkie's Final Testimony

A1 — The Most Important Doctrine I can Declare, and the Most Powerful Testimony I can Bear

B — Shall become as their Maker and Sit with Him on his Throne

A2 — I have thereby Heard His Voice and Know His Word

  C1 — Like Eden. . . like Sinai. . . like Calvary

  D — Mighty Michael who Foremost Fell

   E1 — To Annas, to Caiaphas, to Pilot, to Herod, and back to Pilot

   E2 — His Pain Engulfed Body. . . But He Arose from the Sufferings of the Scourge

    F — The Very God of Nature was in Agony

   E1' — Nicodemus and Joseph of Arimathaea

   E2' — He Took Up that Body. . . Rose in that Glorious Immortality

  D' — As Adam is the Father of Mortality so Christ is the Father of Immortality

  C1' — The Three Gardens of God, the Garden of Eden, the Garden of Gethsemane, and the Garden of the Empty Tomb

A1' — By Christ came Immortality and Eternal Life

B' — In the Coming Day I will Feel the Nail Marks in His Hands and in His Feet and shall Wet his Feet with my Tears

A2' — In the Name of the Lord

The Hymn of the Robe of Glory (AKA, Hymn of the Pearl)

A — Dwelt as Child — Content with Nourishers

B1 — Equipped and Sent

B2 — Load large and light — gold, silver, rubies, agates, adamant

B3 — Took off Robe, Toga — wrote it in my heart that it might not be forgotten

C1 — Maishan, Babel, Sarbug

C2 — Straight to the serpent — single and alone

C3 — Dressed in their Dress

D1 — Son of Kings

D2 — Forgot the Pearl

E1 — Cause

E2 — Deep Sleep

E3 — Letter Written, Signed

F — Letter

E3' — Letter Becomes All Speech

E2' — Arose from sleep

E1' — Result

D1' — Son of Royal Parents

D2' — Remembered the Pearl

D1' — Name of my Father, our Second, my Mother

D2' — Snatched the Pearl

C3' — Stripped off Unclean Dress

C2' — Straight to light of our home — my awakener drew me on

C1' — Sarbug, Babel, Maishan

B1' — Robe and Toga Sent

B2' — Garment Mirror of Myself — gold, beryls, rubies, agates, sardonyres, diamond clasps, sapphire — image of King in full all over it

B3' — Poured itself entirely over me — love urged me to run to meet it and receive it

A' — Worshiped the Majesty of my Father

B3' — He had done what he Promised

A' — I mingled with his Princes — with him in His Kingdom

B4' — Further Promise to go with him to our King

Alma 36, Summary outline

A — Give Ear to My Words

B – Trust in God, Supported in Trials, Troubles, Afflictions

C — I Would Not that Ye Think that I Know of Myself

D – I Arose and Stood Up, and Beheld the Angel

E — Coming into the Presence of My God

F – My Mind Caught Hold, I Cried Within My Heart

E' — Nothing so Exquisite and Sweet

D' – Labored without Ceasing (Bring Souls unto Repentance)
C' — The Knowledge which I have is of God

B' – Trust in Him, Supported under Trials, Troubles, Afflictions
A' — According to His Word

Alma 36, Summary outline – extended

A — give ear to <u>my words</u>;

B1 – <u>keep the commandments</u> of God . . . <u>prosper</u> in the land
 B2 — ye should <u>do as I have done,</u>
  B3 — in <u>remembering the captivity</u> of our fathers . . . they were in *bondage,*
  B4 — none could <u>deliver them</u>
  B4 — he surely did <u>deliver them</u> in their *afflictions.*
  B5 — <u>trust</u> in God
   B6 — <u>supported</u> in their *trials*, and their *troubles*, and their *afflictions,*
  B7 — lifted up <u>at the last day</u>

  C1 — <u>God has . . . made these things known</u> unto me

  D4 — I arose and <u>stood up</u>, and beheld the angel.

   E6 — that I could <u>be banished and become extinct</u>
    E5 — that I might not be brought to stand in <u>the presence of my God</u>
    E2 — I was <u>harrowed up by the memory of my many sins</u>

     F1 — <u>I remembered</u> . . . <u>Jesus Christ, a Son of God,</u>
      F2 — the *sins of the world*
       F3 — 18. Now, as *my mind* caught hold upon <u>this thought,</u>
       F3' — I cried within *my heart*: <u>O Jesus, thou Son of God</u>
      F2' — the everlasting *chains of death*
     F1' — when I <u>thought this,</u> I could remember my pains no more

    E2' — I was <u>harrowed up by the memory of my sins</u> *no more.*
    E5' — <u>God sitting upon his throne</u>
   E6' — my soul <u>did long to be there</u>

  D1' — <u>I stood</u> upon my feet

  C' — the <u>knowledge which I have is of God</u>

B6' — <u>supported</u> under *trials* and *troubles* of every kind, yea, and in all manner of *afflictions*;

B5' — I do put my <u>trust</u> in him,

B7' — he will raise me up <u>at the last day</u>, to dwell with him in glory;

B4' – <u>delivered them</u> out of bondage and captivity

B4' — he has also, by his everlasting power, <u>delivered them</u> out of bondage and captivity,

B3' — always retained in <u>remembrance their captivity</u>;

B3' — retain in <u>remembrance</u>, *as I have done,* <u>their captivity</u>.

B2' — ye ought to <u>know as I do know,</u>

B1' — <u>keep the commandments</u> of God . . . <u>prosper</u> in the land;

B1' — not <u>keep the commandments</u> of God . . . shall be cut off from his presence.

A' — this is according to <u>his word</u>.

Gettysburg Address, Outlined per the Davidic Pattern

A -- Our Fathers
B -- Conceived in Liberty

  C -- A Great Civil War
   D -- To Dedicate

    E -- We Cannot Dedicate/Consecrate/Hallow this Ground
     F -- The Brave Men, Living and Dead, Who Struggled Here
    E' -- What They Did Here

   D' -- To Be Dedicated
  C' -- Great Task Remaining Before Us

 B' -- New Birth of Freedom
A' -- The People

Gettysburg Address, Detail per the Davidic Pattern

a. Four score and seven years ago, our fathers *brought forth upon this continent*

a. *a new nation:*

b1. *conceived* in liberty,

b2. and dedicated to the proposition that *all men are created equal.*

c1. Now we are engaged in a great civil war…

c2. *testing*

c3. whether that nation, or any nation so conceived and so dedicated…

c2. can long *endure.*

c1. We are met on a great battlefield of that war.

d1. We have come to dedicate a portion of that field

d2. as *a final resting place*

d3. for those who here gave their lives *that this nation might live.*

e1. It is altogether *fitting and proper* that we should do this.

e2. *But*, in a larger sense, we cannot dedicate… we cannot consecrate…we cannot hallow this ground.

f. The brave men, living and dead,

f. who *struggled* here have *consecrated it,*

f. far above our poor power to add or detract.

e1. The world will *little note, nor long remember*, what we say here,

e2. *but* it can never forget what they did here.

d1. It is for us the living, rather, to be dedicated here

d2. to *the unfinished work*

d3. which they who fought here have thus far *so nobly advanced.*

c1. It is *rather for us to be here dedicated* to the great task remaining before us… that from these honored dead

c2. *we take increased devotion*

c3. to that cause

c2. for which *they gave the last full measure of devotion…*

c1. that *we here highly resolve* that these dead shall not have died in vain…

b2. that this nation, *under God,*

b1. shall have a *new birth* of freedom…

a. and that *government*

a. of the people… by the people… for the people… shall *not perish from this earth.*

Declaration, Summary outline

A — Unanimous Declaration

B — All men are Created Equal; Life, Liberty, and the pursuit of Happiness

   C — Abolishing the Forms
    D — Their Right; Their Duty

    E — Future Security
     F — Patient Sufferance [List of grievances]

A' — Publish and Declare
B' — Free and Independent States

   C' — Political Connection . . . Totally Dissolved
    D' — Full Power; May of Right Do

    E' — Protection of Divine Providence
     F' — Our Lives, Fortunes, Sacred Honor [List of Names]

I Have a Dream, Summary outline

A — The Greatest Demonstration for Freedom

B — The Emancipation Proclamation

   C — An Exile in His Own Land

    D — Honoring This Sacred Obligation

     E — Stand on the Warm Threshold which leads into the Palace of Justice

      F — Our Struggle on the High Plane of Dignity and Discipline

     E' — Justice Rolls Down like Waters and Righteousness like a Mighty Stream

      F' — Veterans of Creative Suffering. … Unearned Suffering is Redemptive

   C' — Let Us not Wallow in the Valley of Despair

    D' — I Have a Dream

   B' — We Will Be Free One Day

A' — Let freedom ring

Inter-Chiastic Analysis: Declaration of Independence, Gettysburg Address, and I Have a Dream

Davidic Pattern	Declaration of Independence	Gettysburg Address	I Have a Dream
A. Words	**A.** Unanimous Declaration	**A.** Our fathers brought forth upon this continent	**A.** The Greatest Demonstration for Freedom
B. Covenants	**B.** All men are created equal... Life, Liberty, and the pursuit of Happiness	**B.** Conceived in liberty... all men are created equal.	**B.** The Emancipation Proclamation
C. The World	**C.** Abolishing the forms	**C.** A great civil war	**C.** An Exile in His Own Land
D. Servants	**D.** Their right...their duty	**D.** To dedicate a portion of that field... for those who... gave their lives	**D.** Honoring This Sacred Obligation
E. Preservation	**E.** Future security	**E.** We should do this. But...we cannot dedicate... cannot consecrate... cannot hallow this ground.	**E.** Stand on the Warm Threshold which leads into the Palace of Justice
F. The Suffering Servant	**F.** Patient sufferance [List of grievances]	**F.** The brave men... who struggled... have consecrated it	**F.** Our Struggle on the High Plane of Dignity and Discipline
F. Atonement	**F.** Our Lives... Fortunes... sacred Honor [List of names]		**F.** Veterans of Creative Suffering; Unearned Suffering is Redemptive
E. Salvation	**E.** Protection of Divine Providence	**E.** What we say here, but...never forget what they did here.	**E.** Justice Rolls Down like Waters and Righteousness like a Mighty Stream
D. Servants	**D.** Full power... may of right do	**D.** To be dedicated...to the unfinished work... they who fought here have thus far so nobly advanced	**D.** I Have A Dream
C. Overcoming the World	**C.** Political connection... totally dissolved	**C.** The great task remaining before us	**C.** Not Wallow in the Valley of Despair
B. Fulfillment	**B.** Free and Independent States	**B.** Under God... a new birth of freedom...	**B.** We Will Be Free One Day
A. Salvation Song	**A.** Publish and declare	**A.** Of the people... by the people... for the people... shall not perish from this earth.	**A.** Let freedom ring

NOTES: 1.) The A thru F structure of the back side of the Declaration of Independence outline has been inverted for ease of comparison to the themes of the other two examples cited above. 2.) Also, the backside F and E of King's "I Have a Dream" have been inverted here for the same reason.

FOOTNOTES

[1] Starting in 1996 we published upwards of 200 examples of the pattern:

- Old Testament: 50+ examples, including the 23rd Psalm

- New Testament: 40+ examples, including the Beatitudes, the Lord's Prayer, the Prodigal Son, the Great Intercessory Prayer, Ask/Receive, Seek/Find, Knock/Opened

- Book of Mormon: 30+ examples, including Alma's Conversion in Alma 36, and Moroni's Promises in Moroni Chapter 10

- Doctrine and Covenants: 30+ examples, including, a Marvelous Work and Wonder in D&C 4, and the Sacramental Prayers in D&C 20;

- Pearl of Great Price: 10 examples, including the Articles of Faith

- Joseph Smith: 50+ examples, including, the King Follett Discourse, and the Standard of Truth

- LDS authors: 50+ examples, including The Living Christ, The Family--A Proclamation to the World, Hugh B. Brown's Profile of a Prophet, and Elder Bruce R. McConkie's Last Talk

- Non-LDS authors: 20+ examples, including Thomas Jefferson's Declaration of Independence, Martin Luther King, Jr.'s I Have a Dream, Abraham Lincoln's Gettysburg Address and 2nd Inaugural, George Washington's 1783 Prayer for the Nation, The Hymn of the Robe of Glory, Patrick Henry's Give Me Liberty or Give Me Death!, Douglas MacArthur's Duty-Honor-Country.

For more about the pattern, see the following URL: www.davidicchiasmus.com.

* See also Harold B. Lee's article in the New Era and other places, "When your heart tells you things your mind does not know." In it he relates, "When we understand more than we know with our minds, when we understand with our hearts, then we know that the Spirit of the Lord is working upon us." (Harold B. Lee, "When Your Heart Tells You Things Your Mind Does Not Know," New Era, June 2002, 46)

CHIASTIC PATTERNS IN THE PLAN OF SALVATION

By Mark A. Shields

When I was a teenager, my sister and I went to tour a home designed and lived in by the legendary American architect, Frank Lloyd Wright. The home was definitely memorable, and I may never forget the experience of touring it that day. But, besides the architectural marvel, I also remember very vividly a teenage guy who was on the tour with us that day. This slick, tasteful young man was sporting a black t-shirt with a print of the Milky Way Galaxy on the front of it, with an arrow pointing to a spot in that cosmic swirl of stars and planets that read, "YOU ARE HERE." That was funny stuff. I laughed, my sister laughed, and I still remember it to this day.

But I think I remember the shirt after all these years for a different reason besides the chuckle it gave my sister and me back in the day. You see, understanding where we truly stand amidst an infinite expanse is, I believe, one of the great purposes of the restored gospel of Jesus Christ. Hugh Nibley taught that the temple in particular exists to help us "get our bearings on the universe."[1] And while it would be correct to say, like that t-shirt, that we "are here" in this infinite expanse, that knowledge really doesn't do us any good if we don't understand where "here" really is, where we are going or how we can get there. Those lessons are also an indispensable part of the Gospel of Jesus Christ.

If it were possible to map eternity any more precisely or helpfully than that young man's t-shirt tried to do as a joke, the best answer we could likely give would be an assured statement that we are on the Earth in our period of mortality. We learned in Primary that we lived in Heaven a long time ago, and we were sent here so that we could become more like our Father in Heaven and return to him if we are worthy. In fact, this Earth was created just for us so that we could do exactly that. These simple, beautiful truths from Primary are very reassuring and instructive to us because, no matter how much else we learn about where we really are in the expanse of eternity, we know that we have a loving Father in Heaven whose eternal home is waiting for us, and a Good Shepherd in our brother Jesus Christ who can take us there if we will just follow Him.

---

[1] Hugh Nibley, *Mormonism and Early Christianity,* p. 358.

With these simple truths understood, there are actually deeper parts of the lesson on where we are that are actually expressed in chiastic patterns throughout the plan of salvation, throughout eternity. These chiastic patterns are a "YOU ARE HERE" marker in the plan of salvation, but they are so much more than that. Besides telling us where we are, these patterns also teach us our origin, or where we came from. That's an essential understanding of any voyage.

Likewise, they teach us our destination – where we can go, or more correctly, where our Heavenly Father and Savior want and invite us to go.

The final lesson taught through chiastic patterns is *how* we can get there. These patterns, by their very nature, emphasize a central or pivotal point that falls in the middle of the pattern. These central points are a lesson of emphasis and instruction, as they often form the central message of the pattern.

I was introduced to chiastic patterns the last two months of my mission in Lisbon, Portugal. My mission president, R. Douglas Holt, taught us some very "cool" things about chiasmus, and, believe me, missionaries love to learn "cool" things like that. But I soon found that chiastic patterns were more than "cool." Not too long after my mission, I bought a copy of the Book of the Mormon that had been reformatted by Donald W. Parry to emphasize all the literary patterns, including chiastic patterns, that could not possibly have been there by accident. With my eyes more open, I began noticing these patterns not just in short phrases in scripture, but throughout God's creations. Like everything else in this glorious gospel, those chiastic patterns point to the Savior Jesus Christ. They show us "where we are" in the eternal scheme of things, where we came from, where we need to go, and even how to get there.

Mortality in Chiasmus

Our mortal life is part of eternity, something even more vast than the Milky Way. Eternity has no beginning and no end, and such an infinite span is very difficult for us to wrap our finite mortal minds around. In the best terms we can define, our mortal life – how and where we are at this moment in eternity – falls right between a pre-mortal and a post-mortal period. Compared to the pre and post-mortal existence in eternity, our period of mortality is a pinprick in the Great Wall of China or the blink of an eye in the history of humanity. Both ends of eternity, if you could call them that, point to mortal life. As a chiasmus, the pattern would look like this:

PRE-MORTAL LIFE

MORTAL LIFE

POST-MORTAL LIFE

This time and space could also be accurately graphed as follows:

PRE-EARTH LIFE

EARTH LIFE

POST-EARTH LIFE

The Book of Mormon teaches the absolute importance of this little pinprick and blink of an eye as the center and pivot point of our eternity. Because mortality is so short in the expanse of eternity, no one can afford to let a moment pass by without recognizing just what mortality is for and treasuring every minute of it.

And the days of the children of men were prolonged, according to the will of God, that they might repent while in the flesh; wherefore, their state became a state of probation, and their time was lengthened according to the commandments which the Lord God gave unto the children of men. For he gave commandment that all men must repent; for he showed unto all men that they were lost, because of the transgression of their parents (2 Nephi 2:21).

True, eternity hinges on the blink of an eye that we call mortality, but that tiny moment in the expanse of eternity is sufficient for us to do our part to fulfill the great plan that our Father in Heaven has laid out for us. And there isn't a minute to spare.

For those whose mortality is cut too short to receive the necessary ordinances of salvation, we can rest assured that a just God will take care of things in the post-mortal life as only a perfect God could do. As Mormon taught about children who died before reaching the age of accountability and therefore did not receive the ordinance of baptism:

But little children are alive in Christ, even from the foundation of the world; if not so, God is a partial God, and also a changeable God, and a respecter to persons; for how many little children have died without baptism!

. . .

Little children cannot repent; wherefore, it is awful wickedness to deny the pure mercies of God unto them, for they are alive in him because of his mercy.

And he that saith that little children need baptism denieth the mercies of Christ, and setteth at naught the atonement of him and the power of his redemption (Moroni 8: 12, 19-20).

The Prophet Joseph Smith also saw the exalted eternal state of these precious little children in a vision. But Joseph saw that these children are not the only ones whose eternity would be blessed, even if their mortality passed without the opportunity to receive the covenants and ordinances of salvation or exaltation. Joseph's vision teaches clearly that those who treasured their time on earth to prepare for eternity – even if they were not allowed access to the saving covenants and ordinances of the gospel – still will inherit the blessings of a celestial eternity.

The heavens were opened upon us, and I beheld the celestial kingdom of God, and the glory thereof, whether in the body or out I cannot tell.

I saw the transcendent beauty of the gate through which the heirs of that kingdom will enter, which was like unto circling flames of fire;

Also the blazing throne of God, whereon was seated the Father and the Son.

I saw the beautiful streets of that kingdom, which had the appearance of being paved with gold.

I saw Father Adam and Abraham; and my father and my mother, my brother Alvin, that has long since slept;

And marveled how it was that he had obtained an inheritance in that kingdom, seeing that he had departed this life before the Lord had set his hand to gather Israel the second time, and had not been baptized for the remission of sins.

Thus came the voice of the Lord unto me, saying: All who have died without a knowledge of this gospel, who would have received it if they had been permitted to tarry, shall be heirs of the celestial kingdom of God;

Also all that shall die henceforth without a knowledge of it, who would have received it with all their hearts, shall be heirs of that kingdom;

For I, the Lord, will judge all men according to their works, according to the desire of their hearts.

And I also beheld that all children who die before they arrive at the years of accountability are saved in the celestial kingdom of heaven (D&C 137:1-10).

From this revelation, we see that everyone's eternity depends on mortality, even those whose mortal lives were not extended in either time or space enough to allow them to receive the covenants and ordinances of the gospel. The point is, it is mortality where "their works" and "the desire of their hearts" are born and grow and written in the book of life.

Therefore, mortality – our period on the Earth – is still an indispensable part of the plan of salvation for every child of God. It is still the center point of the chiasmus of eternity for every member of the family of Adam.

Adam, Mortality, and a Chiasmus

The scriptures themselves begin with the story of the Creation. First, the Earth was created in five creative periods. Then, the sixth creative period followed with the greatest creation of all: Mankind, our first father Adam, and our first mother, Eve.

Not only do the scriptures begin with the story of the Creation and Adam and Eve, but some of the great missionary experiences in the Book of Mormon also begin with the same account (Alma 18:36;

Alma 22:12). Early in the Book of Mormon itself, we read of Lehi's sons going back to Jerusalem to retrieve the brass plates, which were so important because they contained a history of the Creation (1 Nephi 5:11). King Benjamin's great sermon references the Creation from the start (Mosiah 2). Even the Savior's appearance to the Nephites was introduced with a reference to the Creation (3 Nephi 9:15).

What is so important about the Creation and our first parents that it would be the beginning point of so many great missionary and doctrinal lessons? Quite simply, our first parents' story is *our* story. They are meant to represent us. Their journey from being with God in the Garden of Eden, to being cast out of the Garden, and ultimately back to the presence of God, as shown in Joseph Smiths' vision in Section 138, is our journey as well. Their names and the names of the places in their journey may be different, but they are most definitely our role models.

Adam is also unique because he is revealed in the scriptures and other places as having a second name. The Doctrine and Covenants teaches that Adam's post-mortal name is Michael (D&C 27:11; 78:16).

The Prophet Joseph Smith and the Apostle Bruce R. McConkie have also taught that Adam's *pre*-mortal name is likewise Michael.[1] [2]

Following the same pre and post-mortal chiasmus pattern that centers on mortality, Adam's name progression also reveals a chiastic pattern:

MICHAEL – Pre-mortal name

ADAM – Mortal name

MICHAEL – Post-mortal name

This center point is again a lesson about mortality.

But there is yet another very important chiastic lesson found in the Hebrew meanings for Adam's names. You see, in the native language of the Old Testament, the name "Adam" is not just a name, but it is also a title. More specifically, it is the Hebrew word for mankind.[3] Pehaps equally important, Eve's name is the feminine adjective for "living,"[4] a fitting name for the mother of all living (Genesis 3:20).

Likewise, "Michael" is not just a name. In Hebrew, it quite literally means "who is like God."[5]

As Adam progressed through the pre-mortal life, mortality, and then to post-mortal life, where the Doctrine and Covenants assures us that he has received celestial glory (D&C 137:5), his name was changed in a way that teaches us of our own position in the expanse of eternity. Remember, his story is

---

[1] Joseph Fielding Smith, *Teachings of the Prophet Joseph Smith*, p. 157.

[2] Bruce R. McConkie, *Doctrines of the Restoration*, p. 84.

[3] James Strong, *Strong's Exhaustive Concordance of the Bible*, Hebrew word 120.

[4] James Strong, *Strong's Exhaustive Concordance of the Bible*, Hebrew word 2332.

[5] James Strong, *Strong's Exhaustive Concordance of the Bible*, Hebrew word 4317.

ours. If he is the prototype human whose name reflects on all of mankind, we can rest assured that we too have been, and therefore may become, like God, following Adam's progression and example.

Here we see another chiastic pattern that teaches us of our divine origin as children of God, one more lesson on where we currently are in eternity, and where and how we may become:

MICHAEL – Who is like God

    ADAM – Mankind

MICHAEL – Who is like God

Combining these two chiastic patterns of the prototype man, we see:

MICHAEL – Who is like God – Pre-mortal man

    ADAM – Mankind in mortality on Earth

MICHAEL – Who is like God – Post-mortal man

In what ways was Adam like God in the pre-mortal existence? For one, he was placed on Earth as a child of God, just like us. After all, all children are like their parents if for no other reason than their parents' blood and genetic makeup they carry. Indeed, every prince or princess, as the son or daughter of a king and queen, is no less than a king or queen in waiting.

Adam and Eve were also created in the express image of God (Genesis 1:26-27). The Hebrew word carrying this concept is so direct that it literally means to create an exact duplicate of the original, just as a modern photocopy machine would do with a document.

For all of the divine nature in our first parents (and therefore in each of us) they were still not yet like God in so many other ways. They were not yet tried and tested. They were sorely in need of mortality – the period of Adam and mankind – to become more like God through sweat, work, heartache, and enduring to the end.

But in the end, Adam's progression from Michael to Adam to Michael teaches not just where mankind began, but where mankind may return: Being like God. The Savior in fact commanded all men to follow the Michael-Adam-Michael progression and be like God (Matthew 5:48; 3 Nephi 11:48; 3 Nephi 27:27).

Adam, the Atonement, and Chiasmus

Many times in mortality we are reminded of just how *unlike* God we are. The scriptures are filled with examples of man's sinful nature that makes it very easy to forget who our Father truly is and what we stand to inherit from Him. While the divine nature of our Eternal Father is in us, something must happen here in mortality to help us refine our divine nature and make the return to being like God.

At what point do we cease being so unlike God and begin the transition back to being like God?

King Benjamin teaches that "the natural man is an enemy to God, and has been from the fall of Adam, and will be, forever and ever, unless he yields to the enticings of the Holy Spirit, and putteth off the natural man and becometh a saint through the atonement of Christ the Lord" (Mosiah 3:19). In other words, Adam or mankind will drift further and further away from being like God unless and until he: (A) yields to the enticings of the Holy Ghost; (B) puts off the natural man; (C) becomes a saint through the Atonement of Christ the Lord.

Simply put, the process of following the Spirit, becoming humble, resisting temptation and applying the Atonement is where Adam begins facing a holy direction so that he can again become like God.

As a chiasmus, the pattern looks like this:

MICHAEL – Who is like God

    ADAM – Mankind in mortality before beginning to apply the Atonement

    CHRIST – The Atonement reverses the Fall

    ADAM – Mankind in mortality after beginning to apply the Atonement

MICHAEL – Mankind having applied the Atonement and again being like God

The Savior is the center of this chiastic pattern. In our "YOU ARE HERE" example of eternity, the picture now becomes a little more meaningful and helpful, as we see not just where we came from, where we are, and where we can return, but, at last, where we need to look in order to reach our destination. "And we talk of Christ, we rejoice in Christ, we preach of Christ, we prophesy of Christ, and we write according to our prophecies, that our children may know to what source they may look for a remission of their sins" (2 Nephi 25:26). When we begin to look to that source and apply the Atonement, we begin the journey back to being like God.

Adam and Priesthood Keys

Adam's history also parallels the history of priesthood keys on the Earth. Adam was the first holder of the priesthood here on Earth. From him, the priesthood was passed to his posterity. "The order of this priesthood was confirmed to be handed down from father to son, and rightly belongs to the literal descendants of the chosen seed, to whom the promises were made. This order was instituted in the days of Adam, and came down by lineage in the following manner: From Adam to Seth, who was ordained by Adam . . . " (D&C 107:40-42). From there, the priesthood in this patriarchal order was passed down to Enos, Cainan, Mahaleel, Jared, Enoch, Methuselah, and Lamech (D&C 107:47-51).

This group of patriarchs and priesthood key holders met with Adam at what had to be the greatest priesthood meeting of the dispensation (D&C 107:53-56).

This great priesthood meeting at Adam-ondi-Ahman was a foreshadowing of the great priesthood meeting that will accompany the Savior's return.

> Daniel in his seventh chapter speaks of the Ancient of Days; he means the oldest man, our Father Adam, Michael, he will call his children together and hold a council with them to prepare them for the coming of the Son of Man. He (Adam) is the father of the human family, and presides over the spirits of all men, and all that have had the keys must stand before him in this grand council. . . . The Son of Man stands before him, and there is given him glory and dominion. Adam delivers up his stewardship to Christ, that which was delivered to him as holding the keys of the universe, but retains his standing as the head of the human family.[1]

Not surprisingly, this history of priesthood keys is also a chiasmus. The priesthood keys began on Earth with Adam. They were then passed to his posterity. And they will ultimately be returned to him when the Lord takes His personal return to Earth.

ADAM – Holder of priesthood keys

   FAMILY OF ADAM – Receiving keys from Adam

ADAM AS MICHAEL – Keys returned at Adam-ondi-Ahman

In a very real way, the history of the priesthood on Earth coincides with Adam. All of the children of Adam have been blessed by the priesthood keys that were passed through the hands of Adam. He stands at the head of the human family as its first priesthood holder. We ultimately received our mortal life through him, just as we ultimately received priesthood keys in mortality from him.

But there really is one more person at both the beginning and ending of the chiastic history of the priesthood. It is the Savior Himself.

   CHRIST – The pre-mortal Great High Priest

      ADAM –

         FAMILY OF ADAM -

      ADAM AS MICHAEL –

   CHRIST – The post-mortal Great High Priest returned to Earth

Adam, the Garden of Eden and a Chiasmus

Our chiastic lessons from our first parents are not quite over yet. Adam and Eve's experience in the Garden of Eden also reveals another chiastic pattern. When Adam and Eve were placed in the Garden of Eden, they were told that they were free to eat from every tree in the garden, with one exception

---

[1] Joseph Fielding Smith, *Teachings of the Prophet Joseph Smith*, p. 157.

(Moses 3:16, 17). If they ate from the tree of knowledge of good and evil, they were told that strict consequences would follow (Moses 3:17). Since every tree but this one was available with no negative consequence, it's safe to assume that Adam and Eve were allowed to eat from the tree of life before the Fall. For all we know, this might have been their favorite fruit that they ate regularly.

Symbolically speaking, to eat from the tree of life is to enjoy the presence of God[1], and to eat from the tree of knowledge of good and evil is to enter mortality (2 Nephi 2:23).

But, as we know, after Adam and Eve ate from the tree of knowledge of good and evil, they were not worthy to enjoy the presence of God because they had transgressed. If they had eaten from the tree of life in their fallen state, their judgment day would have been accelerated, and they would have been brought back to the presence of God unworthily, without a chance to repent and grow. As Alma taught, they would have had "no preparatory state" (Alma 12:26). To borrow from our last chiastic pattern of Michael – Adam – Michael, they would have been stuck as imperfect Adam for eternity without the chance to learn, grow and progress with a proper mortality.

As we are told, this would have frustrated the plan of salvation (Alma 12:26), whose whole goal is to bring to pass the immortality and eternal life of man (Moses 1:39).

So, while mankind began prior to mortality with free access to the tree of life, eating of the tree of knowledge of good and evil made them unworthy to eat of the tree of life.

But it remained their goal – and the purpose of all mankind – to eat of the tree of life again one day, for the tree of life represents the presence of God.

In these two trees from the Garden of Eden, we have another chiastic pattern that represents man's origin, his current state, and his divine potential.

TREE OF LIFE – In the Garden of Eden

TREE OF KNOWLEDGE OF GOOD AND EVIL

TREE OF LIFE – The presence of God

At each end of mankind's existence stands the tree of life. In the middle stands the tree of knowledge of good and evil of which we all partake in one way or another each day in mortality. The lesson again in this "YOU ARE HERE" chiastic lesson is where we came from, where we are, where we may return, and the pivotal importance of living each day where we are to prepare to meet God and eat of the tree of life again. If we spend our mortality in search of the tree of life, living each day and preparing to partake of it again, the cherubim and their flaming swords guarding it will one day be seen as our friends and not our enemies.

---

[1]"The Tree of life in Ancient Cultures," C. Wilfred Griggs, *Ensign*, June, 1988.

Saving Ordinances and Chiasmus

With a firm understanding of our divine origin and divine potential, the question then becomes, what do we do to be worthy to partake of the tree of life, to make the transition from Adam back to Michael? The Third Article of Faith gives us the key clearly and unmistakably: By obedience to the laws and ordinances of the gospel, we gain access to the Atonement of Jesus Christ. It is the key to washing away our sins and receiving the blessings of eternity.

Meanwhile, the Fourth Article of Faith tells us more specifically what those ordinances are and what we need to do to receive them: Exercise faith in the Lord Jesus Christ, repent, be baptized by immersion for the remission of sins, and receive the gift of the Holy Ghost.

On this subject, the Savior taught the absolute necessity of being born again, as taught in the Fourth Article of Faith.

Verily, verily, I say unto thee, Except a man be born again, he cannot see the kingdom of God.

Nicodemus saith unto him, How can a man be born when he is old? can he enter the second time into his mother's womb, and be born?

Jesus answered, Verily, verily, I say unto thee, Except a man be born of water and of the Spirit, he cannot enter into the kingdom of God.

That which is born of the flesh is flesh; and that which is born of the Spirit is spirit.

Marvel not that I said unto thee, Ye must be born again (John 3:3-7).

Here, the Savior teaches of a physical birth and then re-birth, of water and the Spirit. Was He speaking of physical birth? Yes. Was He speaking of rebirth through baptism? No doubt.

[I]nasmuch as ye were born into the world by water, and blood and the spirit, which I have made, and so became of dust a living soul, even so ye must be born again into the kingdom of heaven, of water, and of the Spirit, and be cleansed by blood, even the blood of mine Only Begotten; that ye might be sanctified from all sin, and enjoy the words of eternal life in this world, and eternal life in the world to come, even immortal glory (Moses 6:59).

Our physical birth came through the emblems of water, blood and the spirit. Our rebirth at baptism likewise comes through the emblems of the water in which we are immersed and the Spirit that is poured out when we are confirmed and receive the gift of the Holy Ghost. These ordinances and their accompanying covenants give us access to the atoning blood of the Savior.

But baptism and confirmation alone do not carry us through mortality back to the tree of life. There are other births of water and the Spirit that are likewise essential to returning to the tree of life.

Each Sunday, members of the Church of Jesus Christ of Latter-day Saints partake of the sacrament. They eat the bread to remind them of the Savior's torn body. They drink the water to remind them of the Savior's blood, which was shed for them. They promise to always remember Him. In return, they are promised to have His spirit with them (D&C 20:77, 79; Moroni 4:3; Moroni 5:2). Here we have again a very real birth of water and the Spirit.

The books of Exodus and Leviticus speak of yet another birth of water and the Spirit, this one related to the ancient tabernacle or portable temple of the Israelites. "And Aaron and his sons thou shalt bring to the door of the tabernacle of the congregation, and shalt wash them with water. . . . Then shalt thou take the anointing oil, and pour it upon his head, and anoint him" (Exodus 28:4, 7). *See also* Leviticus 8:6, 10-12. In a similar reference, the Savior taught about such a washing, "If I wash thee not, thou hast no part with me. Simon Peter saith unto him, Lord, not my feet only, but also my hands and my head" (John 13:8-9). Likewise, the Lord has revealed that anointing and washing ordinances are part of the restored temple ordinances (D&C 128:39), which ordinances "had been hid from before the world was" (D&C 124:38; 41).

The washing with water is easy to see as a birth of water, if it is essential for us to "have part with" the Savior, as He told Peter.

But what of the anointing with oil? How does it fit as part of a birth of water and the Spirit? Quite simply, oil is a scriptural symbol for the Holy Ghost.[1] Anointing with oil is the essential other half of this birth of water and the Spirit that is central to our returning to the tree of life.

From our mortal birth, to baptism, to the sacrament, to the washings and anointings, we have yet another chiastic pattern of ordinances, of births and rebirths:

PHYSICAL BIRTH

    BAPTISM AND CONFIRMATION

        SACRAMENT

    WASHINGS AND

ANOINTINGS

In this "YOU ARE HERE" map taught through chiasmus, we find ourselves again right in the middle, never more than a few days away from promising again to always remember the Savior so that we may have His Spirit to be with us. Hopefully we are in the very act of keeping that covenant right here and now.

This is yet another pattern within this pattern that reflects not just the importance of the sacrament each week, but the principle of always remembering the Savior and having His Spirit to be with us. You see, in our physical birth, baptism and washings and anointings, the water is *external*. It

---

[1] Joseph Fielding McConkie & Donald W. Parry, *A Guide to Scriptural Symbols*, p. 88.

surrounds us or is applied outwardly. In the sacrament, the water is *internal*. We take it unto ourselves, all so that the Spirit can likewise dwell within us.

> **PHYSICAL BIRTH** – Born into the world surrounded by water
>
> **BAPTISM** – Buried and immersed in water
>
> **SACRAMENT** – Water taken *inside* of us
>
> **WASHINGS AND**
>
> **ANOINTINGS** – Washed outwardly with water

There is something about each ordinance in this chiastic pattern that is designed to place the Spirit of the Lord inside of us, but particularly so with the sacrament. If we keep our sacramental covenant of always remembering Him so that we may keep the commandments He's given us, we are promised that we will have His Spirit to be with us. When Jeremiah taught of a "new covenant with the house of Israel, and with the house of Judah," it was an *inward* covenant, not just an *external* ordinance. "But this shall be the covenant that I will make with the house of Israel; After those days, saith the Lord, I will put my law in their inward parts, and write it in their hearts; and will be their God, and they shall be my people" (Jeremiah 31:33). This process of becoming the Lord's people is based on having his law inside of us, deep in our hearts. If that law is truly in our hearts, it will form the basis not just of who we are but all that we do.

The ordinances of birth and rebirth – of progressing from Adam to Michael, and of moving from the tree of knowledge of good and evil back to the tree of life – are a deep and abiding lesson about taking and keeping the law of the Lord and His Spirit deep inside of us. It should surprise no one that these lessons come to us through chiasmus.

Chiasmus in Applying the Atonement

The first saving ordinance of the Gospel of Jesus Christ is baptism, the first birth of water and the Spirit essential to our salvation. In receiving this ordinance, we take upon ourselves the name of Christ (D&C 20:37. *See also* Mosiah 4:12; 26:18; Alma 5:38; 3 Nephi 27:6; D&C 18:21-25). In other words, our journey back to the Father comes through the act of taking upon ourselves the Savior's name. We apply the Atonement as we take upon ourselves the Savior's name. We further reap the benefits of the Atonement as we honor His name, taken upon ourselves.

As we must take upon ourselves the name of Christ to put the Atonement into practice in our lives, Christ took upon Himself our sins in working the Atonement. So, as the Savior suffered pain beyond mortal comprehension for all the children of Adam, would it not make sense that for some period of time – no matter how short but exquisitely painful – He suffered individually for each of our names as well? If He did not actually take upon Himself *our* name, He surely suffered for the sake of our name as He bled in Gethsemane and hung on the cross in Golgotha. As He knows each of His sheep by name, His suffering was surely associated with our name individually.

In that sense, His suffering for our name's sake should bring new meaning to our taking upon ourselves *His* name.

The chiasmus here is a straight A-to-A-prime pattern:

Baptism – Taking upon ourselves the name of Christ

Atonement – Christ taking upon Himself the sins of our name.

The Earth's Temporal History and Chiasmus

Not only do the chiastic patterns of Adam, Eve and mortality vividly portray the absolute importance of our period of mortality, the Atonement, and the covenants and ordinances that bring us the blessings of the Atonement, but the history of the Earth itself also points to this same period we find ourselves in today, and, by no surprise, to the Savior.

Consider the Earth's creation and history. The Earth was created in a celestial state and dwelt with God. This describes a celestial state (D&C 76:62).

After this, when Adam and Eve were placed in the Garden of Eden, the Earth and its inhabitants had a partial presence of God, but not a full presence. This describes a terrestrial state (D&C 76:77).

After the Fall, the Earth became a telestial dwelling.

With the Millennium, the Earth will be renewed to a terrestrial state. After that, the Earth will return to a celestial state. As Joseph Fielding Smith Jr. wrote, "When our Savior comes, the earth will be changed to a terrestrial condition and will then be made the fit abode for terrestrial beings, and this condition will last until after the close of the millennium when the earth will die and be raised again in a resurrection to receive its glory as a celestial body, which is its final state."[1]

As a chiasmus, this pattern looks like this:

CELESTIAL STATE

    TERRESTRIAL STATE

TELESTIAL STATE (our mortality)

    TERRESTRIAL STATE

CELESTIAL STATE

Once again, our period of mortality, the current telestial state of our Mother Earth, is the focal

---

[1] Joseph Fielding Smith, *Doctrines of Salvation*, Vol. 1, p. 84.

point of the pattern. This is yet another lesson of the importance of mortality.

The Earth's Temporal History, Christ, and Chiasmus

While the Earth is comprised of eternal matter, its temporal existence is defined as comprising seven thousand years (D&C 77:7). Many prophecies of Christ refer to his coming in the "meridian [mid-point] of time" (Moses 5:57; 6:57, 62; 7:46). This time represents the true "high noon" of the earth's history. Not only is it the mid-point, it is the pinnacle. "The meridian of time is the middle or high point of that portion of eternity which is considered to be mortal time. Since Christ lived, ministered, and worked out the Atonement in time's meridian, such era was truly the high point of history."[1]

As a chiasmus, it looks like this:

FIRST THOUSAND YEARS

SECOND THOUSAND YEARS

THIRD THOUSAND YEARS

FOURTH THOUSAND YEARS

FIFTH THOUSAND YEARS

SIXTH THOUSAND YEARS

SEVENTH THOUSAND YEARS

The center point of this pattern is again the Savior Christ, who came at the end of the fourth millennium, or the meridian of time. Elder James E. Talmage has dated the birth of the Savior at April 6, 1 B.C.[2] Presidents Harold B. Lee[3] and Spencer W. Kimball[4] have made similar statements. With these temporal coordinates, there are three millennia on each end of the Savior's advent, pointing to His first coming. Christ's first advent is significantly placed in the fourth of seven millennia, the middle of the chiasmus.

As eternity centers around this time of probation spent on the earth, this time of probation, in turn, centers on Christ.

---

[1] Bruce R. Mcconkie, *Mormon Doctrine,* p. 486.

[2] James E. Talmage, *Jesus the Christ*, p. 104.

[3] *Ensign*, May 1973.

[4] *Ensign*, May 1980.

The Earth's History, the Bible, and Chiasmus

The Bible and its divisions or "testaments" as we call them also form a chiastic pattern. "Testament" (as in Old and New Testament) is the identical word as "covenant" in the Greek language. One of Christ's many titles is the "Mediator of the New Covenant" (D&C 76:69). He is the one to whom the covenants (the Old and New Testaments) point. He is the one who brings the testaments and covenants together.

As a chiasmus, the testaments / covenants look like this:

OLD TESTAMENT / COVENANT

    CHRIST'S BIRTH AND LIFE

NEW TESTAMENT / COVENANT

The coming of our Lord divides the Old and New Testament, just as it divides our reckoning of time between the period of BC, meaning "before Christ," and AD, meaning *anno domini* or "the year of our Lord." Both testaments testify of and point to Christ.

Now consider the primary languages of these Old and New Testaments. The Old Testament comes to us primarily from Hebrew, which reads from right to left, or from east to west if we orient ourselves to the north. The New Testament comes to us primarily through Greek, which reads from left to right, from west to east. As a different kind of chiasmus, it looks like this:

    OLD TESTAMENT - HEBREW

    THE SAVIOR'S COMING

NEW TESTAMENT – GREEK

This pattern is not the typical left side of the chi we might expect in a chiasmus. Instead, it's the right half in the upper register meeting the left half in the lower register, reading from right to left, from east to west. Either way, the halves or the testaments converge in and around the Savior.

The Hebrew Calendar and Chiasmus

The Jewish calendar is remarkable in that it has two separate beginnings and reckoning points: An ecclesiastical reckoning and a civil reckoning. The ecclesiastical calendar begins with the month known as Nisan, while the civil calendar begins with the month Tishri. Nisan is believed by some to be the month or the time at which the universe was created, while Tishri is held in tradition to be the time Adam and Eve were created. While Nisan is the first month on the ecclesiastical calendar, it is the seventh month on the civil calendar. Likewise, Tishri is the first month on the civil calendar and the seventh month on the ecclesiastical calendar. The seventh month was usually the middle point of the year except that the Jewish calendar sometimes had a thirteenth month for the same reason we have leap years under our Gregorian calendar (a full year is not perfectly divisible in whole numbers of days).

The significant Hebrew holy times were based around Nisan and Tishri. Passover falls in Nisan, and Pentecost falls 50 days after Passover (and therefore is reckoned from Nisan). The last of these three major celebrations and holy times, the Feast of Tabernacles falls in Tishri.

If we were to graph these ecclesiastical and civil calendars in chiastic form, it would look like this, with Nisan at the beginning of the ecclesiastical calendar and Tishri at the chiastic center:

Ecclesiastical Calendar

   NISAN

   TISHRI

   ADAR[1]

Now consider the civil calendar mapped chiastically:

Civil Calendar

TISHRI

   NISAN

ELUL[2]

Here, the roles are reversed, with Tishri as the head of the civil calendar and Nisan as the chiastic center. Now, as the two calendars are overlapped, they form a perfect chiasmus, with each chief month forming the other calendar's chiastic center.

NISAN		**TISHRI**	
	TISHRI	**NISAN**	
ADAR		**ELUL**	

This center point is yet another lesson on the Savior. Christ is both a priest and a king, both an ecclesiastical and a civil ruler. He stands at the both the head and the middle of each reckoning of time.

---

[1]This was the twelfth month of the ecclesiastical year and sixth month of the civil year. To account for a full year, a thirteenth month, Adar II or Veadar was periodically added.

[2]This was the sixth month of the year on the ecclesiastical calendar and the twelfth month of the year on the civil calendar.

Under both methods of measuring temporal existence, the Lord is both the beginning and the focal point.

Why Christ?

Where are we? Where did we come from? Where are we going? Our state, our origin and our potential – all of those terrible questions – are answered in the chiastic patterns of the plan of salvation. "WE ARE HERE" in mortality, half-way on a journey from our Heavenly Father and, hopefully, back to Him.

But even the answers to these questions won't help us without one more essential question to answer: How do we get there? That answer is also taught in the chiastic patterns of the plan of salvation: By obedience to the laws and ordinances of the Gospel, by faith in the Lord Jesus Christ, and by repentance made possible through Him.

In the chiastic patterns observed in this chapter, we see two common centerpieces in which the patterns come together: Mortality and the Savior. Mortality is our crucible, our proving ground for eternity. And Christ is the key to our mortality and, therefore, to our *eternity.* Spending mortality in pursuit of His teachings, His example, His qualities, and His gospel will lead us back to Him and to the Father.

As Paul taught of the Savior, "And he is before all things, and by him all things consist" (Colossians 1:17). This word "consist" may also be correctly translated as "hold together." In Christ, the chiastic patterns of the plan of salvation *come* together. By no coincidence, in Christ, all things and all eternity *hold* together. Every detail of every chiastic lesson affirms this simple, beautiful, priceless truth.

CHRIST AS BRIDEGROOM: THE OVERARCHING CHIASM

Lenet Read

Christ as a Bridegroom is the most pervasive and illuminating symbol in the Bible. Considering the great gap between God and man, God's lowering Himself to such a symbol is astonishing. Yet the Lord consistently couched His covenants in terms of this most intimate human relationship. In doing so, He portrayed the deepest love, the awesome beauty, and the breathtaking equality offered in His great work of salvation.

Even more, the Lord revealed His Bridegroom imagery in a chiastic structure, which magnifies its power. He began Biblical events with several witnesses that He would be to us as Bridegroom. He continually reinforced and elaborated on that concept through other events, such as the covenant made at Sinai, and through similitudes and prophecy. When He came as the Christ, He related His words and actions to His role as Bridegroom and to real wedding traditions. This was easy, for the Israelites had *patterned* their wedding traditions after the covenant relationship He, Jehovah, had set. [1]

Jesus Christ's atonement was *the* most critical of all turning points, affecting every man's destiny. This turning point was blazoned with Bridegroom symbolism. And John's "Revelation" shows the Savior's final works will mirror and magnify the Bridegroom/bride panorama first laid out in Genesis.

These are the essentials of a true chiasm. In fact, *it is highly likely that Christ as Bridegroom, with the Turning Point as The Atonement, is the overarching pattern upon which all other Christ-focused chiasmus are based.*

The first half of the chiasm is found in the Old Testament and The Gospels, until the Turning Point of The Atonement. The second half of the chiasm repeats Bridegroom imagery to be fulfilled by

---

End Notes:

[1] Marvin R. Wilson, *Our Father Abraham, Jewish Roots of the Christian Faith,* (Grand Rapids, MI: William B. Eerdman's Publishing Company and Dayton, Ohio: Center for Judaic-Christian Studies, 1989), p. 203.

Christ *after* His Atonement. They are mostly, though not completely, shown in John's "Revelation," which places the bulk of Christ's fulfillment at His Return. However, in other New Testament writings we find parallels of other aspects of the Bridegroom's promises. Importantly, many point to fulfillment in the Restoration.

A. Bounteous dwelling (Eden)	**A' A Far Greater Dwelling**
B. Tree of life; Fountain of waters	**B' More Fruits from Tree; Fountains**
C. Bridegroom reigns	**C' BG to reign with Bride at His side**
D. Bride comes from Bridegroom's side; One	**D' BG to lift Bride up to side**
E. Bride takes Bridegroom's name	**E' Bride to take BG's name**
F. Bride eats forbidden fruit	**F' Bride drinks cup of consummation**
G. Bride to be cast out of God's presence	**G' Bride to re-enter God's presence**
H. Bridegroom to take Bride's guilt	**H' BG to bear Bride's stains**
I. Bridegroom provides covering	**I' BG to provide glorious garments**
J. Bridegroom and Bride cast out	**J' Serpent to be cast out**
K. Bridegroom covenants Home & Seed	**K' Bridegroom prepares Home & Seed**
L. Covenant to be sealed with sacrifice	**L' Sacrifice obtains Christ's covenant**
M. Bridegroom gives waters at well	**M' Bride to give living waters**
N. Plagues, sacrifice free Bride from bondage	**N' Plagues to bring out Final Bride**
O. Bridegroom & Bride betrothed	**O'**
P. Bride is unfaithful	**P' Gentile Bride will be unfaithful**
Q. Bridegroom covenant to Gentiles	**Q' Bridegroom covenants with Gentiles**
R. Bridegroom gives covering for bride	**R' BG's covering lets enter holiest place**
S. Bridegroom purchases bride	**S' Bride to remember she is purchased**
T. Whore cast down	**T' Whore to be cast down**
U. Bridegroom to redeem unfaithful Bride	**U' Former Bride to be redeemed**
V. Bridegroom meets bride at well	**V' BG promises to send waters to Bride**
W. Bridegroom renews covenant	**W' Covenant reviewed to faltering Bride**

X The Atonement

Christ fulfills Bridegroom symbolism as shown in the first half of the chiasm
1. BG offers [cup of] covenant; 2. Bride accepts covenant; 3. BG prays/ works for Oneness;

4. BG purchases Bride; 5. Bride covers Bride; 6. Bride comes from BG side;

7. BG opens Bridal Chamber; 8. Union of BG and Bride; 9. BG meets B at Well; 10. Fruitfulness

Now that we see the overall chiasm, here are the clarifying details.

The Beginning of the Chiasm (For ease in publishing, chiastic points are not in X form.)

A. Bounteous dwelling is created in Eden (Genesis 1:1-25).

B. Eden is gifted with tree of life and living waters (Genesis 2:9-10).

C. The Bridegroom reigns. (Gen 2:15). Adam was a "figure" of Christ (Romans 5:14).

D. The Bride comes from Bridegroom's side; they are One.

E. Bride takes Bridegroom's name; "Woman" taken from "Man" (Gen. 2:23).

F. Bride eats forbidden fruit (Gen 3:1-6). Some Jewish writings say the forbidden fruit

was the grape.[1] The blood of the Savior is likened to wine. It is a chiastic reversal when the fruit cursing mankind becomes its instrument of salvation.

G. Bride to be cast out of God's presence.

H. Bridegroom takes upon himself Bride's guilt (Genesis 3:6, 17).[2]

I. Bridegroom provides a covering for nakedness (Gen. 3:21). While Adam first
emulates the Bridegroom's role, the Lord Himself established this "covering" pattern. By providing a covering, He established a vital role for Israel's Bridegroom.

J. Bridegroom and Bride cast out (Genesis 3:23-4).

K. Bridegroom promises Home and Seed (Gen. 13:15-16). Jehovah covenants

a Heavenly Home and Eternal Seed.[3]

L. Covenant is sealed with blood sacrifice. The Lord solemnized His covenant

by blood sacrifice (Gen 15:9-18), as witness that the breaking of this covenant would

require the shedding of blood [4] (Jeremiah 34:18-20).

M. Bridegroom gives waters of life to bride at a well. Isaac, Jacob and

Moses (Gen. 24:10-51; 29:1-20; Ex. 2:16-21) *all* obtained their brides at wells. In

the latter two cases, the bridegroom removed a stone sealing the well.

N. Plagues and sacrifice free Bride from bondage (Ex. 6-12). Plagues and a blood

sacrifice free Israel to make covenants with the Bridegroom at Mount Sinai.

O. Bridegroom and Bride are betrothed (Ex. 19-20, 24). The covenant at Sinai was a betrothal.[5] Israel was "sanctified" or set apart for the Lord. (Ex. 19:10-11). A betrothal

was considered as sacred as the marriage. Consequences for infidelity were grave.

---

[1]. Hugh Nibley, *Abraham in Egypt* (Salt Lake City: Deseret Book, 1981), 156.

[2] Many miss this meaning in Adam's story. It is one of three levels of meaning. 1. The real events of the historical Adam and Eve. 2. Adam's representation of each of us. 3. Adam as a figure of Christ (Romans 5:14; Ephesians 5:30-32). We miss significant meaning if we do not understand the witnesses here relating to Christ.

[3] McConkie, Bruce R., *Mormon Doctrine*, (Salt Lake City: Bookcraft, 1966) p. 237-238.

[4]. Wilson, *Our Father Abraham*, 206.

[5]. Wilson, *Our Father Abraham*, 205

P. Betrothed proved unfaithful. Prophets called Israel *harlot/adulteress*. "…I sware unto thee, and entered into a covenant with thee, saith the Lord God, and thou becamest mine… And thy renown went forth among the heathen for thy beauty … But thou didst trust in thine own beauty, and playest the harlot" (Ezekiel 16:8,14-15).

Q. Bridegroom's love would extend to Gentiles. Boaz was a similitude of Christ as Bridegroom. He did so by wedding Ruth, a Gentile, who accepted Israel's God.

R. Bridegroom again provides covering for bride. Boaz also covered Ruth with his skirt (Ruth 3:1-9), further testifying of God's role as Bridegroom. "…I spread my skirt over thee, and covered thy nakedness" (Ezekiel 16:8).

S. Bridegroom purchased bride. Boaz paid a bride price for Ruth. "Moreover Ruth … have I purchased to be my wife, to raise up the name of the dead" (Ruth 4:10).

T. Whore, who causes Israel to break covenant, is cast down. Jezebel caused Israel to break covenant (I Kings 16:31-33). She is overcome (2 Kings 9:30-37).

U. Bridegroom will again bring fruitfulness to faithless Bride. "Sing, O barren, thou that didst not bear; … For a small moment have I forsaken thee; but with great mercies will I gather thee" (Isaiah 54:4-8).[1]

The True Bridegroom Appears

The chiasm draws near its center. When Jesus came, His words and works were deliberately set to identify Himself as the Bridegroom.

V. Bridegroom meets bride at a well. He came as Bridegroom to Jacob's well to offer waters of everlasting life (John 4:14). The Samaritan woman received Him.

W. Bridegroom renews the wedding contract (Matthew 5). The Sermon on the Mount was a higher form of the betrothal offered at Sinai.[2] The Bridegroom had come. Who among Israel possessed the necessary light to receive Him? (Matthew 25:1-13).

The Turning Point, When the Bride Is Redeemed and Obtained

The turning point was The Atonement; its central focus was the cross. Remember, *chiasm means cross*. This real chiasm truly turned upon a cross! In reality, Christ's atoning work stretched from the Last Supper through the Resurrection. Because there are so many subtle, powerful meanings to the

---

[1]. Those given are not the only bridegroom images, but the most important.

[2]. John W. Welch, *Illuminating the Sermon at the Temple and the Sermon on the Mount* (Provo, UT: Foundation for Ancient Research and Mormon Studies at Brigham Young University, 1999), 26-32. Welch shows how the Sermon on the Mount contained covenants being offered, as at Mt. Sinai.

atonement, we must show its power through several sub-portions. Nevertheless, they are all part of one vital Chiastic Center.

X1. Bridegroom offers cup of covenant. At the Last Supper, Jesus offered: "This cup is the new [covenant] in my blood" (Luke 22:20). He offered the same cup from which He drank. To drink from the same cup is an act solidifying an alliance.[1] It was the third cup of wine, the "cup of redemption," and related to God's promise, "I will redeem you...and I will take you to me for a people, and I will be to you a God" (Exodus 6:6-7).[2]

X2. The Bride accepts the cup (Mark 14:23). The disciples partook, covenanting to remember Him always and to take upon themselves the name of Jesus Christ.

X3. Bridegroom prays for Oneness (John 17:1-21). Jesus prays earnestly that He and His disciples would be "One." After praying for oneness, He went out to Gethsemane to bring about that Oneness – the final works of the At-One-ment.

X4. Bride is purchased. In His great suffering in Gethsemane, through the scourging, and the crucifixion, Jesus Christ took upon Himself Brides' sins, shed His blood and gave His life. That offering of innocence, blood and life was the price He paid for His Bride.

X5. Bridegroom provides covering. Jehovah gave coats of skin from a sacrificed victim to cover nakedness (Gen. 3:8-12, 21). Providing covering for the bride became the role of the bridegroom.[3] Now this Bridegroom provided His Covering. Scourging ripped open His skin, uncovering flesh. He was crucified in naked shame. He sacrificed *His covering* so His Bride's nakedness could be covered. Now she could re-enter God's presence.

X6. Bride came from Bridegroom's side. The guards pierced Jesus' side; His broken heart shed forth its blood and water![4] Eve had come from Adam's side; now Jesus' wound brought Him *His Bride* --- those who would give their broken hearts in return.

X7. Bridegroom opens entry to bridal chamber. When Jesus died, the veil of the temple was rent. Many recognize here a witness that He had now opened the way for entrance into God's presence.[5] The

---

[1]. Wilson, *Our Father, Abraham,* 211. Wilson also says in modern Jewish ceremonies, when the bride and groom share a cup of wine, it witnesses that though once two people, they are now one, 211.

[2]. Wilson, *Our Father Abraham,* 246.

[3]. Block, "Marriage and Family in Ancient Israel," in *Marriage and Family in the Biblical World,* 44.

[4]. Talmage, *Jesus the Christ,* 668-669.

[5]. Alfred Edersheim, *The Life and Times of Jesus the Messiah* (Peabody, Mass: Hendrickson Publishers, 1993), 893-895 verifies this view; Joseph Fielding McConkie, *Gospel Symbolism* (Salt Lake City: Bookcraft, Inc., 1985), 275, cites Hebrews 10:19, and agrees. "The rending of the veil symbolized the removal of the barrier between man and God, for man was thus enabled 'to enter into the holiest by the blood of Jesus.'"

Holy of Holies signified God's Presence; it also represented the bridal chamber.[1]

X8. Bridegroom knows His bride. Immediately after death, Christ's spirit went to that great holding place of spirits. There many faithful saints with whom He had covenanted became fully His and rejoiced in their salvation (1 Peter 3:19-20; D&C 138:11-15).

X9. Bridegroom meets bride at a well. As the *re-embodied* Christ rose from the tomb, He was met by women (John 20:1, etc.). These represented all the *living* who would inherit His covenant. The grave was the true well, dug in the earth. But the stone was rolled away. Out of the depths had come Living Waters: Christ and Eternal Life!

X10 Fruitfulness ensued.

These mortals who first saw Him hastily went and testified that Jesus the Christ had risen. Thus they immediately manifest the fruitfulness of Living Waters.

After This Great Turning Point, the Bridegroom Imagery Is Repeated

The New Testament covers a very short history, which is also incomplete (1 Nephi 13: 29*). But in larger literary works, only general concepts must be matched in the first and second half of a work to be considered chiastic.*[2]   John's "Revelation" shows how Christ will ultimately complete His role as Bridegroom. John also shows there will not just be parallels, *but a heightening of all things parallel*, a sign of a true chiasm.[3]

While there are indeed impressive parallels, some parallels are not organized in the exact chronology as the first, except at the end of John's "Revelation."

Q' Bridegroom covenanted with Gentiles. The Gentiles received the gleanings of Israel's harvest after Christ's death. "In a truth I perceive that God is no respecter of persons .... Can any man forbid water, that these should not be baptized, which have received the Holy Ghost as well as we?" (Acts10:34, 47).

P' Gentile Bride to prove unfaithful. "If God spared not the natural branches, take heed lest he also spare not thee... If thou continue in his goodness; otherwise thou also shall be cut off" (Romans 11:21, 22).

S' Bride to always remember she is purchased. "... know ye not that your body is the temple of the Holy Ghost ... and ye are not your own? For ye are bought with a price" (1 Corinthians 6:19-20)." "...he hath purchased [you] with his own blood" (Acts 20:28).

---

[1]. See Brown, *The Gate of Heaven,* 136-137 and footnotes 151 and 154.

[2]. Many examples given by Yehuda Raddy in *Chiasmus in Antiquity* of larger works, considered chiastic, do not match every point in a point for point order.

[3] Northrup Frye in *The Great Code* asserted that the Bible is shaped like a U, with the end of Revelation repeating the same elements as Genesis, (which are Bridegroom related). However, there is great evidence the form is actually a chiastic X.

R' Bridegroom's covering will allow entrance to Heaven. "[We have] ... boldness to enter into the holiest [place] by the blood of Jesus... [being able to enter] through the veil [due to] his [sacrificed] flesh" (Hebrews 10:19-20).

W' Covenant reviewed to faltering Saints. With apostasy soon threatening, the Bridegroom warns, "Thou hast left thy first love" (Namely Him! Rev.2:4). He encourages those few still struggling to "Overcome" by reviewing elements of the betrothal. "To him that overcometh will I give to eat of the tree of life, which is in the midst of the paradise of God" (Revelation 2: 7). "I will give thee a crown of life" (2:10). "He that overcometh, the same shall be clothed in white raiment (3:5). "I will write upon him my new name" (3:12). "I counsel thee to buy of me ...white raiment, that thou mayest be clothed, and that the shame of thy nakedness do not appear" (3:18). "To him that overcometh will I grant to sit with me in my throne" (3:21).

V' Bridegroom promises Bride Israel, who has faltered, will yet be redeemed. "... Israel shall [yet] be saved: There shall come out of Sion the Deliverer, and shall turn away ungodliness from Jacob: For this is my covenant unto them, when I shall take away their sins.... they are beloved for the fathers' sakes" (Romans 11:26-28).

U' Bridegroom will send living waters to Bride Israel after apostasy. "For the Lamb ... shall lead them unto living fountains of waters" (Revelation 7:17). The Book of Mormon would fulfill this promise, as living waters of truth, reviving Latter-day Israel in its wilderness (See verification in Isaiah 35:6-7, 10).[1]

T' Whore, who overcomes Gentile Bride, will eventually be thrown down (Revelation 17, 18). "Babylon the great is fallen...all nations have drunk of the wine of the wrath of her fornication" (Revelation 18:2, 3).[2]

The End of the Bridegroom's Work Is the Same as the Beginning

John's "Revelation" continues to show the end of Christ's ministry will repeat the beginning, but it will be magnified, as in any true chiasm.

N' Bride will be brought out by/from plagues (Revelation 9, 16). The plagues of Egypt would be repeated. As plagues helped bring out ancient Israel from Egypt, so would latter-day Israel; "Come out of [Babylon], my people, that ye be not partakers of her sins, and that ye receive not of her plagues" (Revelation 18:4).

---

[1]. LeGrande Richard, *A Marvelous Work and a Wonder* (Salt Lake City: Deseret Book, 1976 printing), 236-242.

[2]. No one organization is intended. "She is a harlot because she and her children have left their true husband --- Christ --- to live with the world. Because they do this for money and power, they have sold themselves." S. Michael Wilcox, "The Revelation" in the *New Testament and the Latter-day Saints* (Orem, UT: Randall Book Company, 1987), p. 365.

M' Faithful Bride Israel will give living waters. "And I saw another angel fly in the midst of heaven, having the everlasting gospel to preach unto them that dwell on the earth" (Rev. 14:6). The Faithful Bride gives others this living water.

L. Saints' sacrifice will obtain Bridegroom's Covenant. "Ye also ...are built up a spiritual house... to offer up spiritual sacrifices...[For] ye are a chosen generation, a royal priesthood, an holy nation,... that ye should shew forth the praises of him who hath called you out of darkness into his marvelous light" (1 Peter 2:5,7).

K' a. Bridegroom prepares covenanted Home. b. In it to be born great Seed.

a. Jesus spoke of *His work* after His ascension. "In my Father's house are many mansions ... I go to prepare a place for you" (John 14:2). Bridegrooms usually built a home for the bride in the "Father's House [compound]." Great deference was given the Patriarch in decisions.[1] Only the Father could judge when that Home was ready. So Jesus said no one knew the time of His return "but my Father only" (Matthew 24:36).

b. The Bridegroom would fulfill covenant of great Seed: "To Him that overcometh will I grant to sit with me in my throne" (Revelation 3:21). Israel's wedding canopy symbolizes the bridal chamber and the Holy of Holies. The ceiling of the canopy was decorated with stars or set up under the stars, reminding of the covenant made to Abraham, Isaac and Jacob, that they should have seed as the stars in the heavens.

J' Serpent will be cast out. The bride and bridegroom were once cast out. The Bridegroom will now cast out the serpent (Revelation 20:2-3).

I' Bride will be covered with glorious garments. "And to [the bride] was granted that she should be arrayed in fine linen, clean and white" (Revelation 19:8). Christ's choice people will be adorned as a bride. Not only will all nakedness be covered, but new glorious garments will be received, as provided by the Bridegroom as her endowment.

H' Bridegroom's garments stained with other's guilt. "And he was clothed with a vesture dipped in blood" (Revelation 19:13). The stained garments represent His blood of salvation for those accepting His atonement, and, symbolically, the blood of the wicked, perishing at His coming.

G. The Faithful Bride enters God's presence. "[New] Jerusalem [is] prepared as a bride adorned for her husband (Rev.21:2-3)."

F. Bride will partake of the cup of consummation at the Wedding Feast. At the Last Supper, Christ did not drink the fourth cup, saying, "I will drink no more of the fruit of the vine, until that day that I drink it new in the kingdom of God" (Mark 14:25). Now the fourth "cup of consummation" would be drunk. "Let us be glad and rejoice... for the marriage of the Lamb is come, and his wife has made herself ready..." (Revelation 19:7).

---

[1]. "Married sons... remained under the authority of the head of the household until he died...." Leo G. Perdue, "The Israelite and Early Jewish Family", 180.

E' Bride will take Bridegroom's name. When the Bridegroom comes, His name, as his love, shall be "faithful and true" (Revelation 19:11). The bride will bear the Bridegroom's name "in their foreheads…" (Revelation 22:4).

D' Bridegroom will lift bride up to His side. When an Israelite bridegroom takes a bride to her new home, she is often lifted up in a bridal chair.[1] Paul testifies, "For the Lord himself shall descend from heaven with a shout … Then we which are alive and remain shall be caught up together with them in the clouds, to meet the Lord in the air: and so shall we ever be with the Lord" (1 Thessalonians 4:16-7).

C' The Bridegroom will reign with His Bride at His side. "I will shew thee the bride, the Lamb's wife…. Having the glory of God" (Revelation 21:9, 11).

B' Bridegroom provides fountain for bride, fruits from tree of life. "I will give unto him that is athirst of the fountain of the water of life freely" (Revelation 21:6). From the union of Bridegroom and Bride will come everlasting fruit, as patterned by the Tree of Life and its great fruitfulness (Revelation 22:2; John 15).

A' New paradise is created --- more glorious than before (Revelation 21:1). The great home covenanted will at last be realized. "The whole earth in that day will be a Holy of Holies."[2] "There are no words in our language that can convey to our earthbound minds the eternal brilliance and shining brightness that prevail where God is."[3]

There are many symbols used to teach of Jesus Christ in the Bible. Through usage of many different symbols, our understanding is opened to many different aspects of Him and His salvation. *But "Bridegroom" is undoubtedly a chief symbol. It is the first, the most pervasive, the sacred Crux, and the joyful last!* This is likely so because it is in the covenant relationship between bridegroom and bride that the most precious bond and the most significant fruitfulness can be realized. Thus, in an amazing way, this imagery contains the most essential and the most glorious aspects of the gospel.

Furthermore, this symbolism, because it is utilized by many prophets throughout the Bible, testifies their writings were guided by His Spirit. For together His works and their writings present a powerful unity, even to the forming of a chiastic structure, testifying this book truly is of God.

Understanding Christ's full role as Bridegroom from this chiastic view greatly strengthens testimony of His unsurpassed and awesome Love.

---

[1].Wilson, *Our Father Abraham,* 213.

[2]. Bruce R. McConkie, *Millennial Messiah, 703.*

[3]. Bruce R. McConkie, *Millennial Messiah,* 702.

CHIASMUS AND THE COVENANT IN THE HUMAN BODY

Yvonne Bent

Years ago I heard Dr. John Welch speak about his discovery of the Hebraic pattern called Chiasmus in the Book of Mormon. I was spell bound to say the very least. Like so many other experiences in my life, it was a precursor to something even more exciting yet to unfold. But it would be years until I could comprehend why Chiasmus appears so frequently in the scriptures. With those extra years of study and divine tutoring, I came to understand the reason why the Book of Mormon has more Chiastic patterns in it than any other document on earth. It is the same reason that Joseph Smith "told the brethren that the Book of Mormon was the *most correct book* of any book on earth, and the keystone of our religion, and a *man would get nearer to God* by abiding by its precepts, than by any other book.[1]" Chiasmus is a precise pattern to get nearer to God by abiding by the precepts of the Gospel in all things. Chiasmus **IS** the pattern of light entering into everything, and what would be the ultimate form but how it enters into man—changing him to becoming like God in the most beautiful of ways!

I love the simple and direct words of God:

*And now, behold, I say unto you: This is the **plan of salvation unto all men**, through the <u>blood</u> of mine <u>Only</u> Begotten, who shall come in the meridian of time. And behold, <u>all things have their likeness, and all things are created and made to bear record of me</u>, both things which are temporal, and things which are spiritual; things which are in the heavens above, and things which are on the earth, and things which are in the earth, and things which are under the earth, both above and beneath: all things bear record of me[2].*

The chiasm is a pattern as well as a symbol, and it also tells a story. It tells the same glorious story over and over again. Not only is it a symbol in the form of an X, but it (the story in the chiastic pattern) encompasses all the geometric figures as symbols in a progressive pattern, both linguistically,

---

[1] *History of the Church* 4:461

[2] Moses 6:62-63

numerically, and physically. They tell the glorious story and promise of the *Plan of Happiness*. It is simple enough for a child to understand, yet deep enough to plummet any earnest seeker into a spiritual case of the bends. Those desirous to comprehend the ways of God can learn the language of chiasmus and begin to identify the Master's clear and glorious signature, as everything truly testifies of Christ.

Seeing Stars, or X's that is

Once I knew how to identify a literary chiasmus[1], I started seeing chiasms all over the place. I began to wonder, 'Why do people write chiastically'? Why does an artist draw chiastically? Or an architect or a musician? Could it be that there is more to chiastic patterns than we have given credence? Could it be that chiasms are in and through every fiber of our being, testifying of a plan that has been imprinted on us or *in us* from before the beginning of time as we know it? Could it be that a chiastic pattern is the mark of the light of Christ, which is in all things?

When I found the magnificent chiasmus in the Articles of Faith[2], I was certain I was the only person living on the earth that knew about it. It entirely changed my view of Joseph Smith, and certainly altered my opinion of the criticism and comments made by many since it was written in 1841.

I started talking about my discovery to anyone who would listen. I had a conversation with Robert Fillerup, who really burst my bubble when he told me that lots of people write in a chiastic form. Being an attorney, he wrote his papers and briefs chiastically, and delivered his arguments in a chiastic outline. And here I thought that everything about chiasmus was pretty much relegated to holy writ!

I figuratively pulled over to the side of the road to ponder his words. My thoughts were, "If all kinds of people were writing chiastically, and not all of them are prophets, then what was the constant in every man that would allow them to write in this pattern?"

After I identified the progressive orderly pattern that is identified in the Articles of Faith, I found it through all generations of scripture, time, and peoples. It is constant in the 10 commandments, the Beatitudes, the Davidic Chiasmus[3], and other great works.[4] It has a beginning, a middle, and an end. It has the necessary male/female component. Because of the simple criteria of the rhythm of life,

---

[1] John W. Welch, Criteria for Identifying and Evaluating the Presence of Chiasmus, Journal of Book of Mormon Studies: Volume - 4, Issue - 2, Pages: 1-14, Provo, Utah: Maxwell Institute, 1995http://maxwellinstitute.byu.edu/publications/jbms/?vol=4&num=2&id=101

[2] See Appendix 1, Comparisons of Chiasmus in Articles of Faith, Sacred Geometry, Ancient Hebrew, and the Davidic Chiasmus.

[3] See Scott Vanatter, The Davidic Chiasmus in previous chapter of this book.

[4] The study of chiasmus is anything but exhaustive. This book and specifically this chapter of the book provides only a partial explanation and sample of the multitude of places where chiasmus can be identified.

it is easily identified in the music of Bach.[1] It is found in the atom.[2] It finds expression throughout millennia of art and architecture. It can clearly be seen in DNA. It continually manifests itself because it is literally ingrained in all creation and bespeaks of the promises of eternity. The center point constantly illustrates a connection with light and testifies of Christ.[3] It is the same Gospel plan that was set forth from the beginning.

Logic and reason dictated to me that since we were Gods in embryo, children of our Heavenly Father, everything in our bodies would testify of this inheritance in a chiastic pattern, even our spiritual DNA, which is *the* constant within all of us. I made it my mission to prove my hypothesis.

Get in shape for Heaven's sake

I am a visual and shapes oriented person. Geometric patterns really speak to me. Not just the shapes, but the function of the shape. I learned that to be able to make a connection of a shape to a word or symbolic meaning; that shape had to have a substantial purpose. I began a process of aligning the geometric shapes with the corresponding Articles of Faith, i.e., the circle or complete round with the number one. The *vesica pisces*, which is two circles drawn intertwining with the number 2, The triangle with the third Article of Faith, etc. This way I had multiple witnesses. I always used the Articles of Faith as a beacon to steer my ship because it was written by our beloved Joseph for us in our day, and through this process I began to see the patterns of connections.

Regretfully, this book does not allow the explanation of each of the Articles of Faith, but suffice to say that I have invested countless hours connecting these witnesses together, and without a single flaw, Joseph Smith understood exactly what he was talking about when he wrote the Articles of Faith as a chiastic pattern to show us how to return home to God.[4]

I, Joseph, the prophet, in spirit beheld, and the eyes of the inner man truly did see, Eternity sketched in a vision from God of what was, and now is, and yet is to be.[5]

As I piece together the clues Joseph Smith has given us, I cannot begin to thank him sufficiently. These gems are like crumbs for little birds dropped along the side of the road. He proves his office as the prophet of the restoration here by seeing deep into a time he didn't live, and knowledge and connections with ancient alphabets, as well as an intense scientific understanding of

---

[1] Too numerous to mention, the pattern of the chiasmus is easily identified in all His works, demonstrating a beginning, middle and end. See *Know Ye not that Ye are the Temple of God (Unpublished work)* by the same author.

[2] Kathryn Paulsen, see Bohr's electron distribution chart. Discovered using the circular periodic table by Helen Pawlowski, *The Visualization of the Atom*, 1987.

[3] The center point of the Chiasmus is always light and often times even denotes an encounter with Christ.

[4] We Believe, Development of the Articles of Faith, by John W. Welch and David J. Whittaker, Ensign, Sept. 1979, Publication of Church of Jesus Christ of Latter-day Saints., see also Elder L. Tom Perry , The Articles of Faith, Ensign, May 1998 Publication of Church of Jesus Christ of Latter-day Saints.

[5] Joseph Smith, *The Vision*, a poem to W. W. Phelps, Esq., This is the only poem extant supposed to have been written by the Prophet **Joseph Smith**. This poem was published in Nauvoo in 1843.

physics. This could only have been achieved by looking into the heavens. His words lend us a great deal of insight when he tells us, "If you could **gaze into heaven** for five minutes, you would learn more than by reading all of the books that had ever been written on the subject."

It is evident to me that he frequently gazed into heaven.[1]

One of the most exciting things about studying chiasmus in the Articles of Faith was discovering the connections in the Hebrew and the sacred geometric shapes.[2]

I was certain that since I already found corresponding witnesses in the geometric shapes and Hebrew, as well as the Davidic Chiasmus[3], I was safe in using this as my measuring stick. (Refer to the format of comparisons at the end of the chapter.) I also started looking at shapes of the Chi, or X's in everything available, including the structure and function of the body, down to the DNA.

"X" marks the spot

The X is an unusually popular letter. X makes a strong statement of identification. Popular in advertising for such items as Xerox, Kleenex, and Clorox, it gave these commodities a dominant position[4] in product placement. These words have actually become the norm for copies, tissue and bleach. You could almost say that they owned the lion's share of the market. I asked myself, "What makes people so drawn to this letter?"

People have been using the "X" to make a mark on a legal and binding document for centuries. The X became a replacement in the Greek for Christ, as in Xmas. But why would X stand for Christ? Why would it become the tenth letter of the Greek alphabet?

Was this "X" actually a mark of what Christ would do for us? Is this His mark on us? Since it is the last letter in the alphabet, and it could stand for the signature of the author, or the artist, couldn't it also stand for His signature in us? Is this what makes us His? Is this what makes us become like Him?

As there is always more than meets the eye, I kept looking for chiasms. Thank the Lord for the internet. I searched for chiasms, chiasmus, and chiastic patterns. I was delighted with what I discovered.

In *The Garden of Cyrus*, Sir Thomas Browne defines the shape of the chiasmus, but calls it the quincunx, because of the five points. And the shape itself is not without the greater importance, which

---

[1] Personages Who Appeared to the Prophet Joseph Smith or Who Were Seen by Him in Vision, *List Compiled by H. Donl Peterson (Used by Permission) See Appendix 2.*

[2] For a complete explanation, see the publication, *Know Ye Not that Ye are the Temple of God*, Yvonne Bent, 2011.

[3] See previous chapter, Davidic Chiasmus. Also see Scott Vanatter's work, http://www.davidicchiasmus.com/.

[4] I first became familiar with this concept in the early 1980's. See *Positioning*, by Al Ries and Jack Trout, McGraw Hill, 2000.

is this crossing point, or emphatical decussation, and it is a *fundamental figure*.[1] Why would the "X" be called a fundamental figure? [2]

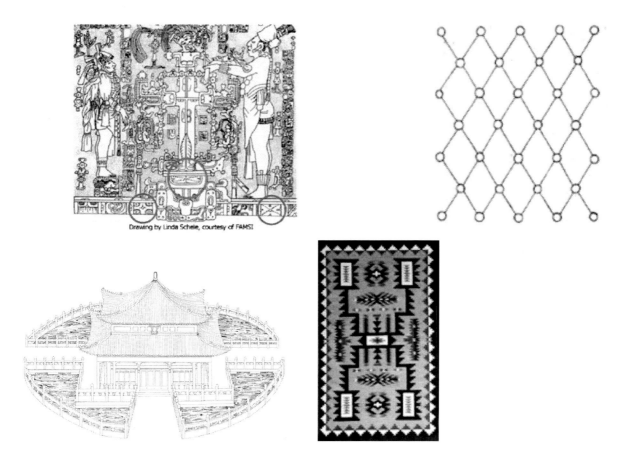

Drawing by Linda Schele, courtesy of FAMSI

Figure 1. Examples of quincunxes[3].

More X's

I doubt very seriously when Rosalind Franklin discovered the diffraction image of DNA, she would have connected it to a Chiastic pattern. But it is obvious that there is a perfect physical pattern of a chiasmus right smack in the middle of DNA.

---

[1] Sir Thomas Browne, *The Garden of Cyrus,* London, 1736.

[2] http://www.soulsofdistortion.nl/great%20celestial%20conjunction%20crosses.html

[3] Meso American Art, Garden Layout, Chinese Temple, Storm Pattern Navajo Rug.

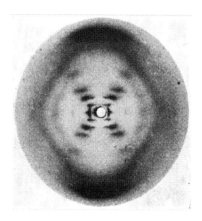

Figure 2. X-Ray diffraction image of DNA, discovered by Rosalind Franklin.[1]

Here was another beautiful chiasm called the optic chiasm. Light enters through the eyes and follows the optic path to meet at the suprachiasmatic nuclei.

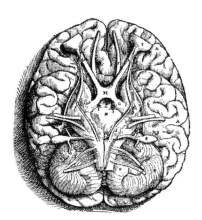

Figure 3. Woodcut from the Fabrica (1555) by Vesalius. Optic Chiasm visable. From Polyak (1957).

'You have, says Coleridge referring to Sir Thomas Browne, 'quincunxes in heaven above, quincunxes in earth below, and quincunxes in the water beneath the earth; quincunxes in deity, quincunxes in the mind of man, quincunxes in bones, in the optic nerves, in the roots of trees, in leaves, in petals, everything. [2]

This was a man after my own heart. The shape of the X is in everything. How marvelously easy; now all I had to do was identify *everything*. But if I took the information that it, the X or quincunx, was

---

[1] http://www.hyattcarter.com/chiasmus_01-04.htm. This is the now famous Photo 51 taken by Rosalind Franklin in Kings College London in 1952. It is an X-ray diffraction image of DNA. This is the X-ray diffraction image of DNA that provided the key missing piece of information for Watson and Crick's discovery of the structure of the DNA molecule.

[2] Biographia Epistolaris, ed, A. Turnbull, London, 1911, 1. Letter 127, 1804.

the pattern in which life responded to light, and Sir Thomas Browne's statement, it shouldn't take me long to put together the answer.

In this paper I use the same criteria set by the Prophet Joseph Smith in the pattern of the Articles of Faith chiasmus. They are set as a pattern of laws and performances, or ordinances, that show a progression and adherence to said laws.

1. All truth is represented in one great whole

2. Male/Female counterpart

3. The Epic Journey of Everyman

4. The World

5. New Life

6. Service/Consecration

7. Convergence or a meeting of light

8. Inversion, the jump to a new level

9. The Priesthood line/revelation

10. The Gathering of Zion

11. A Mighty Change

12. Government

#1: Everything is represented in one great whole

The Word and Light

In the beginning was the *gospel preached through the Son. And the gospel was the word, and the word was with the Son, and the Son was with God, and the Son was of God.*[1]

Joseph Smith was not a scientist, and he made no pretense of solving the scientific questions of his day. However, the Prophet perfectly understood that there was no difference between science and religion.

---

[1] JST John 1:1.

Intelligence or energy was declared by Joseph Smith in May, 1833, to be eternal: "Intelligence, or the light of truth, was not created or made, neither indeed can be." (D&C 93:29.). The Prophet also taught, "The intelligence of spirits had no beginning, neither will it have an end."[1]

Years after Joseph Smith taught us about intelligence; others began to explain their findings of similar properties, but they gave them different words, just as the Prophet said would happen[2].

Walter Russell, (1871–1963) an American polymath, was known for his achievements in painting, sculpture, architecture, and for his unified theory in physics and cosmogony. He posited that the universe was founded on a unifying principle of rhythmic balanced interchange. In 1963, Walter Cronkite in a national television evening news, commenting on Dr. Walter Russell's death, referred to him as "... the Leonardo da Vinci of our time."[7]

Walter Russell had a life changing experience in which he was shown in vision the two shapes in which everything in the world operates. He presented theories on the "fundamental principles of energy dynamics," the nature of matter and the progression of the evolution of matter, and the depiction of the universe as a continuously changing, creating effort sustained by the systematic work effort of the energy of light after this experience. Once, when asked how he acquired his scientific knowledge, he answered: "*...I always looked for the Cause behind things and didn't fritter away my time analyzing Effect. All knowledge exists as Cause. It is simple. It is limited to Light. . . and the electric wave of motion which records God's thinking in matter.*"[3]

Wynn Free references some Russian findings that state, "this spiraling 'torsin' energy could actually be the substance of our human souls, and is therefore the precursor to the DNA molecule ... It already exists in the fabric of space and time before any physical life emerges."[4]

Turn, Turn, Turn

The most popular shape recorded anywhere on earth is the spiral. All nature bears the signature of it.[5] It is the pattern in which all water flows, everything grows, and life responds to light. There is no end to identifying this shape in architecture, entry gates, scrolls, pillar tops, music, jewelry, and tattoos. All nature responds to the call of the light in this fashion and order. The Golden Spiral, or the shape that manifests The Fibonacci Series,[6] is another way of showing response to light.

---

[1] John A. Widtsoe, *Joseph Smith as Scientist*, Bookcraft, 1964 by Mark E. Peterson, pg. 19.

[2] Joseph Smith, Lectures on Faith

[3] Glenn Clark, *The Man Who Tapped the Secrets of the Universe*, The University of Science and Philosophy, pgs. 32-34.

[4] Sol Luckman, *Sound, Intention & Genetic Healing, http://www.bodymindwisdom.com/article_sound_intention.html, 2010.*

[5] Michael S. Schneider, *A Beginner's Guide to Constructing the Universe*, Harper Perennial, New York, NY. 1994, pgs. 145-177.

[6] Leonardo Fibonacci, who was born in the 12th century, studied a sequence of numbers with a different type of rule for determining the next number in a sequence.

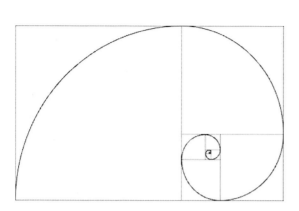 

Figure 1. The Golden Mean Spiral

When you take the golden mean or spiral and turn it into a 3 dimension figure, you have a pyramidal shaped cone. Duplicate and invert it upon itself, you would have the shape of the vortex drawing and collapsing to the center (see above). If you were to take this shape further and try to sketch it in a hieroglyph or symbol, the easiest thing to do would be to draw an "X".

I feel the desire to acclaim the statement made by the Savior when he referred to himself as the Way, the Truth and the Life. He often said He was *The Light*.[1]

Because X stands for 10 in the Greek alphabet, we will use the Tenth Article of Faith as our anchor.

We believe in the literal gathering of Israel and in the restoration of the Ten Tribes; that Zion (the New Jerusalem) will be built upon the American continent; that Christ will reign personally upon the earth; and, that the earth will be renewed and receive its paradisiacal glory.

We not only learn of a return to the presence of Christ, but <u>who</u> will return to His presence. It will be a literal gathering of Israel to Zion. We know it will be those who respond to *The Light*. It is no surprise that Joseph chose to place this shape with its symbolic nature in the perfect place it resides in the Articles of Faith. I believe that the X shape is the very statement of the journey of man back into the presence of light.

I was recently at a fireside where I heard a new convert speak. She was very new to the Church. She had just been confirmed earlier that day. She spoke with amazing power and clarity. She had an assurance unusual for a young woman of only 17 years. She made a profound statement that has stayed in my mind and heart ever since.

---

[1] Statements made by the Lord when He called himself "The Light"; 3 Ne. 18: 16, 24, John 8: 12, John 9: 5, 3 Ne. 9: 18, 3 Ne. 11: 11, Ether 4: 12, D&C 6: 21, D&C 10: 58, D&C 11: 11, D&C 12: 9, D&C 88: 50, D&C 93: 2.

While she was investigating other religions, she observed how those who went in to those churches came out the same way they went in. She noticed that she did not feel any different herself. It wasn't until she had a witness of the truthfulness of the Restored Gospel, and that light filled her heart, that she felt a change. She came out different than she went in. How do we come out different than we go in? And what does that have to do with chiasmus?

We have the Greek Chi or X. Also the Tau or Tav, Hebrew 22nd letter in the ancient or Paleo-Hebrew aleph-beit, is in the form of the X. Here were two things of the same shape, but what about meaning and function?

#2 Male and Female

Evidenced prior to this chapter are multiple witnesses of the Plan of Salvation. This plan is so beautifully expressed to us in *The Family: A Proclamation to the World.*

"All human beings—male and female—are created in the image of God. Each is a beloved spirit son or daughter of heavenly parents, and, as such, each has a divine nature and destiny. Gender is an essential characteristic of individual premortal, mortal, and eternal identity and purpose.[1]

Nephi tells us that there *must* be opposition in all things. There has always been opposition, because this is a law. Opposition is not always a negative thing. We can recognize that all creation is polarized. Chiastic structure must then be constructed with this same principle. There is nothing as critical in chiasmus as the male/female counterpart. The passive/active, masculine/feminine aspect is apparent in all creation down to the atom.

> *Those principles of natural beauty...are all exemplified in the ideally perfect human figure. Though essentially a unit, there is a well marked division into right and left--"Hands to hands, and feet to feet, in one body grooms and brides." There are two arms, two legs, two ears, two eyes, and two lids to each eye; the nose has two nostrils, the mouth has two lips. Moreover, the terms of such pairs are masculine and feminine with respect to each other, one being active and the other passive.[2]*

Marriage, the union of the opposites, is critical, in everything. Celibacy had no recognition within the scripture. Ancient Jewish law and earl Christian law sanctioned and required their disciples to obey the marriage covenant.[3]

---

[1] The Family: A Proclamation to the World—The First Presidency and Council of the Twelve Apostles of The Church of Jesus Christ of Latter-day Saints, 1995.

[2] Claude Bragdon, *The Beautiful Necessity,* Seven Essays on Theosophy and Architecture , *1910.*

[3] Ogden Kraut, *Jesus was Married,* Pioneer Publishing, Genola, Ut, 1969, pg. 27.

I also noticed, especially in the genes themselves, that they were not perfectly symmetrical; the top was a little different than the bottom. It was obvious that there was a male/female element in the DNA.

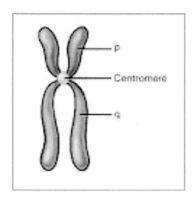

Figure 4. A chromosome, showing upper and lower appendages, and centromere at center.

During an intense study of sacred geometry some years prior to this time, I discovered what I considered a mathematical formula in the scriptures; the human form of man and woman in the divine proportion.[1]

Figure 5. Neither is the Man without the Woman in the Lord.

The definition of geometry comes from the Greek *geo*, which means earth, and *metron*, to measure. The dictionary gives the definition of geometry as the measure of the earth. I believe it is more the measure of *MAN going through his journey on the earth*. Though the divine proportion, or PHI, is seen in many of the body parts, the full body of man or woman is NOT singularly in the divine proportion. It is only when they are together that they comprise the measurement of PHI, or the Divine

---

[1] Avard T. Fairbanks, *Human Proportions for Artists*, Posthumous author, 2005, Fairbanks Art and Books, Bellingham, WA 98226. This work is a compilation akin to the works of Leonardo da Vinci, where the entire human form is measured to display the divine proportion.

Proportion.[1] (See Appendix 3 for comparison to man and woman in the divine proportion and the Salt Lake Temple.)

#3 The Epic Journey of Everyman

Everything wants to be round. The pattern for God is one eternal round. In writing, it is called 'Ring Composition'.[2] It is also called chiasmus, chiastic structure, or simply ring structure. In ring composition, a narrator touches on a number of topics until a significant topic is reached, then continues on in the narrative by retracing in reverse order the topics which were mentioned on the way to the significant point. Ring composition is an important element in epic poetry and every one of us has an epic story of our life.

If you took a simple circle or complete round, such as a rubber band, and twisted it once, you would have the figure 8. There is a lot about this figure 8 in movement, cycles, and journeys. The great anatomist, J. Bell Pettigrew, was very methodical about showing the pattern in forward motion in more than just man.

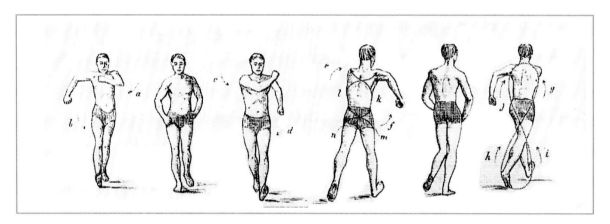

Figure 6. Man walking, seen from before and behind. The double figure-of-8 curves made by the superior and inferior extremities, the double twisting movements occur at the shoulders and hips in walking.[3]

---

[1] Yvonne Bent, *Neither is the Man without the Woman in the Lord*, Copyright, 2004.

[2] Mary Douglas, *Thinking in circles: An essay on ring composition*, Yale Univ. Press, 2007

[3] J Bell Pettigrew, *Design in Nature*, Illustrated by Spiral and other Arrangements in the Inorganic and Organic Kingdoms as exemplified in Matter, Force, Life, Growth, Rhythms, &c., especially in Crystals, Plants, and Animals. With Examples selected from the Reproductive, Alimentary, Respiratory, Circulatory, Nervous, Muscular, Osseous, Locomotory, and other Systems of Animals, Longmans, Green and Company, New York, 1908, pg. 87.

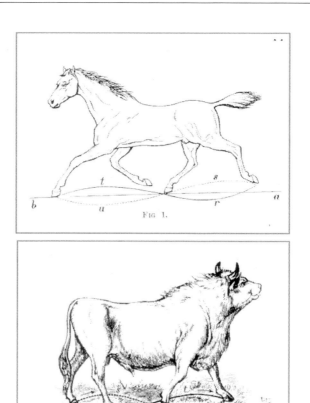

Figure 7. Reveals ponderous body and small extremities and feet adapted for land transit; indicate double curves made by the two anterior extremities, and r, x, those made by the posterior extremities in walking. As the right fore and left hind legs move together to form one step, and the left fore and right hind legs move together to form a second step, the double curves form a figure of 8.[1]

> *Movement at once precedes and follows structure, and the direction of movement in living things is, in every instance, determined by the composition and configuration of the moving parts....There are good reasons why atoms and molecules should arrange themselves, and move in straight lines and in spirals. Straight lines and spirals do not return upon themselves and admit of indefinite extensions, that is, matter can be added in straight lines and in spirals to any amount, and movement in either direction has practically no limit. Those peculiarities of straight-line and **spiral formations and movements are of the utmost consequence in growth and progression**, especially in the locomotion of animals.[2]*

The Hebrew language is a language of forward movement and purpose. Nothing is stagnant and progression is anticipated and expected. It reads from right to left. If you face the North Star to get your bearings and orientation, then the sun would be on your right in the morning and follow you into the west in the evening, which would be to the left. The movement of the sun from the right to the left is the movement even in the reading of Hebrew.

---

[1] Ibid, pg. 89.

[2] Ibid., pgs. 91, 92.

Just a little something about forward movement in life: We know that the family is ordained of God. Marriage between man and woman is essential to His eternal plan.[1] There is no word for bachelor in Hebrew. [2] Brigham Young was quoted to say, "Every man not married and over twenty-five is a menace to the community." Life was meant to be progressive.

The beginning sets the stage. As Mary Douglas outlined in the first of her rules of long ring compositions:

> *Exposition or prologue: There is generally an introductory section that states the theme and introduces the main characters. You can call it a prologue. It sets the stage, sometimes the time and the place. Usually its tone is bland and somewhat enigmatic. It tells of a dilemma that has to be faced, a command to be obeyed, or a doubt to be allayed. Above all, it is laid out so as to anticipate the mid-turn and the ending that will eventually respond to it.*[3]

Life is the Magnum Opus

I have been blessed with beautiful music as a part of my life from the time of my birth. My mother was a classical pianist. It was my orchestral training that helped me to easily see the critical parts of the journey in music. As John Denver said, "Music paints pictures and often tells stories."[4] It was very easy to identify the beginning, middle, and end of a musical composition, especially in a classical concerti composition.

The first movement of a concerto not only sets the tone, but also the melody or story line. This theme will be played often, worked over, around, and upon throughout the entire concerto.

The second movement is indicative of the angst and drama of life's experiences. New themes will be introduced from the short summary of the first movement, which has set the stage. New themes will be combined with the original melody.

The third movement is more animated than the first two. There is a heightened sense of overcoming the previous obstacles (minor key modulations) and success in completion. There is an escalating climactic experience, followed by an anticipated resolve and arrival at a new level.

It was easy to see the beginning, middle and end in an X. But I thought it was important to study the sources of rhythms, since they are critical in a musical composition to give it beauty and meaning. In the human body, these rhythms, or light pulses all originate from the meeting point of the optic chiasm location in the brain coming through the eyes.

---

[1] The Family: A Proclamation to the World—The First Presidency and Council of the Twelve Apostles of The Church of Jesus Christ of Latter-day Saints, 1995.

[2] http://www.tallitministries.com/marriage.htm

[3] Mary Douglas, *Thinking in Circles*, USA, 2007, pg.

[4] John Denver, *The Music is You,* Back Home Again, RCA Legacy, 1974.

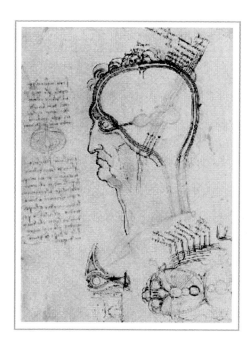

Figure 8. "Brain and Ventricles Saggital View" by Leonardo Da Vinci. Taken from Fincher (1981).

One of the things that really stood out to me was the 3 circular figures or chambers in the brain, shown from the axial view in this particular drawing. Da Vinci calls them the 3 ventricles. I wanted to understand more about them and what was going on inside these chambers.

At the first point of crossing is the circadian "clock" in humans, and is located mainly in the suprachiasmatic nucleus (SCN), which is a group of cells located in the hypothalamus (a portion of the brain).[1]

A circadian rhythm is an approximate daily periodicity, a roughly-24-hour cycle in the biochemical, physiological or behavioral processes of living beings. The term "circadian", comes from the Latin *circa*, "around", and *diem* or *dies*, "day", meaning literally "approximately one day."

The molecular circadian clock can function within a single cell; i.e., it is cell-autonomous   At the same time, different cells may communicate with each other resulting in a synchronized output of electrical signaling. These may interface with endocrine glands of the brain to result in periodic release of hormones. The receptors for these hormones may be located far across the body and synchronize the peripheral clocks of various organs. Thus, the information of the time of the day as relayed by the eyes travels to the clock in the brain, and, through that, clocks in the rest of the body may be synchronized. This is how the timing of, for example, sleep/wake, body temperature, thirst, and appetite are coordinately controlled by the biological clock.[2]

The Pituitary Gland, also located at the midpoint of the optic chiasm. It secrets hormones that are responsible for ovulation, progesterone release, growth factor hormone, testosterone, androgens (male sex

---

[1] http://en.wikipedia.org/wiki/Hypothalamus

[2] http://en.wikipedia.org/wiki/Circadian_rhythm

hormones, like testosterone) ACTH (adrenocorticotropic hormone), which helps prepare the mother for giving birth,[1] just to name a few. Developing physically is part of the journey of man and woman. "God has commanded that all forms of life should multiply and fulfill the measure of their creation, that every form of life might have joy therein."

The Pineal gland is a little gland that does big things. The pineal gland is responsible for sending signals in the form of hormones to different parts of the brain and body for the function necessary to carry out life's responsibilities.

The earth also has a cycle. In a series of studies, Fritz-Albert Popp[2] had one of his assistants -- a 27-year-old healthy young woman -- sit in the room every day for nine months while he took photon readings of a small area of her hand and forehead. Popp then analyzed the data and discovered, to his surprise, that the light emissions from her body followed certain set patterns -- biological rhythms at 7, 14, 32, 80 and 270 days -- and similarities were also noted by day or night, by week and by month, as though the body were following the world's biorhythms as well as its own.[3]

The Hebrew celebrations or festivals are also based upon the earth's cycle. For further information see *The Lord's Holy Days, Powerful Witnesses of Truth*, by Lenet Hadley Read.

#4 The Earthly experience

Continuing on with my quest to learn about chiasms, I went on to research the X in DNA. My experience regarding man on earth always had something to do with the number four, i.e., the four corners of the earth, and most importantly man, which encompasses every nation, kindred, tongue, and people that cover the four corners of the earth. I was thrilled to see multiple witness for the chiasm in DNA.

How beautiful to recognize that this pattern does not leave us wanting with regards to the smallest detail of man. It becomes quadrivial when we learn that palindromes turn up in DNA molecules.

A, T, C, and G stand for Adenine, Thymine, Cytosine, and Guanine, the four nucleotides that form the paired strands of DNA. Like monogamous couples, A always pairs with T and C always pairs with G.

If we let the Greek letter *chi* (χ) indicate a chiasmic structure, then, for DNA —

GATC χ CTAG

Deriving from *quad-*, "four" and *via*, "way or road," **quadrivial** is a Joycean word . . . The word brings to mind a crossroads, four roads that intersect and lead in four different directions. Pointing also in

---

[1] http://en.wikipedia.org/wiki/Hypothalamus

[2] Fritz-Albert Popp

[3] Dan Eden, *Is DNA the next internet?,* http://viewzone2.com/dnax.html.

four directions, and with the same symbolic suggestiveness, is the Greek letter chi, whether in its lower-(χ) or upper-case form (X).

Chi (χ) is suggestive not only of crossroads, but also of the X chromosome, wherein recombinations, or crossings, of genetic material take place, one of the sources of creativity in the evolutionary advance of nature.[1]

The genetic code follows the same rules as all our human languages. [2]The alkalines of our DNA follow regular grammar and have set rules just like our languages. Human languages did not appear coincidentally but are a reflection of our inherent DNA.[3]

To me this was a major milestone. Here was the clue to why so many people write in a chiastic fashion—it 's literally in their genes. The DNA not only looks like an X, but was referred to as a text, a keyboard, and a musical score, and that it could be rewritten. How is it rewritten?

#5: New Life, New Identity

Light and response of DNA, being called of God.

At a genetic level, sound gives rise to light. Fritz Albert Popp's Nobel prize-winning research establishes that *every cell in the body receives, stores and emits coherent light in the form of biophotons.* In tandem with biophonons, biophotons maintain electromagnetic frequency patterns in all living organisms. In the words of Dr. Stephen Lindsteadt, this matrix that is produced and sustained by frequency oscillations "provides the energetic switchboarding behind every cellular function, including DNA/RNA messengering. Cell membranes scan and convert signals into electromagnetic events as proteins in the cell's bi-layer change shape to vibrations of specific resonant frequencies." Emphasizing that every "biochemical reaction is preceded by an electromagnetic signal," Lindsteadt concludes, "Cells communicate both electromagnetically and chemically and create biochemical pathways that interconnect all functions of the body."

Russian scientists Peter Gariaev and Vladimir Poponin have also explored DNA's extraordinary electromagnetic properties. Their research shows that DNA has a special ability to attract photons, causing the latter to spiral along the helix-shaped DNA molecule instead of proceeding along a linear path. In other words, DNA has the amazing ability–unlike any other molecule known to exist–to bend or weave light around itself.

In addition, it appears that a previously undetected form of intelligent light or intention energy (emanating

---

[1] Chiasmus, Chaosmos, Chirality, and Complementarity: Four Intertwining Concepts

[2] Grazyna Fosar and Franz Bludorf, *DNA is influenced by Words and Frequencies,* http://www.soulsofdistortion.nl/dna1.html, 2010.

[3] Mayan Majix , *DNA is Influenced by Words and Frequencies*, October 20, 2005, http://cradle2dagrave.proboards.com/index.cgi?board=FOREVERYACTION&action=display&thread=312, May 19, 2010

from higher dimensions and distinguishable from both gravity and electromagnetic radiation) which Dr. Eli Cartan first termed "torsion" in 1913 after its twisting movement through the fabric of space-time, gives rise to DNA.

Drawing on meticulously documented research, Harvard-trained Leonard Horowitz expertly demonstrated that DNA emits and receives both phonons and photons, or electromagnetic waves of sound and light. In the 1990s, according to Dr. Horowitz, "three Nobel laureates in medicine advanced research that revealed the primary function of DNA lies not in protein synthesis ... but in the realm of bioacoustic and bioelectric signaling."[1]

Research strongly suggests that human DNA is literally a genetic "text"; that chromosomes both produce and receive the information contained in these texts in order to encode and decode them, respectively; and that chromosomes assemble themselves into a holographic grating or lattice designed to generate and interpret highly stable spiral standing waves of sound and light that direct all biological functions.[2]

They found that the ***alkalines***[3] of our DNA follow regular grammar and do have set rules just like our languages. So human languages did not appear coincidentally but are a reflection of our inherent DNA.[4]

Scientists have managed to modulate certain frequency patterns onto a laser ray and with it influenced the DNA frequency and thus the genetic information itself. Since the basic structure of DNA-alkaline pairs and of language are of the same structure, no DNA decoding is necessary. One can simply use words and sentences of the human language![5]

It was apparent that Light was calling, and not only calling, but DNA was responding. This information on DNA and light became proof positive that all things not only testify of Christ, but respond accordingly to the author, just as we respond to the Light of the Gospel.

---

[1] Ibid.

[2] Ibid.

[3] See D&C 89:10-11 And again, verily I say unto you, all wholesome herbs God hath ordained for the constitution, nature, and use of man— Every herb in the season thereof, and every fruit in the season thereof; all these to be used with prudence and thanksgiving. These food substances are high in alkaline based foods, or foods which literally become little time-released capsules of light. Other foods to be eaten sparingly are acid based.

[4] Brazyna Fosar and Franz Bludorf, DNA Can be influenced and Reprogrammed by Words and Frequencies, http://www.soulsofdistortion.nl/dna1.html, 2010

[5] DNA can be influenced and reprogrammed by words and frequencies, http://www.soulsofdistortion.nl/dna1.html, 2010.

#6 Reaching up to the most high

The Dedicated Servant like the Bee

Scientists are reporting evidence that intact double-stranded DNA has the "amazing" ability to recognize similarities in other DNA strands from a distance. Somehow they are able to identify one another, and the tiny bits of genetic material tend to congregate with similar DNA. [1]

How cells "talk" to each other

DNA uses frequencies of every variety as an information tool, this suggests instead a feedback system of perfect communication through waves that encode and transfer information.

When you get a cut or scratch on your skin, the cells that are injured somehow signal the surrounding healthy cells to begin reproducing copies of themselves to fill in and mend the opening, like a fractal. When the skin is back to normal, a signal is sent to the cells to tell them to stop reproducing. Scientists have wondered exactly how this works.

Popp chose to work specifically with UV light because of the experiments of a Russian biologist named Alexander Gurwitsch who, while working with onions in 1923, discovered that roots could stimulate a neighboring plant's roots if the two adjacent plants were in quartz glass pots but not if they were in silicon glass pots. The only difference being that the silicon filtered UV wavelengths of light while the quartz did not. (A quartz is a hexagonal shape, the same shape the bees naturally construct in a bee hive.)

With biophoton emissions, Popp believed he had an answer to this question. This phenomenon of coordination and communication could only occur in a holistic system with one central orchestrator. Popp showed in his experiments that these weak light emissions were sufficient to orchestrate the body's repairs. The emissions had to be low intensity because these communications took place on a very small, intracellular, quantum level. Higher intensities would have an effect only in the world of the large and would create too much "noise" to be effective.

The number of photons emitted seemed to be linked to the organism's position on the evolutionary scale -- the more complex the organism, the fewer photons were emitted. Rudimentary animals and plants tended to emit 100 photons/cm2/sec at a wavelength of 200-800 nm, corresponding to a very-high-frequency EM wave well within the visible range, whereas **humans emit only 10 photons/ cm2/sec at the same frequency.** Here is the number 10 and the CHI in an interesting place.

I could not look at these similarities to healing and communication without being reminded of bees and their respective work in the hives. Bees do communicate in the very same way; on a very small, intercellular, quantum level. The six-sided containers innately designed in a perfect size to accomplish the

---

[1] *ACS' Journal of Physical Chemistry B,* February 06, 2008, http://www.dailygalaxy.com/my_weblog/2008/02/dna-found-to-ha.html

work of the hive and the quartz. The quartz is six sided, which allowed the communication of UV light between the cells. Also because they are able to identify one another, which bees do in their hive, protecting it from any intruders, they serve to nourish the hive, feed the larvae, and help in the development of new life, and in this case, new DNA.

This is a phenomenon called 'photorepair', and it means that there must be some kind of light in the body responsible for *photorepair, or communication and repair in the cell.*

To appropriately demonstrate the role of servant in DNA, I will draw a parallel between the effort of the bees and the change in the DNA.

Joseph Smith and Brigham Young had a very good understanding of bees. Utah was originally going to be named Deseret, which meant 'Honey Bee.'. The product of the bees is the most perfect food on the earth. The Jaredites ate this food while on their journey across the waters in the barges.[1] Lehi and his company carried bees with them to the promised land.[2] There is an obvious message that we must needs have the properties of honey to make this earthly journey with success and health. Our entire physical structure is made of hexagonal shapes, from our bones, to our muscle tissue and everything inbetween. The substance of honey, being in a liquid, but hexagonal nevertheless, would provide the human body with the necessary support because the hexagon if the most sound structural shape anywhere. It is through association and ingestion we benefit from the dedicated service of the bee. We would do well to examine them closer, but for the time being I would like to show how bees are very similar to the incredible tasks performed by our DNA to respond, assist, protect, heal, and elevate.

The parallel of the covenant servant position with those workers in the beehive will serve as a thorough explanation. You could certainly say that bees are covenant workers of the hive. They move in a pattern that is chiastic, as certainly the waggle dance is in the figure 8, which communicates all that is needed to give information of flowers, movement, and danger. They wear their lives out in the service of the hive.[3] Everything the bee does is for the benefit of the hive. All the product the bees deliver, propolis used to protect the hive, royal jelly for the queen so that she can continue in the reproduction and life of the hive, the honey for the life of the bees, the wax for their housing; all this is turned into the good of the hive. Sugars, particularly natural sugars are critical for cell to cell communication as performed by glyconutrients, for without these substances, the body falls into a state of disease.[4]

Light in the DNA does this same kind of labor in behalf of the body, as well as the maintenance for the future of mankind, always maintaining, feeding, protecting, governing, and reproducing.

---

[1] Ether 2: 3 And they did also carry with them *Deseret*, which, by interpretation, is a honey bee; and thus they did carry with them swarms of bees, and all manner of that which was upon the face of the land, seeds of every kind.

[2] 1 Ne. 18: 6 And it came to pass that on the morrow, after we had prepared all things, much fruits and meat from the wilderness, and honey in abundance, and provisions according to that which the Lord had commanded us, we did go down into the ship, with all our loading and our seeds, and whatsoever thing we had brought with us, every one according to his age; wherefore, we did all go down into the ship, with our wives and our children.

[3] Spencer W. Kimball quoted as saying "My life is like my shoes—to be worn out in service" (as quoted in Gordon B. Hinckley, "He Is at Peace," *Ensign,* Dec. 1985, 41)

[4] Glyconutrients reference, 2 June 2010, http://www.glyconutrientsreference.com/whatareglyconutrients/scientificvalidation.html.

Some very interesting things about DNA

In a 1993 study reported in the journal *Advances*, the Army performed experiments to determine precisely whether the emotion/DNA connection continues following a separation, and if so, at what distances? The researchers started by collecting a swab of tissue and DNA from the inside of a volunteer's mouth. This sample was isolated and taken to another room in the same building, where they began to investigate a phenomenon that modern science says shouldn't exist. In a specially designed chamber, the DNA was measured electrically to see if it responded to the emotions of the person it came from, the donor who was in another room several hundred feet away.

In his room, the subject was shown a series of video images designed to create genuine states of emotion inside of his body. The idea was for the donor to experience a spectrum of real emotions within a brief period of time. While he was doing so, in another room his DNA was measured for its response.

When the donor experienced emotional "peaks" and "dips," his cells and DNA showed a powerful electrical response at the same instant in time. Although distances measured in hundreds of feet separated the donor and the samples, the DNA acted as if it was still physically connected to his body.

The Army stopped their experiments with the donor and his DNA when they were still in the same building, separated by distances of only hundreds of feet. Following those initial studies, however, Dr. Backster and his team had continued the investigations at even great distances. At one point, a span of 350 miles separated the donor and his cells.

The time between the donor's experience and the cell's response was gauged by an atomic clock located in Colorado. In each experiment, the interval measured between the emotion and the cell's response was zero—*the effect was simultaneous.*

The experiment showed 4 things:

1. A previously unrecognized form of energy exists between living tissues.

2. Cells and DNA communicate through this field of energy

3. Human emotion has a direct influence on living DNA.

4. Distance appears to be of no consequence with regard to the effect.[1]

"Veljkovic and Cosic proposed that molecular interactions are electrical in nature, and they take place over distances that are large compared with the size of molecules. Cosic later introduced the idea of dynamic electromagnetic field interactions, that molecules recognize their particular targets and vice versa by electromagnetic resonance. In other words, the molecules send out specific frequencies of electromagnetic waves which not only enable them to 'see' and 'hear' each other, as both photon and phonon modes exist for electromagnetic waves, but also to influence each other at a distance and become ineluctably drawn to each other if vibrating out of phase (in a complementary way)."

---

[1]Greg Braden, *The Divine Matrix,* Hay House, Inc., Carlsbad, California, 2007, pgs. 46-50.

All growing matter responds to light. DNA is no exception. The existence of internal photons—internal light— is the basis of virtually all cellular and systemic function, *for all living forms.*[1]

DNA is not only responsible for the construction of our body but also serves as data storage and communication. The Russian linguists found that the genetic code, especially in the apparently useless 90%, follows the same rules as all our human languages. To this end they compared the rules of syntax (the way in which words are put together to form phrases and sentences), semantics (the study of meaning in language forms) and the basic rules of grammar.

One revolutionary corollary of this research is that to activate DNA and stimulate healing on the cellular level, one can simply use words. [2]

What does all this information on DNA have to do with Chiasmus? The power of reading the Holy Scriptures, listening to the voice of the prophets[3], mighty prayer, and singing of the hymns all have a powerful effect upon us. It can have such a profound effect upon us, not only spiritually, but physically. Through these mediums we are called to God. Our very DNA responds to the word. No wonder John tells us that in the beginning was the Word. We responded to it then, and we respond to it now. Our DNA is still responsive to light at great distances, whether it be our deceased ancestors from us, our children away from us, or our distance from God; all are affected by the Light of Christ and can change according to more light.

More on DNA

An **autosome** is a <u>chromosome</u> that is not a <u>sex chromosome</u> – that is to say there are an equal number of copies of the chromosome in males and females. For example, in <u>humans</u>, there are twenty-two (22) pairs of autosomes, and, in addition, there are the <u>X</u> and <u>Y</u> sex chromosomes.[4]

The ancient Hebrew language consists of 22 characters. Understanding that words have a profound effect upon our DNA, the very words of the language given to the covenant people, consisting of 22 characters to effect the transformation and assist in the mission of the Israelites to fulfill their mission on earth is supplied to us here today as we have learned the power of the word on our DNA.

It would then stand to reason that if DNA follows set grammar rules, just like our language, and if it is influenced by words and phrases, then DNA would also influence a person to correspond in like

---

[1] Dan Eden, *Is DNA the Next internet?,* http://viewzone2.com/dnax.html, 2010.

[2] Sol Luckman, *Sound, Intention, and Genetic Healing,* http://www.bodymindwisdom.com/article_sound_intention.html. 2006

[3] Moro. 10: 8, And again, I exhort you, my brethren, that ye deny not the gifts of God, for they are many; and they come from the same God. And there are different ways that these gifts are administered; but it is the same God who worketh all in all; and they are given by the manifestations of the Spirit of God unto men, to profit them. ,D&C 1: 38 What I the Lord have spoken, I have spoken, and I excuse not myself; and though the heavens and the earth pass away, my word shall not pass away, but shall all be fulfilled, whether by mine own voice or by the voice of my servants, it is the same.

[4] Griffiths, Anthony J. F. (1999). *An Introduction to genetic analysis.* New York: W.H. Freeman. ISBN 071673771X. http://www.ncbi.nlm.nih.gov/books/bv.fcgi?highlight=autosome&rid=iga.section.222, 2010.

language—the language and purpose of the DNA. Recurrence is rampant in nature. Evolution relies on gene duplication. It was President Gordon B. Hinckley who described true evolution when he said, "I have become acquainted with what to me is a far more important and wonderful kind of evolution. It is the evolution of men and women as the sons and daughters of God, and of our marvelous potential for growth as children of our Creator."[1]

#7 Convergence, or a Meeting with Light

This is the point in the X which is the meeting point. The word 'decussation' was the description of that meeting point. What did Sir Thomas Browne mean when he referred to it?

Sir Thomas Browne states in The Garden of Cyrus, that this crossing point, or emphatical decussation, is a fundamental figure. Why would the "X" be called a fundamental figure?

The same is also observable in some part of the skin of man, in habits of neat texture, and therefore not unaptly compared unto a net: we shall not affirm, that from such grounds the Egyptian embalmers imitated this texture; yet in their linen folds, the fame is still observable among their neatest mummies, in the figures of Isis and Osiris, and the Tutelary Spirits in the Bembine Table. Nor is it to be over-looked how Orus, the Hieroglyphic of the World, is described in a network covering, from the shoulder to the foot. And the statue face, teraphims[2] and little idols, found about the mummies, do make a Decussation or Jacob's Cross, with their arms, like that on the head of Ephraim and Manasseh, and this deccis is also graphically described between them.

This reticulate or network, was also considerable in the inward parts of man, not only from the first subtegmen[3] or warp of his formation; but in the netty fiber of the veins and vessel of life; wherein, according to common anatomy, the right and transverse fibers are decussated by the oblique fibers; and so must frame a reticulate and quincuncial figure by their obliquations, emphatically extending that elegant expression of Scripture, "Thou hast curiously embroidered me, thou hast wrought me up after the finest way of texture, and as it were with a needle.

Nor is the same observable only in some parts, but in the whole body of man; which, upon the extension of arms and legs, doth make out a square, whole intersection is at the genitals. To omit the fantastical quincunx[4] in Plato, of the first hermaphrodite or double man, united at the loins, which Jupiter after divided.[5]

---

[1] President Gordon B. Hinckley, "God Hath Not Given Us the Spirit of Fear," *Ensign,* Oct. 1984.

[2] Seer stones

[3] Weft, woof, transverse threads woven between warp threads

[4] Quincunx: An arrangement of five objects in a square, one at each corner and one in the middle (thus,); especially, an arrangement, as of trees, in such squares continuously. A collection of trees in such squares forms a regular grove or wood, presenting parallel rows or alleys in different directions, according to the spectator's position. See diagram under quincuncial.

[5] Sir Thomas Browne, The Garden of Cyrus, London, 1736, pg. 34.

We are directed to observe a statement made by Paul:

God has made known to us in all wisdom and insight the mystery of his will, according to his purpose which he set forth in Christ, a plan for the fullness of time, to unite all things in him, things on heaven and things on earth (Eph 1:10)

Webster's Dictionary defines decussation as the act of crossing at unequal angles; the crossing of two lines, rays or nerves, which meet in a point and then proceed and diverge.

Through the study of etymology we learn of the Latin decussare, decussat-, from decussis, the number ten, intersection of two lines (from the Latin decussare, decussat-, from decussis, the number ten, intersection of two lines (from the Romans' use of X for the numeral 10), a ten-as coin : decem, ten; see dekm in Indo-European roots + assis, as (coin). It was a coin value. And it had also evolved from a sealed script to a sinograph in the form of a cross (╋).

Also referred to in the 'X' shape, called a quincunx, was the word 'Paradise'. This Greek word was used in the Septuagint translation of Genesis to refer to the Garden of Eden.

The history of paradise is an extreme example of amelioration, the process by which a word comes to refer to something better than what it used to refer to. The old Iranian language Avestan had a noun pairidaēza-, "a wall enclosing a garden or orchard," which is composed of pairi-, "around," and daēza- "wall." The adverb and preposition pairi is related to the equivalent Greek form peri, as in perimeter. Daēza- comes from the Indo-European root *dheigh-, "to mold, form, shape." Zoroastrian religion encouraged maintaining arbors, orchards, and gardens, and even the kings of austere Sparta were edified by seeing the Great King of Persia planting and maintaining his own trees in his own garden.

As we continue to follow the 10th article of Faith, we can understand this X shape, this quincunx, defined as Paradise to explain… the earth will be renewed and receive 'it's paradisiacal glory'.

Brain decussation is a phenomenon in which the nerve fibers found in one lateral portion of the organ cross another. The status known as pyramidal decussation has to do with the passage of motor fibers from the brain to medulla spinalis and medulla oblongata. The fibers tend to leave the brain in bunches or bundles and cross in the anterior median fissure area of the medulla oblongata.[1]

Nerve decussation is a term that often refers to the crossing fibers within one eye.

I thought I would spend some time studying the optic chiasm and all its component parts with a main focus on the diverging point. I discovered a very beautiful example of this crossing point is shown in the optic chiasm. As Traquair stated…all vision takes place in the form of a pyramid.[2] Light travels in a pyramid fashion through another pyramid structure until it connects together at the optic chiasm. This

---

[1] http://www.wisegeek.com/what-is-decussation.htm

[2] Joel S. Glaser, Romancing the Chiasm: Vision, Vocalization, and Virtuosity, Journal of Neuro-Ophthalmology: June 2008 – Volume 28 – Issue 2 – pp 131-143.

light is responsible for stimulating a myraid of organs responsible for the movement of man throughout his life.

Originating in different places, the optic nerves unite with each other but afterward diverge from each other again...for nature has not interchanged them...the shape of these nerves is very much like the letter chi. If anyone should dissect them rather carelessly, he would perhaps believe that they interchanged...but this is not true; for when they met within the cranium, they united their courses and then again separate, indicating clearly that they came together for no other reason than they might unite their courses...[1]

In the DNA chromosome, the center point is called the centromere. Specific <u>proteins</u> bind to centromeric DNA, forming the <u>kinetochore</u>, which is the site of spindle fiber attachment. The kinetochore is a large multiprotein complex that can be seen in the electron microscope as a platelike multilaminar structure. The center point is not just a passive anchorage site for microtubules: it plays a central role in controlling the assembly and disassembly of the kinetochore microtubules, generating tension in them and, ultimately, driving chromosome movement. [2]

And what does this have to do with binding? It is always about replication, multiplying and repleneshing.

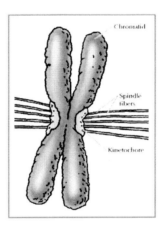

Figure 12 Binding site of centromere with spindle fibers[3]

Not surprisingly, seeing decussations in the human body became a great deal more interesting. I contemplated these crossings and remembered making these quincunxes on a piece of art work I had created several years ago.

---

[1] Ibid.

[2] http://www.ncbi.nlm.nih.gov/bookshelf/br.fcgi?book=cell&part=A4895

[3] http://www.ncbi.nlm.nih.gov/bookshelf/br.fcgi?book=cooper&part=A618

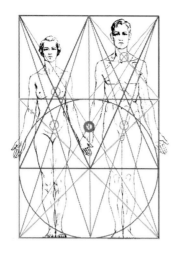

Figure 13. Neither is the Man without the Woman, in the Lord, 1 Cor. 11:11[1].

#8: A New Level

When I was making this piece of art, I tried several times to cut the arms and hands out of glass and solder them together. Every time I did this, no matter how careful I was, the pieces broke at the shoulder or the wrist of the man or woman. After numerous attempts I resolved to place the man and woman together into one piece of glass, with the cut stained glass in the background. It was the only way to keep the man and woman together. They had to be made as one to endure the slightest jar. I found it an interesting parallel between the sealing between the man and woman needing to bind them in a medium that would not separate, so that they could be one and accomplish their divine mission. This would explain why the man and woman were in the divine proportion.

We know that in order to obtain the <u>highest</u> degree of glory, a man (and woman) must enter into this <u>order</u> of the <u>priesthood</u> (meaning the new and everlasting covenant of <u>marriage</u>). The points that decussate on the man and woman show that the new and everlasting covenant of marriage is not just marriage, but the fulfillment of their missions in marriage covenant. (D&C 131:2). They join their DNA and bring together life and light.

The reproductive organs are at a decussate point on both the man and woman. Aside from the brain and heart, the larynx is at the cross point for the man and the heart for the woman. I was delighted to have read about the similarities between the larynx and cervix in The Beloved Bridegroom.[2]

Just as a baby develops in the womb, a testimony develops in the heart. For both a baby and a spiritual witness, a means to deliver a "seed" and a way to "bear fruit" are required. Not surprisingly, the

---

[1] Yvonne Bent, Neither is the Man without the Woman in the Lord, El Cerrito, CA. 2005.

[2] Donna Nielsen, The Beloved Bridegroom, 1999, Onyx Press, pgs. 157-158

body has two parts that are remarkably similar in function and appearance. These two parts are the larynx and the cervix. Medical anatomy books contain pictures of each that show startling similarities.

Larynx	Cervix
Opening to a passage in the throat (neck)	Opening to a passage in the "neck"
Associated membrane covering	Associated membrane covering
Bound with ligaments	Bound with ligaments
Vocal "folds" that open and close	Folds that open and close
Brings forth fruit of the heart	Brings forth fruit of the womb

Tissues from every single body part have distinctive characteristics and can be readily identified with their respective organs. However, the cervix and larynx are the only two parts of the body with identical cell tissue. Although there are variances during the monthly cycle, at any given time identical color and mucus count will be found in both. Samples taken from the larynx and cervix are indistinguishable from each other even under a microscope. [1]

When Joseph was just 14 years old he received the first vision. Fourteen was the age in which he was old enough to be a teacher in the Aaronic Priesthood. Why the age of 14?

Beginning around the age of 14, the larynx (Adam's apple) increases in size. The vocal chords become longer and thicker, and the voice begins to break or crack, then becomes low. Hence, the voice becomes the bass voice.

The Prophet Joseph Smith called upon the choir to sing a hymn, and remarked that, "Tenor charms the ear; bass, the heart."[2] At the age of 14, the voice of a young man has changed, allowing him to preach in a lower voice that would strike the heart.

Many men went to the Prophet Joseph to ask of the Lord what He would have them do, and Joseph returned with the admonition to "Preach Repentance", or in other words, touch the strings of the heart.

Coincidental? I can't believe there is a chance in a billion. Both of these places point directly to both men and women fulfilling the measure of their creation, which is part of the great plan of happiness; women to give life and nurture[3] and men to preach repentance.

When you look at the chiasms previously mentioned, be they the optic chiasm, the DNA, the center point of the heart, the cervix or larynx, there is an element that is crucial in the interpretation of the

---

[1] Ibid. pg. 157.

[2] Joseph Smith, History of The Church of Jesus Christ of Latter-day Saints, 7 Vols. 5:339.

[3] The power of the heart to entrain is profound and too lengthy to cover in this chapter. It is covered extensively in detail in Know Ye Not that Ye are the Temple of God, by the same author.

connection: something takes place that causes a bonding or a sealing. At this point the right and left are inseparably connected.[1]

Alma expresses it most beautifully when he testifies to Korihor, "The scriptures are laid before thee, yea, and all things denote there is a God; yea, even the <u>earth</u>, and all things that are upon the face of it, yea, and its <u>motion</u>, yea, and also all the <u>planets</u> which move in their regular form do witness that there is a Supreme Creator." [2]

"The Logos of him who makes the world is himself the Seal, by which each thing that exists has received its shape...[3] Colossians claims that 'in him all things hold together.' (Col. 1:17) Needed explanation is received when we study about bonds and binding in the scriptures.

The bonds and the binding were the covenant. The verb 'create, 'bara' is used in Genesis 1 (and elsewhere) only for divine activity. . . . The verb is similar to the word for covenant, b'rith, suggesting that the uniquely divine activity of creating was the binding of creation, which was exteded to mean any creative divine act. This was the creation covenant, sometimes called the everlasting covenant and sometimes the covenant of peace. Adam, created as the image, was told to subdue the earth and have dominion over other living creatures (Gen. 1:28), but the word kbs translated 'subdue', means literally to harness or to bind, suggestiong that binding was part of the image. Adam was to maintain the bonds of creation. Throughout the Hebrew Scriptures a creation covenant is assumed, but little noticed nowadays because scholarly interest has been largely confined to the 'historis' covenants: with Abraham, with Moses and with David. The creation covenant appears as the climax of the Noah story: 'my covenant which is between me and you and every living creature of all flesh' 'the everlasting covenant' (Gen. 9:15-16). This was the covenant that bound heaven and earth together, as the Lord declared through Jeremiah; 'my covenant of day and night and the ordinances of heaven and earth . . .' (Jer. 33:24), and it was proof of the Lord's faithfulness to his people.

The bonds of the covenant were secured by The Name, Ha Shem, represented in temple tradition by a diagonal cross. This was the X shaped seal of creation that Justin said was known by Plato. In the ancient alphabet used in the first temple, the letter tau was written as a diagonal cross, which is why Ezekiel saw the faithful marked with a tau: "Touch no one upon whom is the tau' (Ezek. 9:6). The high priest was annointed with The Name, but by the time of the Babylonian Talmud, the ancient alphabet was no longer used, and so the sign of the Name was not described as a tau but as the Greek letter Chi.[4]

Understanding that this is the point of covenant, and Christ always refers to Himself as the Light of the World, it comes as no surprise that at all points of this junction there is some type of exchange of

---

[1] These connecting points are also points where there are Holy of Holies, discussed in a paper by the author entitled Sacred Geometry and the Holy of Holies.

[2] Alma 30:44.

[3] Margaret Barker, Creation, A Biblical Vision for the Environment, Published by T&T Clark International, New York, NY, 2010, pg. 125, quoting Philo, On Flight.

[4] Ibid, pgs. 122-123.

light and bonding, which binds these right and left sides together. In ancient times all covenants were made with salt, which symbolized the binding of the covenant.

One final statement made in lieu of the delight of learning about the joining point.

According to Vesalius, Each nerve of the first pair [optic] under the base of the brain where it rests on the sinus in which the gland which excretes the pituita from the brain is led forward somewhat obliquely, the right nerve extending toward the left and the left toward the right, and then both come together and are <u>intermingled so that in no way can you separate the right from the left</u> so much so that it would be wholly fruitless to attempt to determine whether in this junction the right nerve remains on the right side or is led to the left side by an uninterrupted connection.[1]

What is being connected if not that which is profane with that which is sacred, or heaven and earth, spiritual and temporal, mortal and immortal. All these things are connected inseparably with a power held only by God and put into play by worthy priesthood.[2]

A number of factors are responsible for the stability of the DNA double helix structure, first among them being hydrogen[3] bonds. Internal and external hydrogen bonds stabilize the DNA molecule. [4] Hydrogen is light, and light is the power at the center of everything.

#9 The Gathering and Binding

There has never been a time when inheritance has not been of critical focus. Emphasis has been placed upon being of royal blood lines and the privileges that come with these blood lines throughout all ages, even from the premortal existence. This inheritance was clearly understood and earnestly sought after by the great Patriarch, Abraham.

And, finding there was greater <u>happiness</u> and peace and rest for me, I sought for the blessings of the fathers, and the right whereunto I should be ordained to administer the same; having been myself a follower of <u>righteousness</u>, desiring also to be one who possessed great <u>knowledge</u>, and to be a greater follower of righteousness, and to possess a greater knowledge, and to be a father of many <u>nations</u>, a prince of peace, and <u>desiring</u> to receive instructions, and to keep the

---

[1] Joel S. Glaser, MD, Romancing the Chiasm: Vision, Vocalization , and Virtuosity, The Sixth Hoyt Lecture, Journal of Neuro-Ophthalmology: June 2008 – Volume 28 – Issue 2, pp. 131-143.

[2] D&C 121: 36 That the rights of the priesthood are inseparably connected with the powers of heaven, and that the powers of heaven cannot be controlled nor handled only upon the principles of righteousness

[3] D&C 88, 6, 7, 13: He that ascended up on high, as also he descended below all things, in that he comprehended all things, that he might be in all and through all things, the light of truth;..Which truth shineth. This is the light of Christ. As also he is in the sun, and the light of the…The light which is in all things, which giveth life to all things, which is the law by which all things are governed, even the power of God who sitteth upon his throne, who is in the bosom of eternity, who is in the midst of all things.

[4] D Voet, JG Voet, CW Pratt (1999). Fundamentals of Biochemistry: Biochemical Interactions CD-ROM – J. Wiley & Sons, 2010. Read more: http://www.brighthub.com/science/genetics/articles/23384.aspx#ixzz0rkKCyFT2.

commandments of God, I became a rightful heir, a <u>High</u> Priest, holding the right belonging to the fathers. It was <u>conferred</u> upon me from the fathers; it came down from the fathers, from the beginning of time, yea, even from the beginning, or before the foundation of the earth, down to the present time, even the right of the <u>firstborn</u>, or the first man, who is <u>Adam</u>, or first father, through the fathers unto me. I sought for mine <u>appointment</u> unto the Priesthood according to the appointment of God unto the <u>fathers</u> concerning the seed.[1]

This pattern and importance of passing down the rightful inheritance through the covenant lineage is given a strong level of importance throughout scripture. However, this should come as no surprise because we have a noble birthright from before the beginning of time, and because of the covenant, we can lay claim upon those blessings. Can our pursuit of these blessings coincide with the binding of our spiritual DNA to our physical DNA? So how are we sealed?

A few words about Salt

Figure 14. The character Yan drawn by Beijing salt history professor Guo Zhenzhong, in the Zhuangzi style of calligraphy that was used until about 200 B.C..[2]

Clay Trumbull stated, "It is evident that the true symbolism and sanctity of salt as the nexus of a covenant lie deeper than is yet admitted, or than has been formally stated by any scholar."[3]

Until most recently, salt and water have been king of commerce in the world. Both elements determine life or death. Battles have been fought, won, and paid for in salt. Cities are named for their salt content, such as Salzburg. Salt has been used for years in preservation. The Egyptians preserved their dead in salt. The Hausa used natron (salt) to dissolve indigo so that the color could be fixed.[4] The value of salt has been shown to be greater than that of gold.[5] Salt gives the primal idea of covenanting as a means of life-sharing. There is no life without salt.

---

[1] Abraham 1:2.

[2] Mark Kurlansky, Salt A World History, Penguin Group, (USA) Inc. 375 Hudson Street, New York, NY 10014, USA, pg. 29.

[3] H. Clay Trumbull, The Salt Covenant, 1899, New York, pg. 12.

[4] Mark Kurlansky, Salt A World History, Penguin Book, New York, New York, 2002, pg. 51.

[5] Ibid, pg. 60, Marco Polo's Travels, Col. Yule's translation, II., 29, 35, 36, 37, & notes to Chap. 47.

In Numbers 18:19 we read,

All the heave offerings of the holy things, which the children of Israel offer unto the Lord, have I given thee, and thy sons and thy daughters with thee, as a due for ever; it is a covenant of salt for ever before the Lord unto thee and to thy seed with thee.

"Son of man, cause Jerusalem to know her abominations...As for your nativity [birth], on the day you were born your navel cord was not cut, nor were you washed in water to cleanse you; YOU WERE NOT RUBBED WITH SALT nor swathed in swaddling cloths...No eye pitied you, to do any of these things for you, to have compassion on you; but you were thrown out into the open field, when you yourself were loathed on the day you were born" (Ezekiel 16:2, 4, 5).

Through these two scriptural examples, we can see the power of the use of salt, and the necessity thereof. But the question arises as to why salt is such a necessity?

All the cells in the world contain DNA -- be they animal, vegetal, or bacterial -- and they are all filled with salt water, in which the concentration of salt is similar to that of the worldwide ocean.[1]

The role of salt is to bind with DNA in order to precipitate.[2] If you consider the value of salt throughout all the ages, and the focus on the sealing of the family, it will be easier to understand the critical importance of salt making connections or literally making salt bridges in DNA. DNA contains negative charge with salt and they repel each other, and the salt with positive charge will neutralize some of the negative charge. The salt will eventually cause a long-term tempering, removing impurities which impede the defects in a lattice (the lattice of the DNA is easily visualized, and when DNA replicates, the salt will provide the stability in the lattice, just as the temple sealing provides stability in the bonding relationship through all generations). In a family it causes long term relationships to join. The binding process of salt provides a way for the impurities to be worked out of the relationship, and creates a permanent bond.[3]

Professor Hermann Collitz, of Bryn Mawr, has suggested that the very words in Latin for salt and blood, sal and sanguis, are from the same root. "The Early European word for salt, sal, which probably goes back to the Indo-European period, may be derived from the same root to which the Sanskrit as-r-g 'blood' and Latin s-an-gu-I-s belong...The root es is probably the same from which the word for 'to be' is derived, and the meaning of which seems to have been original, 'to live.'[4]

---

[1] http://fusionanomaly.net/doublehelix.html

[2] Precipitation hardening, called age hardening. A heat treatment technique used to increase the yield strength of malleable materials; relies on changes in solid solubility with temperature to produce fine particles of an impurity phase, which impede the movement of defects in a crystal's lattice. Unlike ordinary tempering, alloys must be kept at elevated temperature for hours to allow precipitation to take place. This time delay is called aging. http://en.wikipedia.org/wiki/Precipitation_strengthening.

[3] A note in passing: The vast majority of salt on this earth today is processed, making it poison to the system. Because most people, particularly those in the areas attended by western medicine, are cautioned to use no salt because of the highly toxic state our bodies reach when imbibing in this substance. Nevertheless, the body has 2 elements it cannot live without; salt and water. Were we to ingest a natural form of salt, our bodies would thrive with their mineral content and a state of health would ensue.

[4] Ibid. pg. 44.

Protein-protein and protein-DNA interfaces contain at least as many water-mediated interactions as direct hydrogen bonds or salt bridges.[1] Think of how often the Savior offered living water.

Water needs to have the correct hydrogen/oxygen relationship to create the lattice formation. When water is ordered it can perform the necessary tasks of nourishing, cleansing, and purifying. Masuru Emoto has been performing studies on the effects of words and music on water. He found that water exposed to music can become ordered. The act of speaking kind words or praying over water, or exposing it to beautiful music (particularly classical pieces by Bach, Mozart, and Beethoven) will cause the water to make beautiful hexagonal crystals which prior to that time were unable to form.[2]

Water in our bodies, carried by blood, sweat, tears, and mucous solution, contain the imprint of the DNA in our bodies. These mucosal fluids, whether through the larynx, cervix, eyes, or heart are balanced with the correct level of salt. This fluid carries an imprint of every genetic marker, as well as emotions, which become a chemical compound in our body, and will become bonded with contact of the heat or light. The exchange of mucus through the act sanctified for marriage is so sacred, for it provides a salt connection, creating the imprint of each person on the other, not only in the act of procreation, but in creating an emotional bonding.

When Christ told His disciples that they were the salt of the earth, perhaps one of the reasons was because they had the power to bind heaven and earth with the priesthood, which is His light.

Salt provides the ability for electricity to send the currents throughout our bodies, making not only the necessary but critical connections. Salt is vital to the nerve cells' communication and information processing. Salt is imperative to preservation; it is a sealer. Salt causes the bonding in the DNA. Just as salt makes the connections in the nerves and seals those connections, we are sealed in the temple through ordinances performed by authorized priesthood who have the authority to call down the power to bind the man to his wife, the bride to the bridegroom.

Consequently, if being like salt was the ability to make a connection of light to make bonds or bridges, the same law would apply to joining families to God. The Latin verb salis has the two-fold meaning "to salt" or "To sprinkle before sacrifice," and "to leap, spring, bound, jump"; the Sanskrit alike.[3]

D&C 2: 1 Behold, I will reveal unto you the Priesthood, by the hand of Elijah the prophet, before the coming of the great and dreadful day of the Lord.

Now that we have focused on the center point for an extended time, the journey moves onward for the remainder of the story. Look at the chiastic structure in the DNA

---

[1] **Energetics of the protein-DNA-water interaction, 2007, http://www.biomedcentral.com/1472-6807/7/4**

[2] Masuru Emoto, The Hidden Messages in Water, Sunmark Publishing, Inc., Tokyo, Japan, 2001.

[3] See Harper's Latin Dictionary, s vv. "sal," "salio," "saltus."

Inversion or a new situation

Palindromes occur in DNA. There are two types.

1. Palindromes that occur on opposite strands of the same section of DNA helix.

5' GGCC 3'

3' CCGG 5'

2. Inverted Repeats, is a sequence of <u>nucleotides</u> that is the reversed <u>compliment</u> of another sequence further downstream.

In these cases, two different segments of the double helix read the same but in opposite directions.

5' AGAACAnnnTGTTCT 3'

3' TCTTGTnnnACAAGA 5'

Inverted repeats at either end of retroviral gene sequences aid in inserting the DNA copy into the DNA of the host and duplicated genes. [1]

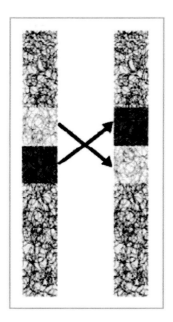

Figure 15. Chromosomal inversion[2]

#11 The Mighty Change

Let us now go to the story of Jacob and the mighty change that takes place when he becomes Israel.

---

[1] http://users.rcn.com/jkimball.ma.ultranet/BiologyPages/P/Palindromes.html, 23 May 2010.

[2] http://www.eurogentest.org/aboutus/info/public/unit6/patientsLeafletsEnglish/chromosoneChangesEnglish.xhtml.

Jacob is the third in line of the Fathers, always mentioned in the Scriptures. He has a very interesting life. He is the twin brother to Esau, through Isaac, the son of Abraham and Sarah. His mother Rebekah knew he was the rightful son to receive the birthright blessing from her womb. After he receives the birthright blessing, it was needful for him to depart his home for his safety's sake. He goes to visit his uncle Laman for a while. During the time Jacob is there, he is betrothed to Rachel. He goes into the situation single, but he comes out very married. Not only does he marry Rachel, but also her sister, Leah, and his wives threw in 2 handmaids for good measure. Before he has left the company of his father-in-law, he is the father of a large brood of 11 children. He is on his way to visit his father when this next event takes place.

And he took them (his family), and sent them over the brook, and sent over that he had. And Jacob was left alone; and there <u>wrestled</u> a man with him until the breaking of the day. And when he saw that he prevailed not against him, he touched the hollow of his thigh; and the hollow of Jacob's thigh was out of joint, as he wrestled with him. And he said, Let me go, for the day breaketh. And he said, I will not let thee go, except thou bless me. And he said unto him, What is thy name? And he said, Jacob. And he said, Thy <u>name</u> shall be called no more Jacob, but <u>Israel</u>: <u>for</u> as a <u>prince</u> hast thou <u>power</u> with God and with men, and hast <u>prevailed</u>. And Jacob asked him, and said, Tell me, I pray thee, thy name. And he said, "Wherefore is it that thou dost ask after my <u>name</u>?" And he <u>blessed</u> him there. And Jacob called the name of the place <u>Peniel</u>: for I have <u>seen</u> God <u>face</u> to face, and my life is preserved. And as he passed over <u>Penuel</u> the sun rose upon him, and he halted upon his thigh.[1]

Some very profound things happen in this event. First, Jacob receives a name change. He has his calling and election made sure, and he sees God face to face.[2]

In Strong's Exhaustive Bible Concordance, we learn the definition for the name Israel, which means, *One who has prevailed*. Margaret Barker also tells us that Israel means seeing God.[3] There is reference to Sar, or prince, where we can see Sarah, or Princess. It means the heir apparent, sons of God. It also means to sing. [4]

The Kingly Line

This might seem like a bit of a diversion, but it is actually quite illuminating. It is established that Israel is a name for a covenant, chosen people. Chosen for their righteousness, and blessed according to that same level of righteousness.

---

[1] Genesis 32:23-29.

[2] In the Standard works there are only a smattering of outright witnesses stating that they saw God face to face: Abraham, Moses, The Brother of Jared, Moroni, Mormon, Nephi, Enos, and Jacob, King Lamoni's entire people, His father, and Joseph Smith.

[3] Margaret Barker, *Christmas, The Original Story* ,Ashfor Society for Promoting Christian Knowledge, London, 2008, pg 89.

[4] PSALM 149:1-2, Praise ye the Lord. Sing unto the Lord a new song, and his praise in the congregation of saints.
Let Israel rejoice in him that made him; let the children of Zion be joyful in their King.

The names Rey, or Reyes, Raj or Maharajah, all stand for a *great king*. The names Rex, Re or Ra all denote kingship. There is not time to go into all the history of these names, but it is apparent that it wasn't the Egyptians that had the corner on this market, but that it has an even greater significance as we see how it appears in the names of 'The Fathers'.

Ab**ra**ham & Sa**rah**

Isaac and **Re**bekah

Jacob (Israel) and **Ra**chel

Joseph & Asanath

Manasseh and Eph**ra**im

You can see that in each of the 3 Fathers, Abraham, Isaac, and Jacob, there is a chiasm in their names. Earlier in this chapter there was mention a decussation or Jacob's Cross, with their arms, like that on the head of Ephraim and Manasseh, and this deccis is also graphically described between them.[1]

After the blessing of Ephraim and Manasseh, when Jacob blesses his grandsons, these two sons come into the birthright position, and Ephraim takes the head, with the RE in his name.

As long as we are going to look through the human body, let us take a look at the circular periodic table, which represents the elements. The human body is made out of only minerals and water, so looking at the elements will tell us some very interesting things about chiasmus.

Here is the periodic table, laid out in a circular fashion. It is much easier to identify the chiastic elements, as they all align themselves on the second ray, or Alkaline elements. Remember that alkali is light.

---

[1] Sir Thomas Browne, The Garden of Cyrus, London, 1736, pg. 34.

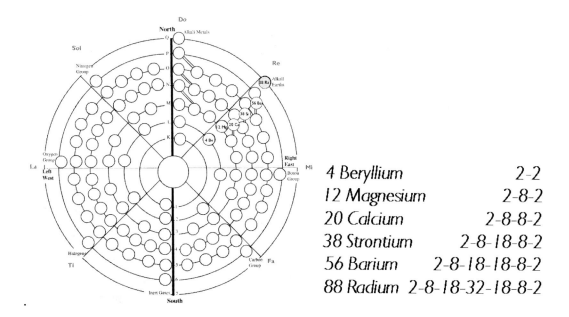

4 Beryllium	*2-2*
12 Magnesium	*2-8-2*
20 Calcium	*2-8-8-2*
38 Strontium	*2-8-18-8-2*
56 Barium	*2-8-18-18-8-2*
88 Radium	*2-8-18-32-18-8-2*

Figure 16 Circular Periodic table[1]

The Re, or second Alkaline earth ray, contains the elements that are chiastic, all running in a direct line. When the body is in a high state of alkalinity, it will conduct light. Each of these elements appears next to the superconducting metal, i.e., copper, silver and gold. These are the metals used to build the sacred temples. Most people would have presumed that these metals were strictly for ornamentation, but it was certainly a secondary use. It was specifically for the conducting of light, to purify us with fire, to make us like God.

When we consider the strong statement made by Paul that we are the temple, that our bodies are temples, it is easier to understand the placement of these chiastic elements in their position. It is necessary to send the charge of light into the entire body and provide immense amounts of light, for refinement, bonding and reduplication of DNA, until it is perfected and capable of being a vehicle that can constantly send off light, being a Christ.

Earlier in this chapter there was mention a Decussation or Jacob's Cross, with their arms, like that on the head of Ephraim and Manasseh, and this deccis is also graphically described between them.[2]Even in the placement of the hands in this blessing gives symbolic message of rays of light, privileged inheritance, and promised blessings.

[1] Helen Pawlowski, The Visualization of The Atom, The Pawlowski Family Trust, Arizona, pgs 21-119.

[2] Sir Thomas Browne, The Garden of Cyrus, 1658.

Figure 17. Jacob Blessing his children.[1]

Moroni teaches us:

Wherefore, my beloved brethren, <u>pray</u> unto the Father with all the energy of heart, that ye may be filled with this love, which he hath bestowed upon all who are true <u>followers</u> of his Son, Jesus Christ; that ye may become the sons of God; that when he shall appear we shall <u>be</u> like him, for we shall see him as he is; that we may have this hope; that we may be <u>purified</u> even as he is pure. Amen. (Moroni 7:48)

How do we get to be called 'Israel'? We will be called Israel because we prevailed with God by our endurance, our obedience. It is because of the amount of light that we have sought for and received that has changed us.

How do we get to be literally gathered? By listening to the still small voice that effects such a profound change upon our hearts, our minds, our bodies, and certainly because of our DNA that calls us and changes us into a Zion people.

How do we come out different than we go in? We can never be the same after we have connected with light, but more importantly, with God. For, as the Brother of Jared's experience with the Lord, he could not be kept from beholding within the veil.

Genesis 28:10-15 JST

And Jacob went out from Beersheba, and went toward Haran. And he lighted upon a certain place, and tarried there all night, because the sun was set; and he took of the stones of that place, and put them for his pillows, and lay down in that place to sleep. And he dreamed, and behold a ladder set up on the earth, and the top of it reached to heaven; and behold the angels of God ascending and descending upon it. And, behold, the Lord stood above it, and said, I am the Lord God of Abraham thy father, and the God of Isaac; the land whereon thou liest, to thee will I give it, and to thy seed; And thy seed shall be as the dust of the earth; and thou shalt spread abroad to the west, and to the east, and to the north, and to the south; and in thee and in thy seed shall all the

---

[1]Giovanni Francesco Barbieri, 1591 –1666, Jacob, Ephraim, and Manasseh, http://en.wikipedia.org/wiki/Guercino

families of the earth be blessed. And, behold, I am with thee, and will keep thee in all places whither thou goest, and will bring thee again into this land; for I will not leave thee, until I have done that which I have spoken to thee of.

When Jacob awoke, he designated the place as "the house of God" and as "the gate of heaven" (Genesis 28:12-17). Describing the second appearance of God to him at Bethel, Jacob mentions the emphasis given to his new name (Israel), the command that he multiply and replenish the earth, and the promises associated with his posterity (Genesis 35:7-12).

The extension of the lower half of the X chromosome, the longer part of the Chi in the chiasms in the human body all lead to the extension of posterity and government. The light that affects the DNA will indeed affect all the functions in the posterity of the world, as well as the mighty change that can take place in us.

Figure 18. Sketch of DNA.[1]

#12 Government

The changed and longer end of the chiasm

I took a look at the longer end of the chiasm, from the Articles of Faith, the optic chiasm, the X chromosome, and the change that took place in Jacob. They demonstrate the same pattern of government as the 12th Article of Faith.

The nerves that lead from the Optic chiasm lead down into the brain stem, possessing the 12 nerves. The X chromosome will include the changes or the inversions that will give strength to the next pairing of DNA. Jacob, with his birthright son Joseph, and Joseph's children, will be called the House of Israel, the governing tribe of Israel, for it was through Israel's birthright son, Joseph, that Ephraim and Manasseh were blessed.

---

[1] Hyatt Carter, Chiasmus, Chaosmos, Chirality, and Complementarity: Four Intertwining Concepts, http://www.hyattcarter.com/index.html, 2010.

Chiasmus and the Covenant in the Human Body

Since we are in the place that speaks of government in through the House of Israel, it is appropriate that we briefly cover government in the human body.

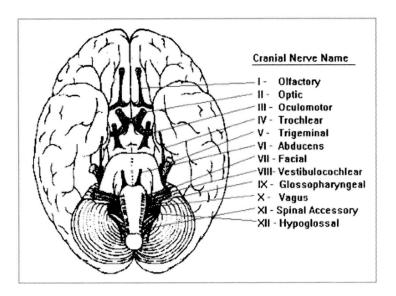

Without the use of our nerves, our muscles and bones would lie inert. So it becomes apparent that our nerves and their signals govern our body. Most of the cranial nerves originate in the brainstem. The brainstem is the pathway for all fiber tracts passing up and down from peripheral nerves and spinal cord to the highest parts of the brain. The cranial nerves are 12 pairs of nerves that can be seen on the bottom surface of the brain. Some of these nerves bring information from the sense organs to the brain; other cranial nerves control muscles; other cranial nerves are connected to glands or internal organs (for example, the heart and lung).

Below is a listing of the cranial nerves and their functions:

Cranial nerve	Function
1. Olfactory Nerve	Smell
2. Optic Nerve	Vision
3. Oculomotor Nerve	Eye Movement; Pupil Dilation
4. Trochlear Nerve	Eye Movement
5. Trigeminal Nerve	Somatosensory information (touch, pain) from the face and head; muscles for chewing
6. Abducens Nerve	Eye Movement
7. Facial Nerve	Taste
8. Vestibulochelear Nerve	Taste
9. Glossopharyngeal Nerve	Taste

133

10. Vagus Nerve	Sensory, Motor and Autonomic Functions of Viscera (glands, digestion, heart rate, etc.)
11. Spinal Accessory Nerve	Controls muscles used in head movement
12. Hypoglossal Nerve	Controls muscles of the tongue

The nerves in the brain control the remainder of the nerves that connect to the remainder of the body and their various functions.

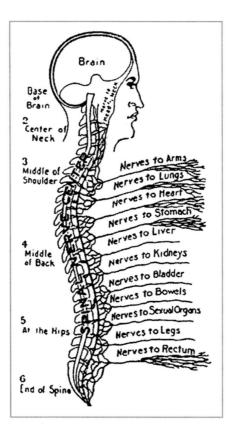

Figure 19 Nerves governing the body.[1]

It is evident that these nerves control or govern the entire body. It is a beautiful thing to realize that all these nerves reside in the brain, which is supported by the neck, and upon the shoulders. With these 12 nerves governing the brain, and the brain sending for nerves to govern the body, how appropriate that we are told that the Government shall be upon His shoulders.[2]   All of the cranial nerves send messages to the body through light signals and the body functions and performs accordingly.[3]

---

[1] http://www.meridianinstitute.com/eaem/renulife/book1/contents.html

[2] Isaiah 9:6, 2 Nephi 19:6.

[3] http://www.thebrainlabs.com/brain.shtml

On and On

I realized that I could go on and on in finding the multiples of chiasms in the body, for the more I researched, I found that truly, they were everywhere. However, for the time being, it is time to call it quits.

To summarize, we have found that:

1. We return to the beginning, the one eternal round, as if we were in the ring composition, or to the ending of our chiasmus.

2. We have a male/female counterpart; we are whole or complete.

3. We have made the journey from the beginning, through the middle, and to the end, or one eternal round. We found the rhythm of life. It takes us full circle and back into the presence of God, and we are changed.

4. We have proven that all action and life is acted upon in a human body

5. We have seen how new life and identity ensues.

6. We have clearly identified the action of service and consecration upon the cells of the body.

7. We have had a mighty change that took place within the middle of the chiasmus; we come out different than we went in.

8. We have reached a new, higher level

9. We have made inseparable connections

10. We can see how this journey has taken us to the Celestial City[1], or to Zion.

11. We can see the possibilities of seeing the face of God and stand in His presence

12. We qualify to be governing bodies

Where do I go from here? I doubt I will ever be able to look at life the same. I used to see these X's, these places of decussation, but now I will look at the symbolism of fishing nets, garden and orchard plots and their layouts. I will think of the Savior telling us 'I am the vine and ye are the tender grapes'. I will look at the tree of life in a more complete way. Above all, I will continue to marvel at the beauty of the pattern in all things, and that, just as the Prophet Alma said, everything does indeed testify of Christ.

---

[1] John Bunyan, *Pilgrim's Progress*, London, 1658.

Chiasmus in the center of Facsmilie #2

Figure 20 Facsimile #2 in The Pearl of Great Price.

Inside the center of the Lotus Blossom is the X.

Appendix 1

Articles of Faith	Hebrew Symbol & Usage	Hebrew	Geometric Form	Value
1. We <u>believe</u> in <u>God</u>, the Eternal Father, and in His <u>Son</u>, Jesus Christ, and in the <u>Holy</u> Ghost.	Aleph : Master, All , Strength, Power, Chief, First Man, first father, Adam, in the express image of the Father, Zion has fled, Number One, patriarch, father of many nations the Son acting in behalf of the father, all knowledge in one whole, The Godhead and the Plan of Salvation	א All Knowledge, One Eternal Round	Monad or Circle	1
2. We believe that men will be <u>punished</u> for their <u>own</u> sins, and not for Adam's <u>transgression</u>.	Beit: House, Doorway, Eve, first woman, womb, to come forth, first residence, multiply sorrow and conception, source, right by birth, a house, garden of the earth, choice, opposites, agency, consequences	ב Agency, opposition, male & female	Dyad	2
3. We believe that through the <u>Atonement</u> of Christ, all <u>mankind</u> may be <u>saved</u>, by obedience to the laws and ordinances of the Gospel.	Gamel or Gimel: To walk, go by foot, carry, Complete journey or round, earth, past, present, & future, being nourished to full maturity, a promising situation for man, a rolling away, courses fixed, camel, the atonement, laws and ordinances	ג The beginning, middle, and end of the journey, the atonement	Triangle	3
4. We believe that the first principles and <u>ordinances</u> of the Gospel are: first, <u>Faith</u> in the Lord Jesus Christ; second, <u>Repentance</u>; third, <u>Baptism</u> by <u>immersion</u> for the <u>remission</u> of sins; fourth, Laying on of <u>hands</u> for the <u>gift</u> of the Holy Ghost.	Daleth : Door, Death, pains of mortality, price of sin, consequence of choice, four angels, four directions, subject to the pains of the earth, gravity, knowledge of good and evil, separation from God, earthly existence, physical body and pathway to return home	ד Earthly physical body, refinement process upon metals	Tetragon, Basic unit of space	4
5. We believe that a man must be <u>called</u> of God, by <u>prophecy</u>, and by the laying on of <u>hands</u> by those who are in <u>authority</u>, to <u>preach</u> the Gospel and administer in the <u>ordinances</u> thereof.	Hey or Hei: Behold, Tree of Life, He shall come down in the meridian of time, to affix, nail in the sure place, the life of the body, fixes stars, rotation of planets by forces that cannot be removed, that which comes down from above, divine decree, covenants, life, callings from God, receiving His permission to act in His name.	ה New life, new name	Pentagon	5

6. We believe in the same organization that existed in the Primitive Church, namely, apostles, prophets, pastors, teachers, evangelists, and so forth	Waw or Vav: Tent Pegs, to secure, Nail, law of God, divine decree, hook, denotes a relationship, that of an arm, service, used to hold or bind Satan, balancing the opposing forces of gravity and repulsion, the force that does not allow planets to wander, organization of callings in the church	ו Covenant workers	Hexagon Structure, Function & Order	6
7. We believe in the gift of tongues, prophecy, revelation, visions, healing, interpretation of tongues, and so forth	Zan or Zijan : Weapon, the flaming sword turns every way to guard the tree of life, that which flows down from above from Heaven, i.e., manna, revelation, blood from a cut, oil, water; divine decree, covenants of God, Spiritual Gifts, Anointed with oil, repentant saints	ז Connection to light	Heptagon	7
8. We believe the Bible to be the word of God as far as it is translated correctly; we also believe the Book of Mormon to be the word of God.	Cheth : Ideogram for life, blessings of the fullness of life, jump to next level, sitting in the presence of God, ladder or gate, tree of life, life of body transcending the earth, blessings from above, completion, throne of heaven, celestial world.	ח Achieving a new level	Octagon	8
9. We believe all that God has revealed, all that He does now reveal, and we believe that He will yet reveal many great and important things pertaining to the Kingdom of God.	Thet : A container made of wicker or clay, Snake, good, some of the story of the seduction of Eve, the tempter, the oppressor, supplanter of his brother, Satan depart, sin taker of agency, renewal, revelation of things hidden and revealed through prophets from the beginning of time	ט Priesthood power to seal	Enneagon	9
10. We believe in the literal gathering of Israel and in the restoration of the Ten Tribes; that Zion (the New Jerusalem) will be built upon the American continent; that Christ will reign personally upon the earth; and, that the earth will be renewed and receive its paradisiacal glory.	Yad or Yod: Life, light and knowledge, male seed, flame of life, power and possession, spirit of life, I see, light & glory, seed of life, restoration of all things, i.e., lost tribes of Israel, Zion will be built upon the earth again, to get light and knowledge, "he shall come down in the meridian of time"	י Gathering of Zion	Decagon, the Pythagorean perfect number, Chiasmus	10

11. We claim the privilege of worshiping Almighty God according to the dictates of our own conscience, and allow all men the same privilege, let them worship how, where, or what they may.	Kaff, Koph, or Kaph: Shepherd's crook symbol of Mercy, to draw down, shepherd of mercy, palm of the hand, palm of Christ, his covering wing to protect, bent horn, strong right arm of the Lord, container, to cover , to hold or possess, wing, coming into the fold of God and His fold, the power to draw in or toward	כ Being in the Presence of God	Hendecagon	20
12. We believe in being subject to kings, presidents, rulers, and magistrates, in obeying, honoring, and sustaining the law	Lamed: Whip or flail, to drive away, scepter of justice, to go, driven forth, whip of justice, on thy belly thou shalt go, ox goad, instructor, justice, arm squared, the left hand, to drive away, negative power, the power of repulsion. Double or confirmed, justice double loaded	ל Government	Dodecagon	30
13. We believe in being honest, true, chaste, benevolent, virtuous, and in doing good to all men; indeed, we may say that we follow the admonition of Paul—We believe all things, we hope all things, we have endured many things, and hope to be able to endure all things. If there is anything virtuous, lovely, or of good report or praiseworthy, we seek after these things.	Mem: The Messiah, the Bird, the hawk, fountain of righteousness, round droplets, one eternal round, waters of life, (doubled means second visitor—Holy Ghost) Prince of Peace, rightful heir, all the sweetness of dwelling in the presence of God and His Holy Son, The protecting wing of the Messiah, who would come at the meridian of time who is in the midst of all things.	מ Head of the Government, Peace	N/A	40

Appendix 2

1. God the Father JS-H 1:17; *HC* 1:5; D&C 76:20

2. Jesus Christ JS-H 1:17; *HC* 1:5-6; D&C 76:20-24; D&C 110:2-10

3. Moroni JS-H 1:30-49; *JD* 17:374

4. Elijah D&C 110:13-16; *JD* 23:48

5. John the Baptist D&C 13; *HC* 1:39-40

6-8. Peter, James, John D&C 27:12; D&C 128:20; *HC* 1:40-42; *JD* 18:326

9. Adam (Michael) *HC* 3:388; D&C 128:21; *HC* 2:380; *JD* 18:326

10. Noah (Gabriel) D&C 128:21; *JD* 21:94

11. Raphael D&C 128:21

12. Moses D&C 110:11; *JD* 21:65

13. Elias D&C 110:12; D&C 27:6; *JD* 23:48

14. Joseph, son of Jacob D&C 27:10

15. Abraham D&C 27:10; *JD* 21:94

16. Isaac D&C 27:10; *JD* 21:94

17. Jacob D&C 27:10; *JD* 21:94

18. Enoch *JD* 21:65

19-27. Twelve Jewish Apostles *JD* 21:94 (Peter, James, and John already counted above.) Names are in Matt 10:1-4 & Luke 6:13-16)

28-39. Twelve Nephite Apostles *JD* 21:94 (Including Three Nephites; names are recorded in 3 Nephi 19:4)

40. Nephi *JD* 21:161; Orson Pratt Letter Box 3/11/1876 (CHO)

41. Seth *JD* 21:94;*HC* 3:388; D&C 107:53-57

42. Methuselah *JD* 21:94; *HC* 3:388; D&C 107:53-57

43. Enos *JD* 21:94; *HC* 3:388; D&C 107:53-57

44. Mahalaleel *JD* 21:94; *HC* 3:388; D&C 107:53-57

45. Jared (Bible) *HC* 3:388; D&C 107:53-57

46. Lamech *JD* 18:325

47. Abel *JD* 18:325; *HC* 3:388

48. Cainan *HC* 3:388; D&C 107:53-57

49. Zelph the Lamanite T&S 6:788

50. Alvin Smith, Joseph's deceased brother *HC* 2:380

51. Mormon *JD* 17:374

52. Paul *TPJS* 180

53. Eve Oliver B. Huntington Diary, Part 2, 214, BYU Library

54. Alma *JD* 13:47.

55. Unnamed Angel <u>D&C 27</u> (Concerning wine in Sacrament) *HC* 1:106

56. Unnamed Angel Sent to accept dedication of Temple. *Life of Heber C.* Kimball, 106; *Temples of the Most High*, pg. 159

57. Unnamed angel Visited Joseph Smith three different times and commanded him to practice polygamy—Eliza R. Snow, *Biography and Family* Records of Lorenzo Snow 69-70

58. "I saw many angels" Warren Cowdery's Account of the First Vision. Joseph Smith's First Vision,

59. Satan, as an angel of Light , *JD* Light (and his associates) 3:229-30, <u>D&C 128:20</u>;

Appendix 3

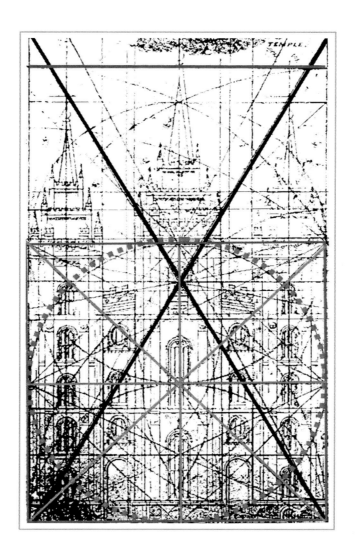

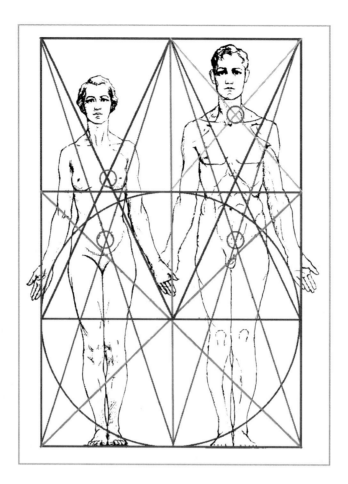

Figure 21. The decussation point (center of the X) at both the temple in the celestial room, and the man and woman, shows the place where the bond originates to become eternal in the new and everlasting covenant.

CHIASMUS AND THE ATOM

Kathryn Paulsen

History has never looked kindly on innovators. It shatters people's paradigms, it threatens the position of those who have a vested interested in being an authority. Galileo was kept prisoner in his own home for the last 8 years of his life. Gutenberg struggled for years to have his printing press accepted by the masses. Morse patiently waited while Congress stalled the access of messages to be sent by electricity. Tesla was a genius, but was hardly recognized. All had the common thread of genius, trying to get a new and important message to the world. There are countless examples regarding this experience, hence, history has many unsung heroes. This paper will address another unsung heroine—Helen A. Pawlowski.

Mendeleev's first sketch of a periodic table of the elements

Great men of science have pondered and obsessed over alchemy for centuries, but it was the scientists of the 19th century that finally put the pattern of the elements into what is today known today as the periodic element chart. It was only after Felix Mendeleev was able to identify the patterns of the octets in the elements that made it possible to construct a sort of edifice, though large parts were missing at the time. Further research and exploration provided the elements that filled in the holes of the original builders of the periodic table of the elements.

These periodic tables, considered a cultural icon, have covered the walls of chemistry classes around the world for decades. These elements, and the symbols that represent them, are a universal language spoken in every science laboratory spanning the globe.

Perhaps Helen Pawlowski was influenced by a statement made by Brigham Young when he said, "To the degree that something is beautiful, it is to that degree true." But when Mrs. Pawlowski[1] , a native Utahan, looked at the periodic chart of elements hanging on the wall of her high school chemistry class, she was aware of one obvious problem: there was an obvious lack of natural beauty in the table. She knew God could not create anything that was not beautiful. With that belief and the fervor of her passion, Helen was to discover the true way in which Heavenly Father would display the 92 natural elements in a more esthetically pleasing way. And not only would it provide a more

---

[1] Helen Ann Williams Pawlowski, born December 16, 1930, Spanish Fork, Utah. Married Engelbert Pawlowski on January 18, 1969. Passed away July 2, 2001 from lymphoma.

delightful way to view the elements, the table and its construction would revolutionize not only the progression of the elements, but it would also explain an absolute placement.[1]

For 35 years, during marriage, children, and the daily motions that make up life, Helen bought used science books and studied atoms, elements, electrons and the periodic chart. She tried a multitude of times in a fashion very similar to Edison and the light bulb, laying out the elements every which way she could think of to make the pattern work. She made as many charts and tables as Mendeleev.

One day in her home she was using gold stickers for electrons and yarn for energy levels. She described her hand being moved in what she later describes as "the flip", which is similar to the eternity symbol (∞). The pattern worked! All the families of elements were lined up on their right order on 8 rays, one ray for each family; transitional elements between the rays. Helen Pawlowski did not measure electrons. She had these ideas flow into her mind after much pondering and studying. It was an incredible moment as all the pieces fit together.

Helen timed it and dated it. She realized this as the pattern of God's revelations and she had received much more than a new periodic chart. She had the exacting position of electrons! She had the Order of the Atom.

I became acquainted with Helen Pawlowski's Circular Periodic Table[2] through her sister, LaVon Finlinson, when my family moved to Arizona during a nine-month work opportunity for my husband. Though the work never manifested itself as a profitable financial move, it certainly turned my life upside down. I had taken chemistry in college, but this was a whole new twist on a subject that I could not wait to finish. As I studied the principles of the atom in this different perspective, it seemed to take over my life. Every night I would get up at 2:00 a.m. and study this material and the connections between God and the great order in the atom.

It became like the school of the prophets for me as I learned about Helen's discoveries of the connections between the atom and religion and how we live our lives. Though I spent only 9 months in Mesa, Arizona, the realization of a circular layout for the elements would change how I saw everything from that time forward.

In every Sunday school class I wanted to teach the principles found in the atom. To say that I had a ripe and anxious audience would have been the antithesis of my experiences. The timing was obviously not right. I would constantly hear the question, "Why do I need to know this? It's not needed for my exaltation. What difference does it make anyway?"

No one will be required to recite the periodic table at the judgment bar. Even so, there is much to be gained by understanding the laws and principles in all things—which certainly focuses on atoms.

I connected with Yvonne Bent during her study of sacred geometry and the Articles of Faith while she was studying the octets in the atoms. She came to a place where she was trying to

---

[1] Absolute Placement

[2] Helen A. Pawlowski, *The Visualization of the Atom*, 1990, The Pawlowski Family Trust, Riverton, Utah. 84065.

understand the patterns of the geometric shapes with the messages in the Articles of Faith. After an answer to prayer, we connected through the hand of the Lord, for it could not have been any other way. When she first saw the circular periodic chart, she exclaimed that she knew what she was looking at was in the correct alignment, as the elements, Gold, Silver, and Copper, were on the north ray. That might not be very significant at first glance, but those are the metals used in the ancient temples, and they are used for the transmission of light. But why would their placement make any difference?

One of Helen's major breakthroughs on the circular periodic table was the placement of copper, silver, and gold. These elements graduate from a place as alkali metals to the top elements on Ray 1.

As we continued to study the table and discuss chiasms, knowing that since the atom was the pattern of all things, I knew there must be chiasms in the atom.

After a lengthy discussion regarding the pattern of chiasmus in all things, I asked the Lord where the chiasmus was in the atom. When I awoke in the morning, into my mind sprang the answer: The second ray of sliders, or super givers, are completely symmetrical or chiasmatic in their electron distribution.[1] I didn't even look at the electron distribution chart at that time. I knew that I had received the answer I was looking for.

The circular periodic table is a delight to examine. It looks identical to a compass, having 8 rays with north and south poles, as well as a right and left side.[2] Everything on the right side is a giver. Everything on the left side is a receiver. There are a number of important things to identify with the periodic table in a circular format.

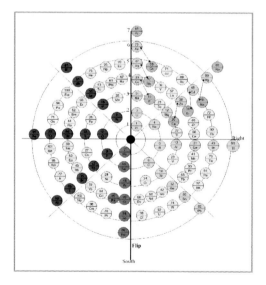

Figure 1 Helen Pawlowski's Circular Periodic Chart

---

[1] See Bohr's Electron Distribution Chart at chapter end.

[2] For a thorough study of the circular periodic table, which answers the questions of quantum and absolute placement, see Helen Pawlowski, The Visualization of the Atom, 1987, 1990.

The entire explanation of the circular motion can be followed in the figure 8 pattern. We will have a very quick overview of some of the myriad of ways in which to study the elements and movement on the table.

First, navigation through the table.

The atom starts with a North South Polarity Line. Add to this an East-West line. Add to this plus sign + two lines, a multiply sign X. These are the eight Rays.

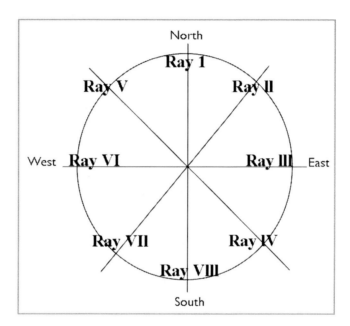

After Ray IV there is a flip taking you back up to the top and starting on the left side. The Pattern is ∞, the number 8 (for octect) and certainly for infinity\

This paper is intended to demonstrate the chiasmus in the atom. It is not intended for a thorough explanation of the elements and positioning. But a brief study the chiastic elements, their location on the periodic table, and their functions and similarities will be illuminating, even for a small moment.

•All the chiastic elements are on the alkali earth ray.

•The alkaline earth metals are more chemically active than most metals.

1.   Beryllium (4) and the distribution is 2-2. The properties of beryllium are high heat absorption and it is perfect as a precipitation hardener in cooper and nickel.

2.   Calcium (20), and the electron distribution is 2-8-8-2. Calcium is very important in our bodies, making strong bones and teeth, and being an alkaline, or an anti-acid, because all acids

are takers. It is also considered a *getter*, which is a substance that removes unwanted elements that would otherwise contaminate the metal.

3.   Strontium (38), and the distribution is 2-8-18-8-2. Finely powdered strontium metal will ignite spontaneously in air to produce both strontium oxide and strontium nitride.

Principal uses of strontium compounds are in fireworks and warning flares and in greases. A little is used as a *getter* in vacuum tubes to remove the last traces of air. Strontium's high-energy radiation can be used to generate an electric current,

4.   Barium (56), which is 2-8-18-18-8-2. Barium is a soft and ductile metal and is used in sparkplugs, vacuum tubes, fireworks, fluorescent lamps. Insoluble barium sulfate is used for body imaging.

5.   Radium (88), which is 2-8-18-32-18-8-2. Radium is known to be radioactive. Purified radium and some radium compounds glow in the dark (luminesce).

Why is this significant? Each of these elements has the ability to be structurally capable of processing light and lots of it. The pattern which can be observed by these chiastic elements is their ability to transfer light and heat, a refining process.

Light is the power by which all things are made; $E=Mc^2$. Energy equals matter times the speed of light. Einstein's relationship converts matter to energy. Those in science have been searching for a mathematical equation equivalent to $E=Mc^2$ for a "Grand Unifying Theory" or "A Theory of Everything" with no success. Helen Pawlowski gave us a picture showing the order of all matter! With this order science will find the Grand Unifying Theory. All energies and all powers are found within the atom, as matter and energy are related to each other.

The spirit and the body are the soul of man (D&C 88:15). The spirit is the light, the life the spiritual part of the soul, and the body is the elements, the atoms, and the matter part of the soul. Inseparably connected, the body and the spirit receive a fullness of joy. Both the physical and spiritual parts must be joined together to bring this joy. And when they become inseparably connected, resurrected, they may receive a fullness of joy.

In examining the circular periodic table, it is interesting to see the perfect balance of giving and receiving, but especially the giving and receiving of more and more light, until the perfect day.

Comprehending the chiasmus in the elements that conduct light throughout the alkali earths makes it easier to comprehend the light flowing throughout the body as the temple. Understanding an atom and the patterns in the microcosm leads to the understanding of things much more complex as in a macrocosm because the same laws govern everything in the same progressive pattern.

It was most interesting to note that upon examining the elements that coincide with priesthood ordinations, there was a decided jump in comprehension. If at the age of 8 a child becomes accountable, meaning being able to account, and oxygen is the 8th element, which causes things to catch on fire and put off light, then immediately one begins to see that it is by the process of giving off light that we become like God.

CHIASMUS IN SACRED ARCHITECTURE

by Val Brinkerhoff

Introduction

Chiastic structure *is* part of the order inherent in inspired sacred architecture the world over, including LDS temples. This special form of symmetry, with a Christ-centered focus, may lie at the heart of three basic archetypes utilized in inspired sacred structures. These include the *square,* where an X marks centrality in *space,* the *circle* – where all revolves around the still center through *time*, and *the vesica pisces* – where *creation* occurs at the intersection of complimentary opposition. How is this done and what does it teach us?

Finding meaning in Latter-day Saint temple worship, and the architecture which houses it, has been a personal focus for some time. For many years, however, my temple experience was unfulfilling. I knew the problem wasn't the temple itself nor God, it was me. I wasn't searching and therefore I wasn't finding. Thus began a long, intensive journey to understand what a temple was and what it was teaching, but primarily from a visual perspective. In addition to immersion in scripture and many good books, this journey of discovery took me around the world to study and experience mostly ancient temples and their symbolic form. I explored pyramids in Egypt and Central America, temple complexes in Cambodia and Myanmar, and standing stone circles in Scotland, Brittany and Portugal. Eventually I turned to historic Christian churches and Gothic Cathedrals in Europe for more Christ-centered connections. Finally I focused on Latter-day Saint temples, while interviewing numerous LDS temple architects. It was during this intensive travel, exploration and research period that various archetypal forms crystallized into recognizable patterns of importance, the most important ones centering on Jesus Christ. One of these patterns is visual chiasmus.

Early on I wasn't sure what the architectural patterns discovered were expressing, but I knew instinctively they were important. Knowing there were patterns, through repeated exposure to them in diverse settings, helped me search out and identify many of them in scripture. Seeing them first in sacred architecture provided an essential key for discovery of their related meaning thereafter in scripture. Rich layers of the gospel, including many deeper doctrines, then began to unfold. Some were hidden in the buildings and scripture all along. Patterns like eight green pillars, for example, surrounding a fifth century baptismal font, appeared to have association with "the eighth day" found throughout scripture; a simple number and color pattern expressing rebirth, renewal or resurrection visually. Temple priests in the Old Testament, or those suffering with leprosy, for example, emerged after seven days of ritual purification – clean and renewed on the eighth day. We know this rebirth is made possible through the mercy of Christ, "the mediator of the New Covenant" (76:69) - through His Atonement and the Resurrection.

Searching Latter-day Saint temples for some of the same forms, archetypes and symbols seen around the world was fruitful. This was especially evident on our most significant structures, such as the Nauvoo Temple, designed under the prophetic direction of Joseph Smith - *the* prophet of the Restoration. Classic archetypes mixed with extensive, unique usage of heavenly motifs is evident there and elsewhere. One of these is the rising sun on the horizon, symmetrically balanced between two pillars; an important architectural motif there and later on Salt Lake Temple, both displaying the chiasmus pattern connecting the structure to the heavens.

The research, in addition to satisfying deeper gospel insights, included a widening circle of friends, those searching for more in their worship and scripture study. One of the first of these new friends was Yvonne Bent. As visual artists, we shared a passion for inspired form wherever it was found, experiencing it initially in the magical order of number, shape and geometry. As our friendship and knowledge expanded, so did our understanding of the order and intelligence of God. Consistent patterns were evident in His creations, but many were expressed in wonderfully different ways, including chiasmus patterns, found not only in scripture, but in the best sacred architecture. Christ was at their center. What are these visual chiasms, and what do they express in association with Him?

Chiasmus: Centrality within Symmetry

The Order of Symmetry   Architecture in general uses symmetry in three basic ways; 1. *Bilateral symmetry,* where two halves of a structure mirror each other, 2. *Spatial symmetry,* where a central object, like an altar, is the central focus of a room or other feature, and 3. *Circular symmetry,* which features movement around a still center, like the planets revolving around the sun. Symmetry in architecture is important in establishing *order.* All of creation is dependent upon order. Vitruvius, the famous Greek trained Roman architect, stated, "symmetry, which is harmony and the basis of architecture, is best represented in the measurement and balance of the human body." [158]This is why so many Greek temples were patterned after the human form. The symmetrical order of the face, typically defines the very essence of *beauty* today. Symmetry, order and beauty thus go together.

Symmetry provides balance, order and beauty in architecture of all kinds, especially sacred architecture. Here usage of an odd numbers of towers provide chiastic symmetry, that focused on the center. Left, Manti Utah Temple; Center, Salt Lake City Utah Temple; and Right, Oakland California Temple

Symmetry in general is often tied to the principle of *complimentary opposition.* In Latter-day Saint theology, opposing symmetry often focuses on male and female as co-creators with God. The enlightened single soul has inner balance, but the exalted man and woman in the unity of the Eternal Covenant, achieve the symmetry and oneness necessary to become eternal creators like God, found at the center of Facsimile Two in the act of creation.[159]

Four of seven classic geometric motifs possessing opposing symmetry in their basic form. Far left, The circle in square; Left, interlocking squares of the Seal of Melchizedek; Right, opposing triangles of the Star of David; & Far right, inverted pentagram in a circle with an upright pentagon at center. Others include the Yin-Yang motif, the vesica pisces, and two opposing spirals. All seven motifs feature duality and are found in or on LDS temples.

Pythagoras recognized the beauty of order in the heavens and in nature. He called it *cosmos*. Aristotle later defined geometric symmetry as the natural order and perfection of the cosmos, that typical of heavenly spheres cycling endlessly above us.[160] Brigham Young equated the order he desired the Saints to have with this kind of beauty. For him, order in art, gardens or temples, revealed God-inspired intelligence – that reflected in the heavens above. Symmetry and order for him was beauty. It invites the Spirit. In inspired Christian architecture, however, the essence of *chiastic* symmetry is a Christ-centered concept, balanced between symmetrical forms on either side of it.

Left, rising sun window between two pillars, Nauvoo Temple Celestial Room; Center, Pyramid of the Niches (Mexico), with the triangular symmetry of scriptural chiasmus from the Book of Mormon (Alma 13:2-9)[161]; Right, Alpha and Omega symbol above a window, Salt Lake Temple. Each features a central focus point in its balanced symmetry.

The Purpose of Chiasmus in Architecture   How is chiastic structure employed for divine instruction in inspired architecture? More importantly, what does it teach us? The answers are diverse and layered. The material hereafter will thus be limited to three elemental archetypes effectively utilizing visual chiasmus for teaching Christ-centered concepts. Our journey begins in the heavens and remains there much of the way.

Left, chiastic three-part symmetry in the Gothic arched doorways of Amiens Cathedral, France. Note the subtle rising sun (Rose window) between two pillars design; Center, octagonal labyrinth at Amiens positioned centrally at the entrance, with a long central axis to the altar in the east- direction of light; Right, North transept circular stained-glass window at Amiens with five-meter inverted pentagram at center – symbol for Christ as the evening and morning star. The Cathedral also references Mary his mother in its name - the Cathédrale Notre-Dame d'Amiens, France

I. The Square & Ancient Centrality: *The Shape of Space*

Chiastic centrality begins with orientation relative to the four points of the compass - *space*, symbolized in the square, and specifically - orientation to the rising sun in the east at the equinoxes, the only time the sun rises and sets due east and west. Diagonal lines crossing the square, mark the two solstices and the two equinoxes - *time*. Before the Latin cross became the dominant symbol in Christianity, the more symmetrical X cross was common for a season. Christ-centered connections to the chiastic X cross may have originated in the heavens, where at least four different crosses are found (the *chi* of chiasmus is the Greek letter X).

Anciently the location of the temple was determined by a priest with a staff or rod, symbol of power. He ceremonially marked the temple's centrality in space and time beneath the heavens. He did so first with a stake or pole driven into the ground. This marked the exact center place for the start of temple's construction. The ancient priest marked the spot for the *templum* by "cutting" it – that is, setting two lines at right angles to one another, an X marking the spot, relative to the four compass points.[162] "The word *templum* signifies space marked for taking observations." The word *tem* has reference to positioning within *horizontal* space, while *plum* has reference to the plumb line - a *vertical*, pole-like line used for measuring. This vertical line symbolized the sacred pillar or tree extending heavenward, connecting the three worlds; the underworld, this world, and heaven, joining past, present, and future. Hence the "cutting" by the priest involved marking the center point of both horizontal sacred *space*, and the vertical pillar of *time*.

At least four crosses appear to be illustrated in the heavens above. Some are connected to the ancient high roads; pathways for heavenly bodies and the spirits of men. All of them call attention to Christ.

A. The Space & Time Cross   The first cross is marked by the intersection of the four directional lines of horizontal, flat *space*. This cross utilizes one line oriented due east and west - the line of the rising and setting sun at the equinoxes (spring and fall). The other line is perpendicular to it, oriented north to south - marking the solstices (summer and winter). A second X overlapping that of the equinoxes and solstices, and perpendicular to it, marks the four in-between cross-quarter days. These two X's and their eight points represent the entirety of space and earthly time. They were used by ancient priests to mark the centrality of the temple, a ceremonial nail driven in the center of the X to hold everything in place. The four-headed figures at the center of most Egyptian hypocephali are symbols of God and his power within this centrality of the four divisions of space and eternal time.[163] According to Nibley, the few hypocephali featuring two-headed gods at center (our own Facsimile Two), symbolize *yesterday - left*, and *tomorrow - right*, the present in between them; thus God's power over all creation within the cosmos.[164] Browne adds that the Hebrew *Tenupha* ceremony involved oblations waved before the Lord by the priest, "unto the four quarters of the world, after the form of a cross; as in peace offerings." He stated that this same X pattern or *Tau* mark was used in the coronation and anointing of ancient kings.[165]

X Crosses, left to right: Church foundation cross, eastern Portugal; Church door cross with opposing spirals, Paris France; Sidewalk marker, Joseph Smith Memorial building, Salt Lake City

The number eight is associated with eternity, especially in the horizontal figure-8 form. Astronomers, for example, have long known of the *analemma*, a figure-8 created by tracking the sun's path over exactly one year relative to the earth.[166] It signals the eternal nature of cyclical time. The figure-8 (two eternal circles joined by a central X) is one of two features in LDS temple Sealing Rooms illustrating the eternal nature of the covenants made there, transcending earthly time. The other is reflecting mirrors on opposing walls, the altar centered in-between them. Both feature visual chiasmus – centrality within opposing symmetry. A chain of figure-8's (in gold-leaf) typically encircle LDS temple Sealing Rooms; the two circles joined at the central X - potentially illustrating two eternities – with mortality on earth in-between them. Bruce R. McConkie stated, "There was a past eternity and there will be a future eternity.   W.W. Phelps, who worked with Joseph Smith as one his scribes on the *Egyptian Grammar and Alphabet* wrote that they had determined from the papyri that the age of our current system was 2,550,000,000 years old (2.5 billion years) and that this represented *one eternity*. Some scientists have calculated that this same time period is required for our universe to make one complete turn or *one eternal round*.[168]

The chiastic X of the figure-8 may also illustrate Christ's mission in the meridian or center place of time; fulfilled in the atonement. It was not long after his death that the X (also called the *tau* mark) became a symbol associated with *protection* through Christ (much like the pentagram and the Seal of Solomon later on).[169] In time the X became a symbol of Christianity on shields in Rome (as found in the equal length arms of the *Chi-Rho* symbol). Still later it was used by the Crusaders.[170] Today the X has been turned vertical, its bottom line elongated, becoming *the* most recognizable Christian symbol – the Latin cross, associated with the instrument of his death, rather than centrality in space and time.

According to McConkie, meridian means, both the center of time and the high point or apex of time, positioned at the center of the earth's *8000*-year existence. He stated that the little season, spoken of by John the Revelator following the Millennium, "is presumed to be another thousand years. The millennial era will be the seventh period of one thousand years of this earth's temporal continuance; thus an added thousand-year period is needed to place the meridian of time in the midpoint in history." [171]

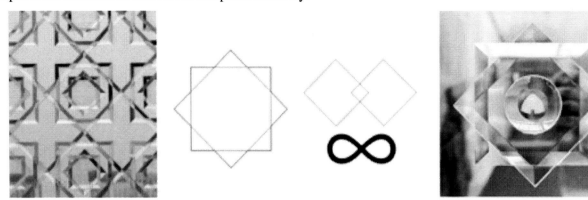

Center, The vertical overlap of the 2 squares of the Seal of Melchizedek may be a modified expression of the horizontal figure-8, both endless and eternal motifs perhaps expressing the eternal nature of time through the sealing power of the Melchizedek priesthood; Left, entrance door motifs of the San Diego California Temple; Right, entrance door motif of the Salt Lake Temple (Annex); Notice also the octagon formed at the center of the motif. As a filled-in star it possesses 8 points, potentially pointing to intersecting space and time: 2 equinoxes, 2 solstices and 4 cross-quarter days.

Time is a component of mortality, a period given us to prove ourselves worthy of God's greatest blessing, eternal life. God said that the "priesthood continueth in the church of God in all generations, and is without beginning of days or end of years" (D&C 84:17). This doctrine, in connection with the priesthood, may be expressed in what some Latter-day Saints today call the Seal of King Melchizedek; an ancient archetype associated with two opposing and overlapping square outlines. It was first seen on an LDS temple at San Diego, and has layered meaning, one of them potentially representing all space and time; its eight points illustrating the two equinoxes, the two solstices and the four cross-quarter days of earth's the time cycle. Time may also be represented folded over upon itself; the past represented below or left, and the future above or right, the present at its chiastic center.

Repeating, horizontal figure-8 designs were found first in LDS context in the Kirtland Temple and continue to be utilized around the upper portion of Sealing Rooms of many modern LDS temples. Intersecting circles also surround the octagonal skylight in the new Nauvoo Temple Celestial Room. Their high placement may express future ascension into the presence of God in *eternity*, signaled by stars. Similar motifs were found on the ancient stonework of Herod's Temple in Jerusalem and in many religious structures the world over.[172]

The Two Seals of the Priesthood   It is more likely, however, that the two squares represent two priesthood seals. God has said that he is the same "from eternity to eternity" (D&C 76:4), and that he is Endless and Eternal (Moses 7:35). The sealing power of the higher priesthood binds or seals families together on earth and in heaven, its power extending into the past (for those who have died), through the present (for those performing the ordinances), and into the future (children born under the covenant). One of Joseph Smith's primary missions in the Restoration was to restore the sealing power as part of the fullness of the priesthood, a mission he attempted to complete before his martyrdom at Nauvoo. This fullness binds families together through all *space* and *time*. According to Joseph Smith, it possesses *two seals*. He stated that the first was, "placed upon a man and woman when they made the covenant [of marriage] and the other was the seal which allotted to them their particular mansion [when they were sealed up to eternal life]." [173] Both seals are recognized on earth *and* in heaven. San Diego Temple Architect Bill Lewis placed some 10,000 of these motifs on the temple. He stated, "The temple itself is a symbol…I just took the dedicatory prayer [by President Ezra Taft Benson], and looked through it for symbols…So the symbol [of the two interlocking squares], for us as members, is certainly the fullness of the priesthood." [174]

B. The Observatory Cross (the horizon & the ecliptic)   A second X above us involves the intersection of the horizontal *horizon line* (where heaven and earth join), which intersects with the vertical line of the *ecliptic* overhead. This specific point on the horizon serves as the rudimentary observatory of the ancients, a natural telescope for viewing the relationship of space and time. The ecliptic is the circular path of the wandering "stars" above us - the moving sun and planets, versus the fixed literal stars behind them. Anciently these were called the seven *planetes* (Greek for "wanderers"), all appearing to move overhead in a single circular pathway from east to west, following the sun's path - sunrise to sunset. This great circle (half of it above us in the day and the other half below us at night), appears to go around the earth. This was the ancient geocentric earth viewpoint of the heavens, one Abraham and the prophets of scripture were shown in vision. The sun's path is also a straight-line from east to west at the equinoxes, also seen when the circular path is viewed from its edge.[175] Thus, a second cross is formed by the intersection of the horizontal horizon line and the vertical ecliptic line - that illustrated in the straight course of the sun each day. This cross, in association with the sun, may be found in D&C 3:2, which states, "His paths are straight, and his course is one eternal round."

*Sacrificial Animals Illustrated in the Heavens: Left, relief of Apis (**bull**-headed figure) between Horus-right and Pharoah-left (courtesy Gunther Eichhorn), Temple of Horus, Edfu Egypt; Center, **lamb** (or **ram** [provided by God in place of Isaac]) stained-glass window, Duomo, Pisa, Italy; and Right, **Pisces** stained-glass window at Chartres Cathedral, France.*

The lower arc of the sun's travel at night is associated with the ancient "underworld" of many cultures, including Native Americans, who believe their ancestors emerged from a previous world (the sipapu of Anasazi ruins, for example). This underworld is the "duat" of the Egyptians, where Osiris battled dark forces before he, like the sun on the horizon each day, was resurrected.

Zodiac Signs   The sun at dawn in the ecliptic, set against the stars behind, as it rises above the horizon on the spring equinox, marks the zodiac sign and time period we are currently in.[176] This chiastic celestial X may also mark God's choice for the animal sacrifices of antiquity. The Savior was born in the age of Pisces – the fish. This sign signaled his birth as Savior and *mediator* of the world. Throughout Christ's life we see the fish playing a dominant role—in the calling of "fishers of men," twice in the miracle of the loaves and the fishes, and in Christ broiling fish after the Resurrection, during His 40-day ministry. Previously, the sun rose against the sign of the ram (or lamb - the age of Aires).[177] And previous to that, from the fall of Adam and Eve to the time of Abraham, the sun rose against Taurus (the bull). It had previously risen against Gemini, the twins (Adam and Eve in the garden before the Fall). We know that the early sacrifice for Egyptians was the bull. According to Huntington, Joseph Smith stated that Adam also offered the bull as his sacrifice. Later the Israelites sacrificed rams or lambs. Thus, the sun rising vertically upon the horizontal horizon, in the vernal equinox ecliptic, set against a particular constellation (the sign), not only signals time (the zodiac sign we are currently in), but apparently God's choice for the ancient sacrificial animal. The sign and the sacrifice are thus both marked by the chiastic cross in the heavens – X marking the spot.[178] Historically, great world cataclysm occurred with the transition from one sign to the next (each lasting about 2200 years). The eminent move from the age of Pisces into Aquarius may thus be ominous – preceding the great and dreadful day of the Lord.

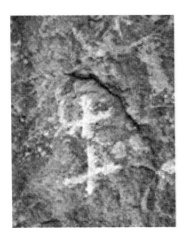   

Left to right: Venus crosses at Parowan Gap in Southern Utah (Piaute), and modern variations in the eight-part stars of the Sacramento and Winter Quarters Nebraska Temples. The two upright crosses of Parowan Gap, one above the other, appear to represent to the two, four-year cycles of Venus (one as morning star and one as evening star, each four years). They mark Venus in connection with the creator God (the Horned Bird Serpent at Parowan & Quetzalcoatl in Central America). He was resurrected as the Morning Star. A number of Latter-day Saint temples feature two, four-part crosses or Venus stars (overlapping one another), like those at Sacramento (right), and Winter Quarters (far right).

C. The Venus Cross   A third cross above is the Venus cross, that created by the criss-crossing patterns of its sophisticated movements, some forming another X above us. Many cultures have documented these patterns, including the Babylonians, the Greeks and the New World Mayans and Native Indians.

God the Father chose the luminous star as the sign to mark the birth of Christ - the light of the world - in the Bible *and* the Book of Mormon. In historic paintings, eight-pointed stars (often featuring two overlapping four-part crosses) typically mark the birthplace of Christ. Venus is the bright and morning star of Revelation 22:16, one of the most luminous "stars" in the night sky. Simple Native American and Mayan rock art crosses symbolize these Venus cycles and its crossing patterns. The time between the first appearance of Venus and its reappearance against the same sign of the zodiac behind, is 1,460 days, or four solar years. This four-year Venus cycle was used by the ancient Greeks as the interval between each of the Olympiades. According to Zehren, "after 1,460 days Venus becomes the Morning star if it was first the Evening star and vice-versa." Thus, the eight-year Venus cycle is equally divided - four years as morning star and four years as evening star.[179]

Native Americans throughout North and Central America have revered Venus, documenting its movements in rock art, associating it with both the cross and the serpent (the feathered serpent of the Mayans [Quetzalcoatl], and the horned bird serpent of the Aztecs and Piautes). Moses may have combined both symbols together when he raised up a serpent upon a pole (perhaps a crossing form at top) for healing purposes in the Old Testament. Both the X-cross and the serpent of the New World were signs for Venus (the evening and morning star), *and* the great white bearded god who visited them and promised to return. It was Christ who stated, "I am the bright and morning star" (Revelation 22:16).

At Parowan Gap in Southern Utah, the Piautes observed the complex criss-crossing of Venus in the night sky, using a variety of X patterns to mark these movements. In addition, two upright rock art motifs next to each other appear to represent the two, four-year Venus cycles. Like the creator God Quetzalcoatl of the Mayans, it was the horned bird serpent of the Piautes who was resurrected as the Morning Star.[180] Two of these crosses near the V-Gap glyph are part of eight different rock art panels at "the Gap" appearing to symbolize the eight-year Venus cycle. This important eight-year resurrection date featured Venus (as *son*) rising in conjunction with the sun (father) and moon (mother) at the Spring Equinox (start of a new growing season, and for some cultures – the New Year). Archeologist Garth Norman believes this important Venus event was discovered some 250 years before the Mayans did so in Central America. His research suggests this Venus knowledge may have transferred to the Mayans via turquoise trading routes in 777 A.D. (the eighth century).

Eight-part stars are common on historic religious architecture and some LDS temples. Some feature two overlapping stars, each with four points, such as those at Sacramento and Winter Quarters. They appear to represent the two, four-year cycles of Venus, eight years total. The Nauvoo Temple also features the inverted pentagram, an ancient archetype formed in the heavens by the path of Venus over an exact eight-year period. It is the only known heavenly body to do so. Venus as a type for Christ is thus symbolized by the cross, the eight-part star, and the pentagram. The Venus oriented numbers 5 and 8 are also frequently illustrated in Native American rock art.[181]

Ancient Swastika   A variation of the Venus cross, with bent ends, is the swastika; a representation of the turning cosmos. It suggests the four cardinal directions of space – and on land, *migrations by Native American ancestors,* to the four compass points, and then back to a central, chiastic gathering place.[182] The Hopi's migrations include a variation. They currently inhabit the fourth world, having "emerged" into it from a previous lower world. With the next future cataclysm, they will "emerge" into a fifth world and age, when Masaw the creator will return. The Fire Clan was given a two-sided sacred stone tablet (about four inches square) by Masaw (Christ) to guide them. Like other clans, they were directed to "migrate" north, south, east and west, before settling on a permanent home. Their combined travel routes formed a great cross at the final gathering place - Oraibi on third Mesa in the southwest. These four directional migrations are symbolized in the four arms of the swastika decorating their pottery and clothing, in their use of four colors, four-day purification ceremonies, the four pillars holding up kiva roofs, etc.[183]

The Squared Circle   Latter-day Saints today utilize a similar 4-part spatial symbol with very similar meaning, the squared circle motif, found on Stake Centers and temples to illustrate a similar concept; the gathering of the elect to the stakes of Zion – and to God. The Kirtland Temple featured the first gathering symbol on a latter-day temple, the squared circle – another rudimentary X, representing gathering to God from the four points of the compass. Kirtland was the first such physical gathering place for the Saints. Joseph Smith explained, "…God gathers together His people in the last days, to build unto the Lord a house to prepare them for the ordinances and endowments, washings and anointings, etc." [184]

This gathering is from the four corners of the earth – where the Remnant (Native Americans of the Book of Mormon) migrated to. The Book of Mormon is written to them first, then to Jew and Gentile (Title Page of the Book of Mormon). Eventually the Remnant will construct the New Jerusalem Temple at the earth's center place, thought to be the original Garden of Eden – the earth's first temple. After great judgments pronounced upon the Gentiles, the remaining righteous Gentiles will assist the Remnant in this construction (see 3 Nephi 16, 20 & 21). Some believe this temple will be erected in the Rocky Mountains, home of most Native Americans today, the tops of the mountains of Isaiah.

Centrality in the Salt Lake Valley   Just four days after arriving in the Salt Lake Valley, Brigham Young took his cane (formerly "the rod" owned by Oliver Cowdery) and forcibly struck it to the ground, marking the exact center spot, like ancient priests, for the future Salt Lake Temple, stating: "Right here will stand the great Temple of our God." Brigham Young later had Elder Orson Pratt (Apostle and astronomer) use the base meridian stone near the temple's southeast corner to survey and lay out all city streets from the temple, the center place of Zion. Elder Pratt also built a small observatory near this stone. It became the center place for the mapping of the entire Great Basin, later completed by the federal government in 1870. The centrality of the new temple, combined with Joseph Smith's ordered, square grid system planned for the City of Zion in Missouri, ensured that all city streets in Salt Lake, extending from the temple, possessed cardinality to the four compass points.

In addition to its literal centering in horizontal space, the Salt Lake Temple also makes use of Polaris as a symbolic "centering" motif in the vertical dimension. High atop its west central tower is the Big Dipper, featuring seven, six-pointed stars. They point to Polaris in the northern heavens, suggesting that the temple is a centering place for the Saints, for the things of God available in the order and fullness of the priesthood.

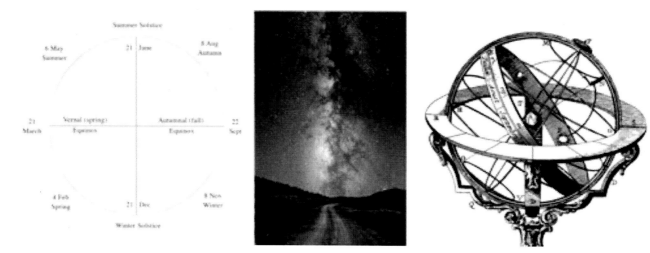

Left, The eight parts (two X's) of the Circle of Time (two equinoxes, two solstices and four cross-quarter days); Center, The Milky Way, a blue river of stars, one of the ancient "high roads. The ecliptic intersects this river forming another cross (Milky Way illustration courtesy Larry Landolfi);" Right—Armillary sphere with celestial equator (horizontal circle around the center of the earth). Note the near vertical ecliptic overhead with zodiac signs and the seven "planates"- including the sun (courtesy Wikipedia Commons). The ecliptic is now tilted 23.5 degrees off the vertical axis towards Polaris in the north. Some believe this shift occurred at the Fall of Adam and Eve, changing the climate as well.

D. The Light over Water Cross   A last, fourth cross is found in two intersecting pathways above, that of light (the sun) in the *ecliptic*, crossing over water (the Milky Way) east to west each day. The *Milky Way* (a blue river of stars running south to north) represents an important ancient pathway in the heavens. The Maya viewed the impressive Milky Way as a great river—a pathway for departed spirits on their journey back to God. He was thought to dwell in the northern heavens (see Isaiah 14:13). The Egyptian Pharoahs were thought to travel these celestial highways (like the Nile itself), doing so in a heavenly boat or bark (see the barks in Facsimile 2) on their journey back to God. Few see the impressive beauty of the Milky Way today due to light pollution and lack of interest. On a dark clear night, however, this luminous river of stars is bluish, the color associated with water and heaven, and priesthood in scripture.

Each day the sun and the planets cross over this river westward in their ecliptic journey. This chiastic X crossing is reflected on earth below, appearing in eight different water-crossings in scripture. Each is a cleansing, accomplished by the miraculous crossing of a great river, sea, or gulf by "*the chosen*," often on dry ground east to west. We read in Alma 26:20, that God's mercy "hath brought us over that everlasting gulf of death and misery, even to the salvation of our souls." Each of the miraculous crossings is part of a great *migration*. (It should be remembered that the number eight symbolizes rebirth throughout scripture and sacred architecture, often in connection with the cleansing power of *water*). Joshua, crossing the Jordan River westward, with the Israelites into the Promised Land, represents one example of the chosen crossing over cleansing water into land promised their posterity. Another is that of Lehi and his family crossing the great gulf of the ocean to the only other Promised Land of scripture - America. An 8th, last crossing is yet to come.[185]

Most of these migrations were east to west, the pathway of the sun in the ecliptic crossing the Milky Way. *Westward* direction in *movement* is consistently tied to righteousness throughout scripture, eastward movement (rather than orientation) is tied to sin.[186] This pattern of light crossing water may reflect being reborn - of water (the Milky Way) - and the spirit (sunlight); a Baptism of Fire and the Holy Ghost, symbolized in the sun.[187]

Left, the Milky Way, running south to north at Parowan Gap, Utah, between the north peak (bottom) and the south peak (top); Right, side view of the south peak profile of the God Tobats, who faces Polaris centered over the north peak.

Crosses on Earth: As Above – So Below

The Temple Cross & the Axis Mundi   The most sacred place within the ancient temple, including the Jerusalem temples was the holy of holies, the navel of the earth, the *omphalos* - X marking *the* spot. This cube-shaped room (representing the presence of God) rested at the center of another square in the ancient temple layout. Next to it, eastward was the square of the courtyard. At its center was the square altar of sacrifice. An implied X cross for Christ thus marked the spot for both altars, a reflection of those found above.

Anciently, the exact site for the Holy of Holies for Solomon's Temple appears to have been marked by the bedrock foundation of the threshing floor of Arauna (Ornan the Jebusite). Situated atop the temple mount (thought to be just north of the octagonal Dome of the Rock today), this central stone was used to thresh grain. It featured one or more oxen pulling a millstone around a central axis, grinding wheat into flour. The cycling motion of the threshing oxen revolving around the central vertical axis, mirrored that of the constellation signs revolving around the north celestial pole—the cosmic axle of the Axis Mundi. This pillar stretches from the chaotic waters of the underworld below, through the earth, and up into the ordered heavens above. This great threshing rock was the "foundation stone" of the Holy of Holies for the ancient Jews.[188] It capped and controlled the waters of creation below it. It is thought that the Holy of Holies of Solomon's Temple was built atop this chiastic central spot.

According to Barker, the great foundation stone, replacing the Ark (the altar of the Second Temple), "was the bastion against ever threatening chaos. Evil and disorder...were represented by the subterranean waters of the great deep, waters which had to be driven back before the creation could be established and God's people live in safety."[189] The light of continuing rituals re-enacted in the temple thereafter, were thought to sustain and renew creation, keeping these forces at bay.[190] Ritual dances and prayer in circles (like that of the Hopi and other cultures today) may help to maintain and renew creation, sustaining order amidst encroaching chaos.

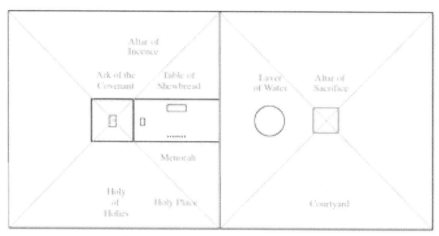

Chiastic centrality of the ancient Tabernacle, with the Ark of the Covenant and the Altar of Sacrifice both centered. The measurements of the tent Tabernacle and Solomon's Temple were 10 x 30 cubits, the Holy of Holies 10 cubits square. These were doubled in Herod's Temple. The Holy Place was a rectangle consisting of two, 10x10 cubit squares. The vertical axis mundi or pillar of fire was most likely positioned directly over the Ark in the Holy of Holies (left). Note how the square with cross resembles an aerial view of an Egyptian pyramid.

Prior to Solomon's Temple, the Israelites kept the ancient tent Tabernacle at the center of their camp as they wandered in the wilderness for forty years. At each stopping place, the tribes camped in an outer area; three tribes at each of the four compass points. The Levites were placed in a more central location, with the temple at center.[191] These four concentric *square* areas reflected a general progression of holiness, from the general population of all Israel in the outer areas, to those responsible for conducting priesthood ordinances (the Levites), and finally to the presence of God - symbolized in the cubed-shaped Holy of Holies. Both Ezekiel's visionary description of the temple, and descriptions found in the Dead Sea Scrolls, reveal a pattern of three concentric zones of increasing holiness, often connected with the square and its four compass points.[192]

Left, Squared circle window at the Kirtland Ohio Temple; Right, Centrality of the ancient temple in Jerusalem. Both feature centrality within the four cardinal directions of space.

The Straight and Narrow Way Back to God

The Two Ways – A Chiastic Return   The return to God involves choice – to go forward or back - a straight and narrow path in two directions. It is a chiastic straight line, centered on alignment to God and our return to Him. We once dwelt with Him, and though now in mortality, our objective is a return to Him. This is symbolized in the linear layout of the ancient Tabernacle, Solomon's Temple, and many modern single floor LDS temples (like the Billings Montana Temple - it is oriented eastward, and movement through its ordinance rooms is from east to west, the Celestial Room at the far end of the straight line westward). Adam and Eve were expelled from the presence of God in the Garden *eastward*. Our symbolic return to God is back, through the long, linear pathway of the ancient temple *westward* – a representation of the Plan of Salvation (see below). The ancient High Priest passed by eight items on this journey, each symbolizing the Great Mediator Jesus Christ.[193] This mirrors the straight-line course of the sun from east to west. Potentially created to withstand the Flood, the Great Pyramid of Egypt also has a single long straight and narrow entrance passage. It ascends to Polaris in the north, and descends to the bottomless pit (below ground level) in the south.[194]

The Temple as a chiastic design displaying the Plan of Salvation, Illustration courtesy David Christensen

Throughout scripture movement eastward is connected to sin, whereas movement westward is connected to righteousness.[195] These opposing directions are also a part of ritual circumambulation – the perceived circular course of the sun around the earth, as clockwise movement around a centralized object is connected to *blessing* (temple cornerstone dedication ceremonies), whereas counterclockwise movement is connected to *cursing* (the walls of Jericho). Both types of movement may be reflected in D&C 3:2, which reads, "his paths are straight, and his course is one eternal round."

God is at the center of the chiastic choice of life, a five-fold covenant path, known anciently as the doctrine of the two ways.[196] There were five lamp-stands on either side of "the way" leading to the Holy of Holies of Solomon's Temple (the presence of God). This appears to be another chiastic visual presentation of the way back to God, made possible in the five portions of the New and Everlasting Covenant of the gospel today. We read in 2 Nephi 33:9, "…be reconciled unto Christ, and enter into the narrow gate, and walk in the strait path which leads to life." The ancient doctrine of the two ways presents us two choices (the law of opposition in all things); the way of life or the way of death. In the New and Everlasting Covenant *of the gospel* first given Adam and Eve, we have laws and ordinances presenting salvation and exaltation – *the way*. In this eternal covenant, made new with us again today, we have opportunity to enter into five total covenants embracing both salvation and exaltation, seen clearly in the temple endowment. These five covenants (foundational pillars of the gospel) represent five points of fellowship between man and god, fully realized in the sacred embrace of antiquity, illustrated on many Egyptian pillars.

In addition to the five pillar-like lampstands lining both sides of "the way" in Solomon's Temple, God directed Moses atop Sinai to use five pillars at the entrance to the ancient Tabernacle (Exodus 26:27); again potentially referencing the five covenants of the temple, covenants critical to our return. They pertain to 1. obedience, 2. sacrifice, 3. the gospel, 4. chastity, and 5. consecration. The principles of obedience and sacrifice, are part of the law of the gospel, seen in the concepts of faith, repentance, baptism and sacrifice (time, tithing, etc.) are part of the salvation or Aaronic portion of the everlasting covenant. Two more Melchizedek Priesthood covenants are added in the temple. These pertain to exaltation and are associated with chastity and consecration. The law of consecration is the great separator. The early Saints had a very difficult time with it, yet scripture informs us that it is law of a Zion people, and of the Celestial Kingdom (D&C 78:7). All covenants made previous to it are preparatory. Pres. Ezra Taft Benson stated, "Until one abides by the laws of obedience, sacrifice, the gospel, and chastity, he cannot abide the law of consecration, which is the law pertaining to the Celestial Kingdom." [197] Two groups of people in scripture demonstrate the final result of the choice between the two ways - life and death. They are the people of Enoch and the people of Noah; the first group was translated, the other destroyed in the Flood.

Cruciform Design   Many Christian churches and Gothic cathedrals are constructed in basic X or cruciform shape – the long nave, typically running west to east, intersected by the shorter transept, running south to north. The long straight line axis typically leads to the altar in the east, reflecting the straight-line path of the sun, part of its circular travel overhead in the ecliptic.

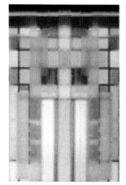  

Cruciform Designs: Left, Stained-glass window, Boston Mass. Temple; Middle, Cruciform created by the intersection of the nave and transept at Amiens Cathedral, France; and Right, aerial view of an LDS church, Elk Ridge, Utah. All three feature the Latin cross, a modern variation of the X above, featuring an elongated bottom line.

The elongated cross of the Gothic Cathedral nave and transept reflects the manner of the Savior's torture at Golgotha rather than the four X crosses above us. The Latin cross is not used by Latter-day Saints because of its connection to torture and death. Instead, the Saints prefer Gethsemane as the symbol of the Atonement – becoming one again with God through Christ. [198] Subtle crosses are found in some Latter-day Saint temples and churches, however. The Mount Timpanogos Temple, for example, features a cruciform shaped Celestial Room ceiling, whereas the Boston Temple features stained glass windows with subtle embedded crosses. Many LDS churches are also cross-shaped from an aerial perspective. Their spires (positioned at the crossing X area) transition from a square at bottom, through an octagonal mid-section, ending with a circle at top. This common transition of shape appears to symbolize the perfecting process, made possible through Christ, the great mediator of the covenant at center.

Some believe church spires echo the pillar of circling fire atop the ancient Tabernacle, or the one seen above the Kirtland Temple at its dedication. They are comparable to the axis pole of the threshing floor of Arauna, upon which the Holy of Holies of Solomon's Temple was built.[199] Such a pillar may have been originally symbolized in the Provo and Ogden Utah temple towers, before the Moroni statues were placed atop them. These spires were originally yellow in color (like fire), resting above what resembles the white cloud shape of the temple below.[200]

II. The Circle: *Shape of Time*

From the stable, static, earth-oriented square with its center X, we turn now to the symmetrical circle, associated with the eternity of heaven, God and light, and cycles of time. The circle is the only shape universally acclaimed as perfect, hence its use as the geometric symbol for all things divine the world over. The circle is a graphic expression of not only chiastic centrality, but movement and harmony. It is endless, appearing to be in perpetual motion, yet it possesses a still center around which all things revolve – the place where time stands still. The circle symbolizes the number one; the chiastic center place, as well as unity.[201] Of all shapes, the circle provides the greatest internal volume with the smallest external perimeter. Various rituals in many ancient cultures involved the circle, mirroring and harmonizing with, the circling heavens above. Some feature joyful singing, music, worshipful prayer or dance. Such circles also interface with the square, as they are conducted within the four cardinal directions of space; participants often facing each of the four compass points. Some cultures believed these ritual circles aided the opening of a fiery pillar of light to God in the north, a vertical Axis Mundi connecting the three worlds.

For millennia the circle has had association with physical and spiritual *protection,* and with sacredness. The most sacred ordinances are tied to it, including the early covenant rites of circumcision, and baptism in circular temple fonts today. Blessings surrounding the sick are in a circle, as are temple cornerstone dedication ceremonies which circumambulate the building clockwise. The most sacred prayers are often in circles.[202] We find spiraling ascension in temple staircases at Nauvoo and Manti, and spiraling movement through ordinance rooms in the Salt Lake and Cardston Temples.

Chiastic, Sun-Centered Zodiacs. Left, Beit Alpha zodiac, 5th-6th century, Israel. The Sun god Helios is depicted at center in a chariot drawn by four horses. The four seasons are found at the four corners; Nisan (Spring); Tamuz (Summer); Tishri (Autumn) and Tevet (Winter). Right, zodiac with eight-part sun at center, Library of Congress, Washington D.C.

Many historic cathedrals make use of circles in their great overhead domes. Some feature circular stained-glass windows with a rose or pentagram at center. Others have circular labyrinths on floors just inside their front doors. The common Gothic arched doorway and window (also seen in the Kirtland Temple) make use of two intersecting circles, forming the *vesica pisces* at center; a motif focused on *creation* (discussed later on). Ultimately the chiastic symmetry of the never-ending circle focuses on God at center, whether seen in the circling stars of the zodiac around the sun, or Christ in the midst of the Apostles in an ancient prayer circle. Both feature twelve around one – the number 13 centered on Christ.[203] The circle around a chiastic central point is the Egyptian symbol for light.[204] Faith has always centered on God, our communication with Him and eventual ascent to Him. The very center scripture of the Bible, Psalm 118:8, encourages us to trust in the Lord – not man.[205]

Three Connections to the Circling Heavens

Inspired sacred architecture is connected to the heavens. Ancient standing stone temples like Stonehenge mark sacred *space*, and are tied to the heavens via the eternal nature of cyclical *time* above them.[206] Time was marked and symbolized on many temples anciently to establish times for important rituals and ordinances, connecting them to the past, present and future. Modern temples interface with the heavens as well, and remain a key in understanding the space-time relationship. Connections between the earthly temple and the circling heavens are both symbolic and literal, revealed in three ways.

Measure of Space & Time   The first of these is the *measure* of *space* in inches, feet or sacred cubits, for example, often symbolizing *measured time*. This is often done in a circle, representing, for example, the solar year or the great year (the precession of the equinoxes). The Great Pyramid of Egypt utilizes measure well to illustrate both of these years and much more. The measure of its circumference at ground level (the first course of the masonry) in pyramid inches, for example, matches the measure of the length of the earth's *solar year* (a cycle of time on earth). These ordered numbers (36524246) correspond to days, hours, minutes and seconds in our year. In addition, the circumference of the pyramid at the 50th course of its masonry, marking the all-red King's Chamber inside, matches exactly the length of *the Great Year*, more commonly known as the Precession of the Equinoxes (a foundational cycle of time in our galaxy – the time it takes all twelve signs of the zodiac to circle back to the same point in the night sky - 25,826.54 years). This is also the exact number of pyramid inches provided in the sum of the two crossing diagonal base lines of the Great Pyramid - the X-cross of its foundation. There are many such space-time correspondences in measure in this, one's of the earth's oldest and most impressive structures. It is thought by some to be a pre-Egyptian memorial to the resurrected Christ.[207]

Heavenly Symbols   A second connection to the heavens, also making use of the space-time relationship, is the use of symbolic sun, moon and star motifs on two early historic LDS temples, for example, symbolizing advancing space and the slowing of time as one vertically ascends each of their pillar-like pilasters (30 at Nauvoo and 50 at Salt Lake, symbolizing the eternal covenants made inside their great circle). Circumambulating the Salt Lake Temple's moon phases - clockwise, we complete one solar year. Ascending its pilasters vertically, we experience earthly weeks (earthstones), lunar months (moonstones), solar years (sunstones), and finally the realm of the gods in the stars of eternity (starstones). This is the ancient eighth heaven, beyond the seven heavens (the rotation circles of the six known "planets", including the sun). Saturnstones were in the original plans for the Salt Lake Temple (above the sunstones at the top of the temple's walls), and would have marked the jump off point from earthly time to the eternity of the stars beyond, as anciently Saturn was also known as *Kronos* (chronograph – watch), a last outpost for time.

Physical Connection to Light   A third heavenly connection is literal or physical, featuring direct contact normally with the light of the sun, via temple orientation eastward, for example (the Great Pyramid also interfaces with the stars, via four shafts, pointing to Polaris and Orion). Each day the rising sun on the horizon symbolizes life, hope and resurrection – all embodied in Jesus Christ. At the spring equinox, the resurrection of the sun on this date marks the ancient New Year (April General Conference for Latter-day Saints today); a time to gather and renew covenants with him in His temple. The rising sun on the horizon is the most common architectural motif on both the Nauvoo and Salt Lake Temples, seen above nearly every door and window of both structures – inside and out – pathways for light. It is an important symbol of His light, and a reminder of the invitation to enter into it.

All three of these space-time markers serve as heavenly witnesses of creation and the Great Creator, but only for those with sufficient understanding to recognize and appreciate their great order and beauty.

Horizontal Cyclical Time   Important events occur at important points in cyclical time; time marked by the heavens – both the sun and the moon. Anciently, the sun marked *the season* for the ancient Hebrew holy days (such as spring equinox), whereas a specific moon phase following it, marked the *exact day* for its start (full moon for Passover, the new moon for the Feast of Trumpets). According to Nibley, "The all-important timing of rites and festivals required close observation of the heavens." [208] The Holy days were ancient set times for man's appointments with God at the temple, where important rituals and ordinances were performed. [209] The two equinoxes divided the year symmetrically in half – marking two sets of three holy days each, centered on *mercy* (the spring holy days), and *judgment* (the fall holy days). (The fall equinox marked the civil New Year in ancient Israel, the spring equinox marking the sacred New Year. The Lord reversed these two New Years dates after the Babylonian captivity.) Pentecost was in-between them (7 holy days total). The authors of Hamlet's Mill have pointed out that many ancient cultures believed portals opened at these two mid-points in the circle of time; to heaven above at the spring equinox, and to the underworld below at the fall equinox. Events in early Church history appear to reflect this, the equinoxes connected to important events associated with the Prophet Joseph Smith and the *Restoration*, including the First Vision (at or near the spring equinox), and Moroni's repeated visitations to the young Prophet as part of the Coming forth of the Book of Mormon - all on the fall equinox, a book speaking about future judgment, from the dust—*the past*). [210]

The symmetry of the equinoxes also marked the two most important holy days – Passover and Tabernacles. The start of Passover (like most of the holy days) was marked by the full moon, occurring approximately two weeks after the spring equinox (and new moon). This coincided with April 6th at the time of the Savior in the meridian of time, and was the key date for a number of events in His life.

Today, these 'set' times for temple rituals are most often illustrated by the clearest time-centered sphere on LDS temple architecture; the moon in its changing phases. A number of LDS temples feature advancing moonstones around their horizontal perimeter. On the Salt Lake Temple this is done through four repeating moon phases, illustrating monthly cycles through an entire year. [211] The moon phases on the east and west central towers mark two symmetrical mid-points in the modern yearly cycle of time: April and October, our general conference dates. These correspond to the two important solemn assembly dates in ancient Israel—Passover and Tabernacles respectively. They divide the year in half. Its circle is made up of four seasons, each thirteen weeks in length. At the Palmyra New York Temple, the advancing moon phases not only express one calendar year, but two of its moon phases mark three dates of historical importance. The birthday of the Savior is marked by an April 6 moon phase, which is also the dedication date of the temple. This moon phase is located over the south Tree of Life window (the exterior of the Celestial Room). The martyrdom date of the Prophet Joseph Smith (June 27th) is marked by another moon phase directly opposite the Sacred Grove on the west side of the temple.

Left, Chiastic symmetry of the Salt Lake Temple, aligned to equinox sunrise and sunset; Right, The east central tower of the Salt Lake Temple features the moon phase for April 6, 1878 as observed by Apostle and astronomer Orson Pratt. Note also the central Alpha keystone atop the Omega arch with five-part star at center. It also resembles a half-circle rising sun on the horizon between two pillars. Each of these symbols is Christ-centered.

April was the time of the early planting season in ancient Israel; a period of springtime rebirth and renewal. It is also the birth month of Jesus Christ, the great High Priest, and the time of many important events in the Savior's life, including his baptism, death and resurrection, all at Passover – events centered on *mercy*. Church history has witnessed a number of important events on these two seasonal dates marked by the heavens. Those in the spring include the organization of the Church in 1830, the dedication of the Church's first temple at Kirtland, and the dedications of many temples, including the Salt Lake, St. George, and Palmyra Temples. This season centers on hope and rebirth. Moroni's repeated visits to Joseph Smith, however, exactly at the fall equinox, center on coming judgments in the last days, as evidenced in his quotes of Malachi, etc., and the consistent warnings to the gentiles in the Book of Mormon – its central message being repentance.

The Salt Lake Temple is positioned relative to the sun in symmetrical fashion. Its west central Aaronic priesthood tower features an October moon phase, as identified by astronomer, scientist, and early Apostle Orson Pratt.[212] This was the birth month of John the Baptist. October coincided with the fall harvest season in which three of the seven Hebrew holy days were celebrated; all of them connected to *judgment* (the Feast of Trumpets, the Day of Atonement, and the Feast of Tabernacle (in connection with repentance, judgment, and the return of the king respectively). The east central Melchizedek priesthood tower (6 feet higher than the west towers and facing the origin of light) features an early April moon phase. April occurs *6 months* after October and is the birth month of Jesus Christ – signaled in the April 6 moon phase on the east central tower (the temple has 50 total moon phases). The springtime festivals are connected to God's mercy (*Passover, Unleavened Bread,* and *Firstfruits,* in connection with atonement, purification, and resurrection respectively).[213] April 6 was the dedication date for the southeast cornerstone of the temple in 1853, and the final dedication of the temple when the capstone was placed 50 years later in 1893. Pentecost (the presence of the Lord's Spirit) is centered within the seven holy days between the three spring and three fall holy days, coming 50 days after Passover). Thus the great outpouring of the Lord's spirit at Pentecost was also chiastic.

The Salt Lake Temple exterior showcases movement of heavenly bodies, indicating centrality in space and time. The moons feature four different phases (months) starting with April on the east central Melchizedek priesthood tower. This phase represents the Savior's birth month, the organization date of the Church, its dedication date, Passover, and April General Conference. Proceeding around the temple 180 degrees to the west central Aaronic priesthood tower is the October moon phase, John the Baptist's birth month, corresponding to Tabernacles and October General Conference. One solar year is thus indicated by horizontal movement around the temple; six months between April and October; both are near the equinoxes. Illustration by Michael P. Lyon, courtesy The Neal A. Maxwell Institute for Religious Scholarship

Circumambulation   Like the orbit of the earth around the sun and the advancing moon phases around some LDS temples, circular movement in a flat horizontal plane, called circumambulation, is seen throughout the ancient world and in LDS tradition today. In ancient Egypt, for example, sites were given special protection and *blessing* in this fashion. According to Lundquist, this was done, "by a rite of circumambulation by the gods, in which statues or images for all gods for whom the temple was being built were carried around the site, clockwise. Circumambulation is a ritual act that commemorates the journey of the sun god through the heavens, and thus further cosmicizes the building."[214] In the Old Testament, ritual circumambulation was also employed in ritual fashion for *cursing* Jericho (thought to be in reverse direction). During the Feast of Tabernacles circumambulating the altar by priests on the eighth or Great Day of the Feast was associated with *blessing*. We also find circumambulation in the sprinkling of blood from the sin offering in the Mosaic Law, where it was placed on each of the four horns of the altar of burnt-offering, starting with the north-east corner, at specific points in time.[215] Some ancient Hebrew marriage ceremonies also involved the bride circling her new husband seven times.[216] Movement in circles, focusing on the chiastic center, remains a part of LDS temple practice, appearing in a number of ordinances.[217]

Dedication of LDS Temple Cornerstones   Dedication of a temple's four above ground cornerstones also proceeds in a great symmetrical circle. This priesthood ceremony is symbolic of the first stones laid at the temple, marking this important point in time – the first major step in creating the temple – and pointing to the very foundation of it, Christ.[218] The date for a cornerstone ceremony is often carefully chosen to coincide with important events in the Savior's life, such as April 6th (of 1853 for the Salt Lake Temple), as Christ is the solid foundation for the gospel itself.

Jackson County Missouri was the site of the Church's first temple cornerstone dedication ceremony. The Prophet Joseph Smith had twelve men, representing the 12 tribes of Israel, lay the symbolic foundation stone for the future city of Zion on August 3, 1831. The four cornerstones were dedicated at the Center Place temple site, starting with the northeast stone.[219] The land was then dedicated and consecrated for the gathering of the Saints. It was later at Kirtland, however, that the advancing clockwise priesthood order was fully established, starting at the southeast corner: a practice based on the origin and strength of the most light, above ground. This tradition continues today.[220] (The Holy of Holies of the Salt Lake Temple is in the southeast corner of the third floor. The offices of Joseph Smith were typically in the southeast corner of the historic buildings he occupied. Increased light is the key for both.)

Cornerstone and Capstone at the Salt Lake Temple: The cornerstone dedication ceremony (April 6, 1853) marked the start of a temple's construction – the first stones laid, whereas the capstone ceremony represented the last stone placed (forty years later, April 6, 1893). Both are relic chambers (today called time capsules); Left, the recordstone is near the southeast cornerstone; Middle, Capstone chamber below Moroni; and Right, southeast corner earthstone.

The cornerstones of temples are typically large blocks of pure stone placed above ground level at the four corners of the building, symbolizing the first stones laid. After the southeast stone is dedicated, the remaining three are then dedicated in clockwise fashion, mirroring the path of the earth around the sun. Each cornerstone dedication is individual, featuring remarks, mortaring, a song, and prayer by different priesthood holders: Melchizedek priesthood holders in the east, and those of the Aaronic order in the west, the year again divided in symmetrical form.[221] A total of 24 priesthood brethren are required to mark the intersection of *space* (stones rising from darkness below ground into light), with important points in *time* (the symbolic beginning of temple construction). The number 24 may mirror two quorums of the Twelve—one in the western hemisphere and one in the eastern hemisphere—established as part of the kingdom of God and his two great world headquarters. This number may also represent the Twelve with their wives.

In addition to symbolic connections of the southeast stone to Christ and His light, President Hinckley stated that the four cornerstones of the Salt Lake Temple specifically symbolize four *gospel* cornerstones: the southeast cornerstone—the Savior Jesus Christ; the southwest cornerstone—the First Vision; the northwest cornerstone—the Book of Mormon; and the northeast cornerstone—the restoration of the priesthood with associated keys and offices.[222] The capstone (the ball underneath the Moroni statue) laid on April 6th of 1893 was the last stone laid at the Salt Lake Temple, signaling completion. The laying of the cornerstone and capstone were thus alpha and omega events as part of the temple's creation.

Creation at the Center   The building of a temple is symbolic of creation generally, as indicated in the Lord's questions to Job: "Where wast thou when I laid the foundations of the earth? declare, if thou hast understanding. Who hath laid the measures thereof, if thou knowest? or who hath stretched the line upon it? whereupon are the foundations thereof fastened? or who laid the corner stone thereof; When the morning stars sang together, and all the sons of God shouted for joy" (Job 38:4-7). Nibley stated that, "The foundation of the sanctuary coincides with the foundation or creation of the earth itself: 'The first fixed point in the chaotic waters…which becomes the earthly seat of the world-order, having its palladium in throne and altar.'"[223] Circles point to cycles, the most elemental being creation. The creation drama presented inside our temples is tied to the earth's seasons and the cycles of the heavens. The drama itself is cyclical, performed over and over, year after year, according to Nibley, "Because the Divinity—the First Father of the Race—did so once in the beginning, and commanded us to do the same."[224] The renewal of covenants we enter into there appear to stabilize creation and renew it, keeping darkness and chaos continually at bay. This may be a primary reason for continuing ancient Native American circle dances (like those of the Hopi), a form of ritual prayer.

In addition, both Joseph Smith and Brigham Young stated that cornerstone ceremonies (specifically those at Nauvoo and Salt Lake) were designed to remedy the Savior's statement that "he had no place to lay his head."[225] When Joseph Smith dedicated the southeast cornerstone of the original Nauvoo Temple, he pronounced a benediction upon it addressing this theme. "This principal corner stone, in representation of the First Presidency, is now duly laid in honor of the great God; and may it there remain until the whole fabric is completed; and may the same be accomplished speedily; that the Saints may have a place to worship God, and the Son of Man have where to lay his head."[226]

Just as the cornerstones are the foundation of the temple, the Savior is the foundation of the Church and the center of our lives: "It is upon the rock of our Redeemer, who is Christ, the Son of God, that ye must build your foundation" (Helaman 5:12). He is the stone, "which the builders rejected, the same is become the head of the corner?" (Luke 20:17; see also Acts 4:11). It is noteworthy that the first or Initiatory ordinances of the temple, also began on stone in the Nauvoo Temple,[227] as did ancient coronation rites in Egypt (upon "the Stone of Truth"). So too crowning of kings in England (upon the "Coronation Stone"). Christ is also symbolized by light in connection with this ceremony. It is found in greatest quantity in the southeast. In breaking ground at the southeast corner of the Manti Utah Temple, Pres. Brigham Young chose twelve noon to knell and pray, bringing together time, space, and brilliant sunlight in a cosmic, symbolic relationship.[228] The ceremony started at the southeast corner because of its connection to light.[229] Peter also prayed at twelve noon upon his housetop, receiving the vision to take the gospel to the gentiles (Acts 10:9). Pres. Gordon B. Hinckley stated, "We preserve the symbolism of the cornerstone in remembrance of the Son of God upon whose life and mission this Church is established. He, and He alone, is the Chief Cornerstone. There is built upon Him a strong foundation of Apostles and prophets and above this 'all the building fitly framed together' to constitute The Church of Jesus Christ of Latter-day Saints."[230]

Spiraling Ascension: Ritual Ascent to God

We experience the symmetry and centrality of the time-oriented circle inside temples as well, often in a spiral, via progression through spiraling staircases and through successive ordinance rooms. This spiraling ascension may represent the last of eight divisions of sacred space, those intersecting space and time simultaneously in heavenward spiraling progression. These include the four horizontal spatial dimensions (north, south, east and west), plus the three vertical, time-based divisions of *past* (the Baptistery), *present* (the Endowment Room), and *future* (the Sealing Room). The spiral intersects both horizontal space and vertical time simultaneously, focusing attention on the chiastic center point; God in eternal time at the center of the great turning wheel of the spinning cosmos.

The expanding phi-proportion spiral is the most common shape in the universe, its golden proportion seen in the tiniest DNA molecule, as well as in huge expanding galaxies many light years across. The unique microscopic makeup of the double helix spiraling DNA molecule, in the temple of the human body, is reminiscent of Jacob's Ladder in its ordered form.[231] This creation symbol is embedded in our 23 pairs of chromosomes. According to one source, its biological order appears to be part of an elemental sacred language of letters used and spoken by God *for* creation.[232]

Spiral staircase at the St. George Utah Tabernacle, dedicated 1867

The ascending motion of spiraling movement in temples may initially reflect the ascension of the ancient sacred mountaintop (like Sinai, a natural temple), and to the dwelling place of God via the opened fiery conduit of light. The mountaintop is reached by movement upward, around, and inward to the chiastic center place, the apex of the mountain—the symbolic presence of God. (Ascension of the great mandala-like stupa at Borobudur is accomplished in this pattern.) The spiral may thus symbolize man's progressive ascent to God through the trials of life, and the saving, perfecting and exalting covenants of the temple. Nibley referred to the spiral form as one eternal round in connection with our progression, "as typified by the sun in its course, but instead of an eternal return to the starting point, the course is depicted as an ever mounting spiral, eternal progression."[233]

Spiraling Staircases   The two spiraling staircases at Nauvoo and Manti may have originally been created to use one staircase for ascending and the other for descending (combing both directions in Jacob's Ladder). Such staircases are often opposing (symmetrical) in their directional turn at LDS temples, and mirror dual pathways (one up, one down) from ancient myth.[234] A similar, but flattened pattern of opposing spirals (in 13 parts) face each other on all windows at the new Draper Utah temple. These have potential association with the sun and moon anciently, and more specifically to man and woman in the new and everlasting covenant of marriage, where creation of offspring is part of the couple's eternal posterity and their kingdom. While horizontal circles express the *cyclical* nature of time, the ascending spiral inside some temples appears to also express the eternal *progression* of time in association with purification; enduring the trials of this life to the end, choosing between good and evil, and eternal progression beyond. Such movement purifies, as seen in some water purification systems which utilize spiraling movement to cleanse.[235]

The spiral serves as an excellent symbol for the ritual ascent to God, made possible by the step-by-step ordinances and covenants of the temple. The Archimedes-style spiraling staircases at Nauvoo, Manti and elsewhere feature ascension in three divisions of space: upward and around, with an inward focus, symbolically progressing through time—the past, present, and future. Solomon's Temple appears to have featured at least one spiral staircase (1 Kings 6:8). Ezekiel's visionary temple also featured a spiral staircase (Ezekiel 41:7), as does the Temple Scroll from Qumran.[236] The Manti Utah Temple has two beautiful, handcrafted spiraling staircases gracing its west end. Only one other building in the United States features comparable freestanding historic craftsmanship.

The related Gothic cathedral labyrinth has similar associations to the ascending spiral staircase. It too is symmetrical. Labyrinths are usually flat Archimedes spirals that use linear movement in two dimensions to potentially symbolize the literal three-dimensional ascent to God. They too are representative of trials and testing, of ascension and resurrection, finally realized in personal rebirth after traveling to the center and back out again. Some believe they serves as a substitute for the pilgrimage to Jerusalem. Many are octagonal, illustrating their connection to rebirth, transformation at the eighth level, or ascent to the kingdom of the gods in the stars.

Centralized spiraling labyrinths left to right: Chartres Cathedral and Amiens Cathedrals labyrinths in France, Cologne Cathedral labyrinth, Germany, and San Vitale labyrinth, Ravenna, Italy.

The labyrinth at Chartres features 11 circuits or paths in 12 concentric circles; potentially pointing to the moon and therefore female symbolism, as there are 112 lunations at the edge of the outer circle. (There are 28 days of a lunar month.) This labyrinth also features 180-degree turns (other parts of Chartres Cathedral are tied to the sun).[237] The oldest Labyrinth may be that of Ammenemhet III of Egypt (12th dynasty). Pliny described this Labyrinth, according to Lundquist, as "constructed in a maze-like fashion, analogous to the mandala.

Spiraling Ascension Through Ordinance Rooms   Progression as a theme in LDS temples is sometimes done via ascension in upward spiraling form (clockwise) around a chiastic center. At the Cardston Alberta Canada Temple, this center is the Celestial Room – symbolizing the presence of God. At least two other LDS temples feature upward, spiraling movement involving the eight divisions of sacred space: the St. George (1877) and Salt Lake (1893) Temples, both designed by Truman O. Angell under the direction of Pres. Brigham Young (changes have since altered this pattern at St. George).

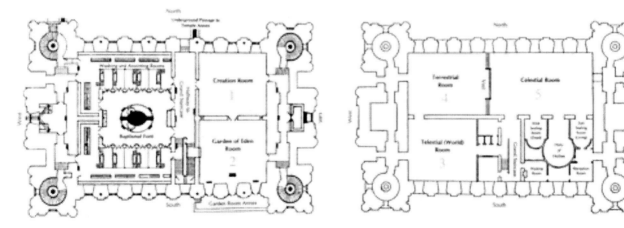

Spiraling Movement through 5 Ordinance Rooms within the Salt Lake Temple: Left, First floor and right, second floor. Such movement intersects both space and time while progressing heavenward. Five covenants are made as part of the Everlasting Covenant. The number five is chiastic, used prominently throughout the culture of ancient Egypt.

Patrons at the Salt Lake Temple, for example, progress in a perfect circle, ascending one floor from the plain, lower lit Creation Room, to the fully illuminated and intricately decorated Celestial Room higher up. Initiates begin this symbolic journey facing east in the lower level of the temple and end up facing east again as they pass from the Terrestrial Room into the Celestial Room, the symbolic presence of God. Passing through the veil is done eastward, in a straight-line axial path, like the ancient temples (the early LDS temples combined both circular and axial movement – D&C 3:2).[238] According to former temple architect Keith Stepan, progression through the three vertical floors of many larger temples, or through the three successive ordinance rooms (in horizontal fashion in the smaller, single floor temples) symbolizes travel through the past, the present, and the future. "Even if the temple is on one level, it was always a progression from one end through to the other, with the sealing rooms on the far end."[239]

Ascension in the Fiery Pillar of Light   Perhaps the most important of all associations made with the common spiral is the whirling conduit or pillar of light or fire experienced by many in scripture, taking worthy souls to the throne of God and into His presence. This conduit (often accompanied by the sound of *mighty* wind) was seen at the dedication of the Kirtland Temple, opened via the will of God, and aided through the *mighty* prayer of the faithful. Ancient May pole ceremonies, labyrinths in Gothic cathedrals like Chartres, Hopi snake dances (coiling upward), and Jacob's vision of the ascending ladder in Genesis, all appear to represent a similar ritual circular ascent to God, made graphic in the spiral.[240]

One Eternal Round: The circle is the symbol of cycles of time on earth, of the eternity of heaven, and of all things divine, heavenly, or God-like. Left, eight-hour star trail above an Anasazi mountain-top prayer circle or vision-quest site in southern Utah; Center, Gustave Doré's "White Rose," illustration for Dante's Divine Comedy, Paradiso; and Right, Dome of the Pantheon, Rome Italy. Light is central to the chiastic symmetry of each.

The single fiery pillar resting above the ancient tabernacle appears to have been a spiraling conduit opening between heaven and earth, where God could visit and instruct Moses. It was potentially represented in the Egyptian *Djed* pillar, symbolizing stability and duration. This pillar was a kind of nail, fastening or holding everything in a sure place.[241] Isaiah spoke of it stating, "And I will clothe him with thy robe, and strengthen him with thy girdle, and I will commit thy government into his hand...And the key of the house of David will I lay upon his shoulder; so he shall open, and none shall shut; and he shall shut, and none shall open. And I will fasten him as a nail in a sure place" (Isaiah 22:21-23). These verses may refer to Christ as the guardian and sentinel of "the Way", the mediator who opens and shuts the portal, based on our worthiness and light. The way of the fiery pillar connecting heaven and earth, rested above the ancient tabernacle and the Kirtland Temple at its dedication. It is seen in other places in scripture and Church history, including the Sacred Grove. Some ancient cultures believed Polaris, the North Star (also called "the Nail" by some) was the direction to which this pillar opened – the potential home of God.

Fiery light is central in each of these examples, and to creation itself, represented in the sun, the primary symbol of God. It is His light that dispelled darkness and chaos at creation, animating matter, providing life throughout the cosmos. Light is also the binding and sealing power of the Order of the Priesthood. This appears to be suggested in chiastic form in the sun's central position between two covenant-oriented pillars on the early LDS temples; pillars representative of the eternal covenant renewed each day in the resurrecting sun. Light is elemental to creation, symbolized in the vesica pisces.

III. The Vesica Pisces: *Creation via Complimentary Opposition*

The vesica pisces (horizontal or vertical) makes use of two intersecting circles, the overlapping center area forming a vertical almond shape. This ancient archetype utilizes the principle of *complimentary opposition* to bring forth the chiastic central concept of *transition* or *creation*. Literally translated the "bladder of the fish," the vesica pisces is found in the fish-shaped pointed-arch windows and doors of many Gothic cathedrals and other sacred buildings around the world, including many historic European cathedrals. The Kirtland Ohio Temple makes use of Gothic arched windows.

The Vesica Pisces, left to right: Chartres Cathedral, France; Ely Cathedral, England; Strousbourg Cathedral, France; and Church Window, Brussels, Belgium. Christ or His mother Mary are typically found at their center.

The vertical almond shaped portal at center represents the place of transition or mediation. Christ, often located in this central position, is the mediator between worlds in the everlasting covenant (D&C 76:69). He is also the great creator. The vesica pisces resembles openings in the human body, some of them horizontal, including the eye, a doorway for light, hidden knowledge, and the "mysteries." Both the all-seeing eye and the Egyptian *wedjat* eye (or Eye of Horus) are good examples.

Vertical Portal   This *vertical* almond-shape typically represents a sacred *threshold* or *portal* formed by the intersection area of the two interlocking circles—one the sacred spiritual sphere inside the building (heaven) and the other the profane physical sphere outside it (earth). Passing through an entry portal of this shape into a sacred structure (like a Gothic Cathedral) signals this transition. In an LDS temple context, the ordinances of the temple bridge these two worlds, symbolized by the vesica pisces—that of the *living* and the *dead*. Entrance through this shape may thus represent movement from the profane world outside to the sacred world inside via this symbolic transitional portal or *threshold*.

The number two in connection with this motif also has association with the principle of *complimentary opposition*, most often connected to *creation*; the two leading to three - father, mother and centralized son.[242] Christ is the firstborn son of our two heavenly parents. He is often portrayed within the womb-like portal of the vesica pisces, typically in European Gothic structures named after His mother; part of the cult of the Virgin. Mary is thus sometimes placed inside it rather than Christ.[243]

Horizontal Fish   As discussed earlier, Christ was born in the age of pisces – the fish (the horizontal vesica pisces shape). This is when the precession of the equinoxes revealed the sun rising against the constellation Pisces at the vernal equinox sunrise. Previously, again due to the precession, the sun rose against the ram (or lamb - the age of Aires). From the fall of Adam and Eve to the time of Abraham, the sun rose against Taurus (the bull).[244]

Time was thus not only signaled in the heavens (each of these signs averaging 2200 years in length), but in the sacrificial animals illustrated there as constellations. In the meridian of time (the age of Pisces) we see the fish playing a dominant role—in the Savior's calling of "fishers of men," twice in the miracle of the loaves and the fishes, and in Christ broiling fish after the Resurrection, during His 40-day ministry, etc.[245] The fish motif on many born-again Christian bumper stickers is a horizontal version of this archetype, calling attention to His mission in the chiastic meridian of time.

Gothic style window arches at the Kirtland, Ohio Temple, dedicated 1836.

Creation and Two Pillars

Pillars are symbols of covenant-making, first seen when Jacob set up a "stone for a pillar" at Bethel in Genesis (28:18, 22). His single stone "set up for a pillar" was a memorial, witness and marker for his temple experience with God – the vision of the ladder with God its top. Scripture affirms that truth is established "in the mouth of two or three witnesses," a principle common in a court of law or in any establishment of truth (1 Timothy 5:19; Deuteronomy 17:6). The use of two pillars at entranceways to many temples, like Jachin and Boaz at Solomon's Temple,[246] symbolizes many concepts, beginning with *two guardians*[247] (to the sacred threshold of God), and *two witnesses*[248] (of the covenant making occurring inside temples). Joseph and Hyrum Smith once stood in the east niches of the Salt Lake Temple, for example, symbols of two important upright leaders - pillars of the Restoration.[249] They are also associated with *memorials*.[250] Some have associated the two pillars of Solomon's Temple and those fronting the ancient tabernacle in Exodus, with the pillar of the cloud by day and the pillar of fire by night. Many associate two pillars with two great trees—the Tree of Knowledge (of Good and Evil) and the Tree of Life (like those of the Salt Lake Temple Garden Room). Ultimately, chiastic creation itself may be symbolized in them, through association with the basic elements of creation - male and female.[251]

The Egyptian temple city of On may have been a primary influence for usage of pillars at Israelite temples in connection with the concept of creation—a primary theme of the temple today. Nibley stated that the two famous pillars fronting the entrance to Solomon's Temple (2 Chronicles 3:17) "belonged to the solar cult of On…The Djed-pillars of Egypt were popular in Palestinian and Phoenician temple architecture, they were the pillars of the cosmos…symbols of permanence for the reckoning of the Equinoxes… Since the Temple was oriented in a west-east direction, the Sun at the Equinoxes must rise between the pillars."[252]

Set atop one great obelisk at the great temple at On (the City of the Pillar) or Heliopolis (Greek for "sun-city") was a greenish-black meteorite, the triangular Ben-ben stone. (Heliopolis is mentioned three times in Facsimile

Two of the Book of Abraham. None of the other 125 known hypocephali do so.) The first and last rays of sunlight struck this tall pillar each day (light was an ancient male symbol of creation). The Ben-ben stone and its pillar eventually became the standard Egyptian obelisk, often with phallic associations.[253]

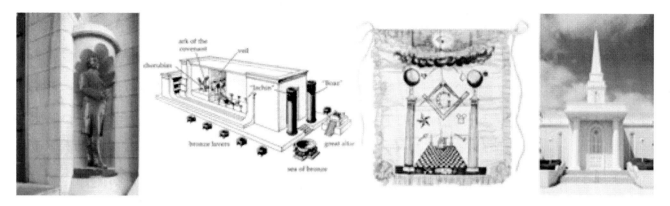

Far left, Statues of Joseph and Hyrum Smith were originally placed in the two east niches of the Salt Lake Temple. These two pillars of the Restoration were removed in 1911 and placed in-between the temple and the south visitor's center; Left, Jachin and Boaz were two free-standing brass pillars standing at the east entrance of Solomon's Temple. Their symbolism possibly included that connected to witnesses, guardians and leadership (as king and priest); Right, Joseph Smith's Masonic Temple Apron with two pillars, symbolizing that knowledge and other 'mysteries' were available beyond the pillars, as part of Freemasonry tradition; Far right, Two pillars at the east entrance to the Orlando, Florida LDS temple. Apron photographed by Val Brinkerhoff, used by permission of the Community of Christ.

Chiastic Symmetry in Creation: Father, Mother and Children   The symmetry of two symbolizes male and female becoming one in creation. Many early Church leaders believed the Savior was married with children, potentially to more than one wife.[254] The Nauvoo Temple iconography may be a representation of the eternal family of God, among other things (an illustration of the church of the Firstborn); the sun and moon symbolizing man and woman, with stars representing children. Heavenly bodies on temples have layered meaning, most Latter-day Saints looking no deeper than post resurrection glory for them (see D&C 76). Joseph (sold into Egypt) had a dream as a youth that included representation of his father as the sun, his mother as the moon, and his 11 brothers as stars, all of them bowing in homage to him (this occurred later in Egypt, Genesis 37:9-10). His father Israel clearly made these heavenly connections.[255] Beyond space (kingdoms) and their intersection with time, the celestial motifs at Nauvoo potentially point to God (sunstones), our Mother in Heaven (moonstones), and their elect sons and daughters, as joint heirs with Christ of all they have. They may be represented in the 144, 5 pointed upright solid stars at the top of the temple's octagonal tower, a symbol of endless posterity as part of the doctrine of the new and everlasting covenant of marriage—a doctrine presented to the general body of the Saints for the first time at Nauvoo. The number 144 also connects them to the special missionary force (potentially translated), who as members of the Church of the Firstborn, seek out and / or administer sacred rites to others, after bringing them to Zion.[256]

Family unity and physical salvation was preserved for Israel and his family by Joseph's service in Egypt. Eternal family unity is preserved for all who enter into and honor the New and Everlasting Covenant of Marriage. Children as numerous as the stars are promised righteous married couples as part of the Abrahamic Covenant portion of these priesthood promises and their associated ordinances: "I will make thy seed to multiply as the stars of heaven" (Genesis 24:60; 26:4). Procreation in the next life is only possible for those so blessed. This may be one interpretation of the plural "lives" in scripture.[257]

The parents of the human race also appear to have been represented by the sun and moon. When Adam and Eve left the Garden of Eden, they settled in the hills of Adam-ondi-Ahman and the nearby plains of Olaha Shinehah.[258] In the Doctrine & Covenants we read, "Is there not room enough on the mountains of Adam-ondi-Ahman, and on the plains of Olaha Shinehah, or the land where Adam dwelt" (D&C 117:8). The meanings for these ancient words are found in Abraham 3:13, where the Lord states that "Shinehah" is the name given to the sun and "Olea" (a variation) is the name given to the moon. The Lord appears to have named these plains after Adam and Eve as creators, the sun and moon – parents of the human race.[259]

Two pillars as part of chiastic symmetry, also combined with the symbolism of two witnesses or male and female. Left to right: Twisting pillars with Mary at center, Amiens Cathedral, France; Confessional with two female witness figures and two outer twisting pillars, St. Michael and St. Gudula Church, Brussels, Belgium; Mary and Christ Duomo, Florence, Italy; Two towers, Westminster Abbey, England; and Two towers, Chartres Cathedral, France (the left tower features a sun atop it, the right tower features a moon atop it).

Historic Sacred Marriage Symbols   Sacred architecture in a number of later cultures appears to also connect sun and moon symbols with the sacred marriage of men and women. The Gothic cathedral builders, for example, made use of them in two ways. This may be seen first in the two great towers of differing height (asymmetry) at the entrance of Chartres and Amiens Cathedrals in France. The tallest north tower at Chartres has a sun-symbol weathervane atop it, while the shorter tower features a moon-symbol weathervane.[260] The labyrinth just inside Chartres also features 11 circuits or paths in 12 concentric circles, with a potential tie to female - moon symbolism, as there are 112 lunations at the edge of the outer circle.[261]

French gothic cathedrals with potential man (sun) and woman (moon) symbolism; Left, Amiens Cathedral with two towers of differing height; Right, Chartres Cathedral with higher sun weathervane tower and lower moon weathervane tower. Inside the 16-rayed sun symbol is a crown. Below it are many intertwined serpents. The moon tower is 28 feet shorter than the sun tower (there are approximately 28 days in a lunar month). Notice the chiastic sun symbol (Rose window) between the pillars, echoing the Egyptian rising sun on the horizon between two pillars, also found at Nauvoo and Salt Lake.

The length of this important structure appears to be a male - solar year representation at 365.25 feet. Round rose windows are positioned in between their pillar-like towers, mirroring usage of the Egyptian rising sun on the horizon motif (*aht*), between two pillars; an ancient design also utilized extensively inside and out at both the Nauvoo and Salt Lake Temples.

The Marriage Huppah: Jerusalem Windows at Nauvoo and Salt Lake   The curving arch or half circle (rising sun) motif, positioned atop nearly every rectangular doorway and window (earth), is extensive throughout the Nauvoo and Salt Lake Temples. There are also visible in all interior doorways at the Salt Lake Temple, each featuring opposing spirals nested in a fully risen sun symbol.[262] These windows are sometimes called "Jerusalem windows," their arched shape mirroring the marriage *huppah*, a bridal canopy or "wedding house." The huppah was considered a sign of God's presence and in Hebrew meant "that which covers or floats above."[263] The entire display of heavenly motifs on the Nauvoo Temple displays the church of the Firstborn, the Bride of the Lamb. Its half-circle rising sun windows also resemble the marriage huppah.

Other Chiastic Marriage and Creation Symbols

Two Opposing Spirals   The basic crossing form of the single ancient swastika has association to *creation* and the spinning cosmos (a spiral), as well as the slow turn of the precession of the equinoxes.[264] According to Hall, when two swastikas or spirals appear in symmetrical opposing orientation (facing each other), they represent the sun and the moon.[265] Brenan states, "In the sky imagery [of ancient passage mound rock art] the sun and moon [opposing spirals] represent the two opposite principles and the stars represent multiplicity. Together they make up time and space and the entire universe." [266]

Left: Newgrange passage mound entrance with curbstone and opposing spirals (right side of stone), Ireland, 3100 BC. Right: Knowth passage mound and entrance, 3000 BC. Both the symbolism of light entering a dark, inner, womb-like chamber on one day per year (normally the winter solstice sunrise), and opposing spirals, signal creation and male and female at these temple-tombs. Similar light-based symbolism pointing to creation is found around the world.

At Newgrange, Ireland (3000 BC) a large curbstone at the main entrance to this huge passage mound is carved with opposing spirals.[267] The curbstones at the perimeter of this and other ancient temple mounds feature rock art with celestial motifs, including suns, moons, and stars—similar to other temples. These ancient temple-tombs appear to feature a number of male–female symbols in addition to opposing spirals, including light and darkness, and tall phallic-like pillars. The ancient Chinese yin-yang symbol has similar connotations. The Endowment Room of the Bountiful Utah Temple features small yin–yang motifs on its walls.[268] Opposing spirals are found on some LDS temples, including the pulpits and interior pilasters of the Kirtland Temple,[269] the Nauvoo Temple,[270] and the Salt Lake Temple[271] (in the Terrestrial Room). In temple settings these opposing forms appear to signal a sacred union resulting in endless offspring into the eternities as part of the New and Everlasting Covenant of Marriage.

Light Entering a Dark Inner Chamber   On the winter solstice sunrise, light enters the dark inner sanctum of Newgrange, penetrating the mound's long passageway, striking a chiastic standing stone at center. Light thus marks creation, a male symbol, the dark inner chamber, the female womb. The pillar centered inside Newgrange has 3 sets of opposing spirals carved in it. A basin or altar is nearby.

At Cairn L, Loughcrew, Ireland, a white central free-standing stone is struck at sunrise, again only on or near the winter solstice sunrise, lighting both the celestial rock art on this stone, and reflecting light throughout much of the mound's interior. This light-based creation event is thought to have marked the birth of the new year, when the return of light is symbolized on longer days after the winter solstice—the shortest day of the year (Joseph Smith was born just after the winter solstice, signaling the return of light in the Restoration). According to Brenan, the winter solstice sunrise in such settings is a "symbol of creation and the power of light over darkness." [272] The Irish passage mounds pre-date most of the pyramid temples in Egypt by a thousand years or more and continue to effectively mark time and creation via light.

Center, Opposing 13-part spiral motifs on south windows at the Draper Utah Temple. The white rectangle at center (lighter from the inside) may point to Christ at the center of the Twelve, a potential symbol of divine government or a prayer circle. This temple was dedicated at spring equinox (March 21-22, 2009), the sacred New Year's day in Israel.

Modern Opposing Spirals   Newer LDS temples also feature opposing spirals, including the Draper Utah temple, where each of the exterior windows feature opposing 13-part squared-spirals at their top and bottom. Each also features a 13th lighter facet at the chiastic center, surrounded by 12 slightly darker ones. This may illustrate Christ in a form of divine government, surround by the 12 Apostles in a prayer circle. There are 13 windows on the temple's south wall, the direction of most light (the number 13 is closely tied to Christ).[273]

Opposing spirals and swastikas are extensive at the Kirtland Temple, the first temple of the Restoration. Left, Opposing spirals atop the 12 pulpit-altar pillars; Center, Opposing spirals atop pillars beneath the second floor rising sun window. This window and the altars were built by Truman Angell, later architect of the Salt Lake Temple. Similar opposing spiral motifs are found on pillars inside the Terrestrial Room of the Salt Lake Temple (see Abraham 3:13; Genesis 37:8-10). Notice also the Tree of Life motif positioned within the Chiastic central keystone, and the True Vine on the arch of the rising sun, all of them positioned symmetrically between and atop two pillars. All motifs are Christ-centered.

Opposing spirals also resemble the curving horns of rams. Horns have ancient association with fertility and creation. At Pres. Brigham Young's Beehive House in Salt Lake City, two bed headboards feature prominent sun symbols on them, one in rising form. Both have opposing spirals left and right of the sun.

Sunlight entering a dark inner chamber is the key creation symbol, an archetypal representation of the complimentary opposition necessary for creation, in male and female, the sun and moon, light and darkness. Not only is this ancient symbol found in the sun entering the passage mounds of Ireland (on the winter solstice sunrise), but it is found in the rising sun on the horizon passing between the two pillars in Egypt, between the two mountains of Parowan Gap in Southern Utah, and between two pilasters in the temple architecture of the modern Nauvoo, Salt Lake, or Mount Timpanogos Temples (each of these at the vernal equinox). All of them signal man and woman in creation, along with other concepts such as rebirth and resurrection – symbols of the Great Creator, Jesus Christ.

Fertility Symbols left to right: Pomegranate crown-like top or calyx (with numerous seeds inside); Hindu Yoni & Linga, Holy of Holies area, Angkor Wat, Cambodia; Vesica pisces shape, Duomo, Florence, Italy; and menhir, east Portugal

Other Opposing Creation Motifs   Opposing mirrors on either side of a centralized altar in LDS temple sealing rooms (in connection with the figure-8 motifs encircling the room above), represent yet another chiastic temple motif featuring complementary opposition in connection with marriage. According to Seaich, ancient Coptic texts reveal that mirrors were part of the ancient bridal chamber.[274] They may also be connected to patriarchal and matriarchal concepts in the higher priesthood. Additional opposing motifs seen in sacred architectural settings include female *Asherah* pillars in opposition to the male altar,[275] and opposing Egyptian *Wedjat* eyes as seen in Facsimile 2 of the Book of Abraham.[276] Other temple creation motifs feature connections to fertility, including the pomegranate, fig, grape, olive, the number 5, and the Hathor cow at the female bottom half of Facsimile Two.[277]

The Chiastic Rising Sun Between Two Pillars

The heavenly path of the sun rising vertically on the horizontal horizon is one of four chiastic X crosses above us – the Observatory Cross. This cross was illustrated in different ways by the Egyptians of the old world (the Egyptian *Aht* Motif – the rising sun on the horizon), and the Native Americans of the new world (a simple X cross in rock art). This vertical, rather than horizontal, circle of time is a flat line when viewed on its edge, and is endless in its cycling rhythm—one eternal round. The sun rises up from the underworld below at sunrise, and then re-enters the underworld at sunset. This appears to be symbolized in sun symbols (rock art) near caves at the east and west ends of the Gap. They may mark the exit and entrance points for the sun from the underworld up into this world (*east* cave), and entrance down into the underworld from this world (*west* cave).[278]

The important moment of creation and renewal each day at the eastern sunrise was represented by the Egyptian *aht* or *Re-Harakkhty* motif; a half-circle rising sun resting on the flat horizon, set between two pillars, pylons or mountains. This motif was representative of the place or gateway of transition, symbolized in the half sun disk on a horizontal line. The line of the horizon was between the upper and lower worlds (representing body and spirit) —being in both at once for the a magical moment—the supreme moment of resurrection—the unthinkable instant representing the passing of time from the past to the future.[279] The intersection point is the horizon – this world. The Native American "Gap" temple space at Parowan may be a kind of east-west *duat*, lined up perfectly to the rising and setting sun.[280] Its north and south mountains mirror the two pillars or obelisks of many Egyptian temples; symmetrically balanced points through which the sun rises and sets due east and west at the equinoxes.

In Malachi 4:2 we read, "But unto you that fear my name shall the Sun of righteousness arise with healing in his wings." This scripture may illustrate the pervasive Egyptian gold sun disk with wings (suggesting travel in the heavens). The horizon in Egypt also represented the point of transition from the *past* (the underworld, or *duat* of the Egyptians), to the *future* (heaven) at the exact moment of stillness in this, the *present*, central world. The rising sun symbolized rebirth and resurrection, representing not only the sun in its daily course, but the important Egyptian god Osiris - a type for the resurrected Christ.

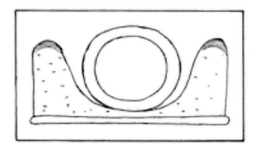  

Left: The Egyptian Aht hieroglyph illustrates the resurrecting sun rising between two pillars or mountains; Left, Cairn marker for viewing the setting sun at Parowan Gap, Southern Utah (it features a north and south mountain which the rises and sets between at the equinoxes); Right, Two Doric style pilasters framing the 1ˢᵗ floor assembly room window of the Nauvoo, Illinois Temple (note the half-circle rising sun with rays) in-between them.

In ancient Israel, the rising sun marked the sacred New Year's date at the spring equinox as it rose over the Mount of Olives. Two weeks later, the full moon at this same position, marked the start of Passover (our April 6 at time of Christ's crucifixion); both heavenly bodies thus marked the exact time for the start of this important Hebrew Holy Day. Margaret Barker has suggested that during the fall equinox at Solomon's Temple, "the rays of the rising sun would have shone through the gate and illuminated the great golden throne in the *debir* [the Holy of Holies]. This symbolized the coming of the Lord to his people." [281]

This same rising sun on the horizon motif is utilized throughout both the Nauvoo and Salt Lake Temples, found in half-circle forms atop most doors and windows, inside and outside of both sacred structures. It is especially apparent in the personified sunstones at Nauvoo, a symbol of creation, God's light, and his resurrection and His future millennial return. It may be the most important of all chiastic temple symbols – centered on Him and His light.

Two prophecies of the Lord's millennial return are instructive relative to light. First, Ezekiel saw "the glory of the God of Israel" come from the east and enter the eastern gate of the temple "and, behold, the glory of the Lord filled the house" (Ezekiel 43:1-5; see also 1 Kings 8:10-11; D&C 84:5). Second, Joseph Smith's inspired translation of Matthew states, "as the light of the morning cometh out of the east, and shineth even unto the west…so shall also the coming of the Son of Man be" (JS-Matthew 1:26). Both orientation and movement relative to the light of the *sun* are signaled in these two important verses. They also potentially point to the chiastic return of the gospel to the Jews (and the Remnant) in the later days, after the Gentiles reject the fullness of the gospel (3 Nephi 16:10); an offering of light first to the Jews, then the Gentiles, and finally to the Jews once again – the first being the last.[282] This return of light to the Jews in the last days is much like the symbolic return to God generally, marked by the chiastic expulsion of Adam and Eve from the Garden temple eastward, and then the invitation for them and all of us to return to him westward, through the ordinances and covenants of the temple.

Other connotations exist for the sun rising between two pillars in sacred architecture, the pillars tied to covenant-making throughout scripture, for example.[283] The chiastic center is sunlight, symbolizing God's power, intelligence and presence. In addition, the light of " the mysteries" is available only for those passing between the two covenant-oriented entrance pillars, as seen in Solomon's Temple and early Egyptian temples. The blessings of this "light" (knowledge, intelligence, the Spirit of God, and ultimately His personal presence) are realized as we honor covenants made in the temple. "Light beyond the pillars" symbolism has been utilized by the Egyptians, Native Americans, and Freemasons. Joseph Smith's inspired design of the Nauvoo Temple connects it to coming into the Lord's presence in this life - the Second Comforter, in D&C 93:1 and other scriptures. Coming into His presence lies at the very heart and center of the gospel of Jesus Christ.

Modern Variation   This ancient light-based chiastic pattern is found in the first temple of the Restoration at Kirtland and inspired modern temples today, including the Mount Timpanogos Temple. On April 6th the sun rises over Mount Timpanogos (aligned to the temple due east), striking the roundel atop the Celestial Room's east Jacob's Ladder window.[284] This window rests atop two covenant-oriented pillars on the east side of the temple. Sunlight then travels the long axis of this room westward (like the Tabernacle and Solomon's temple), within the Celestial Room (in cruciform shape), striking perfectly a circle in square motif (symbol of the temple – where heaven and earth meet). This archetype also rests between two covenant-oriented pillars.[285] The whole luminous room is surrounded by pilasters, eight of them; two in each of the four cardinal directions.

Setting for acceptance of the Kirtland Temple by Christ at Passover and the day of His resurrection, Easter Sunday, March 27 of 1836 (one week after the Spring Equinox); West, Melchizedek Priesthood Pulpit-Altars, 1ˢᵗ Floor, Kirtland Ohio Temple. Note the rising sun on the horizon design between the two pillars atop the pulpit-altars. Keystones and other symbols are found in this important setting, directly behind where the Savior (and other heavenly beings) appeared to Joseph Smith and Oliver Cowdery (enclosed within a lowered veil), all near its dedication date.

The temple is also aligned directly south to Mount Nebo—the highest mountain in the county, some 100 feet higher than Mt. Timpanogos. Latter-day Saint Archeologist V. Garth Norman found that the temple is in near-perfect alignment with both mountains along with two others, being aligned diagonally to Squaw Peak at the winter solstice sunrise (from the northwest to the southeast corner of the temple), and to Mahogony Mountain at the summer solstice sunrise (using a line drawn midpoint from the west center of the temple to its northeast corner).[286] Similar alignments to nearby important mountains, at specific points in time, are found at Izapa in southern Mexico, also researched by Norman.[287]

In addition, The Mount Timpanogos Temple features another ancient alignment pattern; vertical alignment over living water below (and to light above) – ancient male and female symbols. A natural spring—living water is a trait common in many ancient Meso-American temples, as well as the early Utah Temples, including those at Nauvoo, St. George, Manti and Salt Lake. This appears to be part of an inspired temple pattern.[288] Space here does not allow for a thorough discussion of these sacred architecture alignments, those of vertical and horizontal nature.[289] Such alignments are also dependant on proper timing as indicated in the heavens.[290]

The east ends of both the Nauvoo and Salt Lake Temples feature rising sun motifs between two pillars. Both temples, along with the Kirtland Temple, also feature eastern Holiness to the Lord plaques, featuring two strong Doric pillars framing gold words - statements of ownership and sacredness.

Alpha and Omega motifs as part of windows at the Salt Lake Temple (left), the Kirtland Temple second floor east rising sun window (middle), and Manti Temple window (right). Each features a central keystone and half circle rising sun shape

The Related Alpha & Omega Symbol   The Alpha and Omega motif found on many LDS temples is directly related to this rising sun symbol. It features classic visual chiasmus, connected to Christ and creation. It is located above all doors and windows on the exterior of the Salt Lake Temple – entrance points for light. Christ may be symbolized in the central, inverted *Alpha* keystone, balanced within the visual symmetry of two *Omega* endpoints. The symbolism of light, creation and keys center on Him in this motif.

Light   We first notice that this symbol is placed above all places of light entry (windows and doors) at the Salt Lake and other LDS temples. Light is the elemental symbol of God - His power and intelligence. Alpha and Omega represent the beginning and the end - of light in sunrise and sunset each day. Observe also that it resembles the Egyptian *aht* motif; representing rebirth and the resurrection of the sun each day, and that of Osiris. We all are reborn through Christ as mediator, and look for the return of the resurrected Christ in the millennium.

Creation   At the top center of the half-circle sun is a keystone, an inverted A; the first letter of the Hebrew and Greek alphabets. It is associated with God as the first, the creator. *Alph* (symbolizing God) and *Beth* (symbolizing house, womb or creation) are the first two "parent" letters of the Hebrew alphabet, representing male and female.[291] Anciently, the inverted A (the Keystone) resembled, and was associated with, a bull head with horns (symbols of power and fertility). It symbolized God as the great creator bull in ancient Egypt. The bull (Taurus) was the first animal of sacrifice in many ancient cultures, including early Egypt. According to one historic source, Joseph Smith stated that Adam (the first earthly father) offered the bullock as sacrifice upon leaving the Garden with Eve. Latter God provided Abraham a ram as the new sacrifice (Aires).[Mark] The words on the outer circle surrounding Facsimile Two refer to God as the great creator in reference to a bull. He is the father of the human race, planted here and elsewhere by him.[292]

Keys   The chiastic keystone at center is key to the stability and strength of the sun-like arch stones. Christ is the strength of His church. As the great High Priest, he provides the keys of the priesthood. He is also the key that opens and closes "the way" – the pathway home through the stars. The return to his presence, passing all sentinels along the way, is via the fiery pillar of light - the axis mundi, ladder or tree. It is literally and symbolically only through Him that we have salvation and exaltation.

Summary

Chiasmus is found in the basic form of sacred architecture, including the intersecting X-cross diagonals of the spatial square, the center point of time-oriented circles and the creation focus of the vesica pisces. It is also found in many other temple motifs, including opposing spirals and the rising sun on the horizon motif, positioned centrally between two upright pillars. This light-oriented motif, covering Joseph Smith's inspired Nauvoo Temple, may be the most important visual chiasm on Latter-day Saint sacred architecture. It suggests the primacy of light in all of creation, symbolized by the sun - God. It is His light that dispelled darkness and chaos at creation, animating matter, providing life throughout the cosmos. Light is also the binding and sealing power of the Order of the Priesthood, keeping all things from descending into darkness and a return to chaos. This and other meaning appears to be suggested in its chiastic center - the sun - positioned between two symmetrical, covenant-oriented pillars; pillars representative of the Eternal Covenant, renewed each day in the resurrecting sun. The complimentary opposition of this motif also signals male and female – in creation – a primary temple theme connecting us to the Great Creator. Chiasmus is symmetry, balance and unity. It is also beauty and order - the Order of the Priesthood. This and much more can be discovered as we seek God in the form and symbols of the most inspired sacred architecture.

Examples of Chiasmus in Sacred Architecture

Centrality within Symmetry

The Heavens: As Above So Below

> The rising sun on the horizon between two pillars
>
> Twelve around One: the sun surrounded by twelve zodiac signs, thirteen-part stone circles, thirteen-part Draper Temple spirals, etc.
>
> Four X-Crosses in the heavens
>
> Polaris with circling stars

Basic Temple Form

> Linear layout of Solomon's Temple: The expulsion from, and the return back into, the presence of God
>
> Altar between two mirrors in Sealing Rooms

Symbols

> Figure-8
>
> Alpha and Omega
>
> Vesica Pisces
>
> Symmetry (opposition with a central theme)

> Inverted pentagram with upright pentagon, Star of David (two opposing triangles), Yin -Yang, Two opposing spirals, Seal of Melchizedek (two opposing squares), circle in the square, vesica pisces

End Notes
[1] What follows is an excerpt from my book *The Second Comforter: Conversing With The Lord Through the Veil*, © Denver C. Snuffer, Jr., 2006, 2008, Mill Creek Press.

1   [1]Matt. 23: 1-3: "Then spake Jesus to the multitude, and to his disciples, Saying, The scribes and the Pharisees sit in Moses' seat: All therefore whatsoever they bid you observe, that observe and do; but do not ye after their works: for they say, and do not."

2   [2]The whole of the book is a chiasm, although its author refers to his discussion in terms of "loops."

3   [3]Chiasmus is an ancient sentence structure in which the pattern reaches a central point, then reverses. The pattern can be summarized by the example: ABCDCBA; where the concept in "A" appears in the first and again in the last sentence. Similarly concept "B" repeats in the second to the first and second to the last sentence, and so on.

4   [4]Bongard developed a series of tests involving patterns and shapes. The discussion uses Bongard's tests to demonstrate analytical and reasoning issues relevant to the text. They depend upon abstract reasoning, but also require an ability to find the simple patterns within a complex set of problems.

5   [5]It was John Welch who discovered chiasmus in the Book of Mormon while a missionary in Germany. He has written about the subject, including *Chiasmus in Antiquity.* Edited by John W. Welch. Provo: The Foundation for Ancient Research and Mormon Studies, 1981. One of the longest examples of a chiasm in the Book of Mormon is found in Chapter 36 of Alma. The entire chapter is a lengthy form of this pattern of writing.

6   [6]See Exo. 25: 32: "And six branches shall come out of the sides of it; three branches of the candlestick out of the one side, and three branches of the candlestick out of the other side."

[2] See The Church of Jesus Christ of Latter-day Saints, Standard Works, which include the Old and New Testaments, The Book of Mormon, The Doctrine and Covenants, and The Pearl of Great Price.

[3] Marvin R Wilson, *Our Father Abraham: Jewish Roots of the Christian Faith* (Grand Rapids, MI: William B. Eerdmans Publishing Company and Dayton, Ohio: Center for Judaic-Christian Studies, 1989), p. 203.

[4] For ease in publishing, chiastic points are not set up here in their x form.

[5] Hugh Nibley, *Abraham in Egypt* (Salt Lake City: Deseret Book, 1981), 156.

[6] Many miss this meaning in Adam's story. It is one of three levels of meaning. 1. The real events of the historical Adam and Eve. 2. Adam's representation of each of us. 3. Adam as a figure of Christ (Romans 5:14; Ephesians 5:30-32). We miss significant meaning if we do not understand the patterns relating to Christ.

7 . Some may be disturbed with the Bible's continually imaging Christ's people as His Bride, since it contains both men and women. This must not be construed as promoting homosexuality, as the Lord makes quite clear throughout His scriptures that such is not according to His plan. Here, from the very beginning, we see that the major focus of the Lord's covenant is to bless His covenanted people with Eternal *Seed*. This is a major reason why homosexuality cannot fit into the Lord's overall plan for exaltation.

8 John W. Welch, *Illuminating the Sermon at the Temple and the Sermon on the Mount* (Provo, UT: Foundation for Ancient Research and Mormon Studies at Brigham Young University, 1999), p. 32. Welch shows the Sermon on the Mount was a covenant making event as at Mt. Sinai.

9 Wilson, *Our Father Abraham,* 211. Wilson also says in modern Jewish ceremonies, when the bride and groom share a cup of wine, it witnesses that though once two people, they are now one, 211.

10 Wilson, *Our Father Abraham*, 246.

11 Daniel I. Block, "Marriage and Family in Ancient Israel," in Campbell, *Marriage and Family in the Biblical World,* p. 45.

12 David W. Chapman, "Marriage and Family in Second Temple Judaism," in Ken M. Campbell, ed., *Marriage and Family in the Biblical World* (Downers Grove, IL: Inter Varsity Press, 2003), 190.

13 Boyd K. Packer, "Who Is Jesus Christ?" *Ensign,* March 2008, p. 15.

14 Daniel I. Block, "Marriage and Family in Ancient Israel," in Campbell, *Marriage and Family in the Biblical World,* p. 44.

15. Alfred Edersheim, *The Life and Times of Jesus the Messiah* (Peabody, Mass: Hendrickson Publishers, 1993), 893-895; Edersheim gives many witnesses of the rending of the veil and this interpretation, and suggests, referring to Acts 6:7, it was likely the rending of this very heavy veil that caused many priests to thereafter join Christ's Church, for they realized this rending could only have occurred at the hand of God; p. 895, f. 85. See also, Joseph Fielding McConkie, *Gospel Symbolism* (Salt Lake City: Bookcraft, Inc., 1985), 275. He cites Hebrews 10:19-20, and says, "The rending of the veil symbolized the removal of the barrier between man and God, for man was thus enabled 'to enter into the holiest by the blood of Jesus.'"

16. Many examples given by Yehuda Raddy in *Chiasmus in Antiquity* of larger works, considered chiastic, do not match every point in a point for point order.

[17] Prior to a similar mass outpouring of the Spirit at the Kirtland Temple, the prophet's prayer held this same Bridegroom imagery, "Remember … That thy church may… be adorned as a bride" (D&C: 109:72-76).

[18] For one in-depth study of connection between early Christian and latter-day tokens of the covenant, see Matthew Brown, *The Gate of Heaven* (American Fork, UT: Covenant Communication, Inc., 1999), pp. 165-247.

[19] This ties to imagery in Isaiah of "the thirsty land [becoming] springs of water" fulfilled by the Restoration of His Church in the last days. In reality *The Book of Mormon*, coming out of the earth contains living waters of truth now reviving and re-gathering Israel from their previous barren existence (See Isaiah 35:6-7, 10).

[20]. "Exalted beings --- who shall sit with God on his throne and be as he is --- shall go to the highest heaven in the celestial world. … There they will have eternal increase, meaning spirit children in the resurrection forever and ever." Bruce R. McConkie, *The Millennial Messiah* (Salt Lake City: Deseret Book, 1982), 707.

In addition to the above sources I must give credit to Northrop Frye, whose work *The Great Code* pointed out the overall unity of the Bible. However, he said it had a U form. I came to see it was actually a chiastic X.

I also credit Donna B. Nielsen, whose research on how Christ fulfilled many Hebrew wedding traditions led me to some good sources. See **Beloved Bridegroom,** Onyx Press.

[21] Hugh Nibley, *Mormonism and Early Christianity*, p. 358.

[22] Joseph Fielding Smith, *Teachings of the Prophet Joseph Smith*, p. 157.

[23] Bruce R. McConkie, *Doctrines of the Restoration*, p. 84.

[24] James Strong, *Strong's Exhaustive Concordance of the Bible*, Hebrew word 120.

[25] James Strong, *Strong's Exhaustive Concordance of the Bible*, Hebrew word 2332.

[26] James Strong, *Strong's Exhaustive Concordance of the Bible*, Hebrew word 4317.

[27] "The Tree of life in Ancient Cultures," C. Wilfred Griggs, *Ensign*, June, 1988.

[28] Joseph Fielding McConkie & Donald W. Parry, *A Guide to Scriptural Symbols*, p. 88.

[29] Joseph Fielding Smith, *Doctrines of Salvation*, Vol. 1, p. 84.

[30] Bruce R. McConkie, *Mormon Doctrine,* p. 486.

[31] James E. Talmage, *Jesus the Christ*, p. 104.

[32]*Ensign,* May 1973.

[33]*Ensign*, May 1980.

[34]This was the twelfth month of the ecclesiastical year and sixth month of the civil year. To account for a full year, a thirteenth month, Adar II or Veadar was periodically added.

[35]This was the sixth month of the year on the ecclesiastical calendar and the twelfth month of the year on the civil calendar.

[36] Helen Ann Williams Pawlowski, born December 16, 1930, Spanish Fork, Utah. Married Engelbert Pawlowski on January 18, 1969. Passed away July 2, 2001 from lymphoma.

[37] Absolute Placement

[38] Helen A. Pawlowski, *The Visualization of the Atom*, 1990, The Pawlowski Family Trust, Riverton, Utah. 84065.

[39] See Bohr's Electron Distribution Chart at chapter end.

[40] For a thorough study of the circular periodic table, which answers the questions of quantum and absolute placement, see Helen Pawlowski, The Visualization of the Atom, 1987, 1990.

[41] *History of the Church* 4:461

[42] Moses 6:62-63

[43] John W. Welch, Criteria for Identifying and Evaluating the Presence of Chiasmus, Chapter 2?

[44] See Appendix 1, Comparisons of Chiasmus in Articles of Faith, Sacred Geometry, Ancient Hebrew, and the Davidic Chiasmus.

[45] See Scott Vanatter, The Davidic Chiasmus in a previous chapter of this book.

[46] The study of chiasmus is anything but exhaustive. This book and specifically this chapter of the book provides only a partial explanation and sample of the multitude of places where chiasmus can be identified.

[47] Too numerous to mention, the pattern of the chiasmus is easily identified in all His works, demonstrating a beginning, middle and end. See *Know Ye not that Ye are the Temple of God* by the same author.

[48] Discovered by Kathryn Paulsen in 2009 using the circular periodic table by Helen Pawlowski, *The Visualization of the Atom*, 1987. See also Bohr's electron distribution chart for chiastic elements.

[49] The center point of the Chiasmus is always light and often times even denotes an encounter with Christ.

[50] We Believe, Development of the Articles of Faith, by John W. Welch and David J. Whittaker, Ensign, Sept. 1979, Publication of Church of Jesus Christ of Latter-day Saints., see also Elder L. Tom Perry , The Articles of Faith, Ensign, May 1998 Publication of Church of Jesus Christ of Latter-day Saints.

[51] Joseph Smith, *The Vision,* a poem to W. W. Phelps, Esq., This is the only poem extant supposed to have been written by the Prophet **Joseph Smith**, and published in Nauvoo in 1843.

[52] Personages Who Appeared to the Prophet Joseph Smith or Who Were Seen by Him in Vision, *List Compiled by H. Donl Peterson, See Appendix 2.*

[53] William H. Brownlee, *Principles for Biblical Interpretation among the Sectaries of the Dead Sea Scrolls,* BA 14 1951, pg 54-76.

[54] For a complete explanation, see the publication, *Know Ye Not that Ye are the Temple of God,* Yvonne Bent, 2011.

[55] See previous chapter entitled Davidic Chiasmus. See also http://www.davidicchiasmus.com/.

[56] I first became familiar with this concept in the early 1980's. See *Positioning*, by Al Ries and Jack Trout, McGraw Hill, 2000.

[57] Sir Thomas Browne, *The Garden of Cyrus*, London, 1736.

[58] http://alignment2012.com/mothfath.htm

[59] Sir Thomas Browne, *The Garden of Cyrus*, London, 1736

[60] Ming Tang Chinese Temple, http://luoshu.com/book/part_one/chapter_nine/temple_building.

[61] Storm Pattern Navajo Rug, http://www.navajorugrepair.com/regionalrugs.htm

[62]This is the now famous **Photo 51** taken by Rosalind Franklin in Kings College London in 1952. It is an X-ray diffraction image of DNA. This is the X-ray diffraction image of DNA that provided the key missing piece of information for Watson and Crick's discovery of the structure of the DNA molecule, http://www.hyattcarter.com/chiasmus_01-04.htm.

[63] Vesalius, Woodcut from the Fabrica, 1555, from Polyak, 1957.

[64] Biographia Epistolaris, ed, A. Turnbull, London, 1911, 1. Letter 127, 1804.

[65] JST John 1:1.

[66] John A. Widtsoe, *Joseph Smith as Scientist*, Bookcraft, 1964 by Mark E. Peterson, pg. 19.

[67] Glenn Clark, *The Man Who Tapped the Secrets of the Universe*, The University of Science and Philosophy, pgs. 32-34.

[68] Sol Luckman, *Sound, Intention & Genetic Healing*, http://www.bodymindwisdom.com/article_sound_intention.html, 2010.

[69] Michael S. Schneider, *A Beginner's Guide to Constructing the Universe*, Harper Perennial, New York, NY. 1994, pgs. 145-177.

[70] Leonardo Fibonacci, who was born in the 12th century, studied a sequence of numbers with a different type of rule for determining the next number in a sequence.

[71] Some statements made by the Lord when He called himself "The Light"; 3 Ne. 18: 16, 24, John 8: 12, John 9: 5, 3 Ne. 9: 18, 3 Ne. 11: 11, Ether 4: 12, D&C 6: 21, D&C 10: 58, D&C 11: 11, D&C 12: 9, D&C 88: 50, D&C 93: 2.

[72] The Family: A Proclamation to the World—The First Presidency and Council of the Twelve Apostles of The Church of Jesus Christ of Latter-day Saints, 1995.

[73] Claude Bragdon, *The Beautiful Necessity, Seven Essays on Theosophy and Architecture*, Manas Press, Rochester, New York, 1910.

[74] Avard T. Fairbanks, *Human Proportions for Artists*, Posthumous author, 2005, Fairbanks Art and Books, Bellingham, WA 98226. This work is a compilation akin to the works of Leonardo da Vinci, where the entire human form is measured to display the divine proportion.

[75] Yvonne Bent, *Neither is the Man without the Woman in the Lord*, Copyright, 2004.

[76] Mary Douglas, *Thinking in Circles: An essay on ring composition*, Yale University Press, 2007

[77] J Bell Pettigrew, *Design in Nature*, Illustrated by Spiral and other Arrangements in the Inorganic and Organic Kingdoms as exemplified in Matter, Force, Life, Growth, Rhythms, &c., especially in Crystals, Plants, and Animals. With Examples selected from the Reproductive, Alimentary, Respiratory, Circulatory, Nervous, Muscular, Osseous, Locomotory, and other Systems of Animals, Longmans, Green and Company, New York, 1908, pg. 87.

[78] Ibid, pg. 89.

[79] Ibid., pgs. 91 & 92.

[80] The Family: A Proclamation to the World—The First Presidency and Council of the Twelve Apostles of The Church of Jesus Christ of Latter-day Saints, 1995.

[81] http://www.tallitministries.com/marriage.htm

[82] Mary Douglas, *Thinking in Circles*, Yale University Press, USA, 2007, pg. 36.

[83] John Denver, *The Music is You,* Back Home Again, RCA Legacy, 1974.

[84] Leonardo Da Vinci, from Fincher, 1981, http://www.cerebromente.org.br/n10/opiniao/cairasco/art_i.htm.

[85] http://en.wikipedia.org/wiki/Hypothalamus

[86] http://en.wikipedia.org/wiki/Circadian_rhythm

[87] http://en.wikipedia.org/wiki/Hypothalamus

[88] http://www.wddty.com/human-energy-fields-fritz-albert-popp.html, Sept. 2010.

[89] Dan Eden, *Is DNA the next internet?,* http://viewzone2.com/dnax.html.

[90] Chiasmus, Chaosmos, Chirality, and Complementarity: Four Intertwining Concepts, http://www.hyattcarter.com/index.html, September 2010.

[91] Grazyna Fosar and Franz Bludorf, *DNA is influenced by Words and Frequencies,* http://www.soulsofdistortion.nl/dna1.html, 2010.

[92] Mayan Majix , *DNA is Influenced by Words and Frequencies*, October 20, 2005, http://cradle2dagrave.proboards.com/index.cgi?board=FOREVERYACTION&action=display&thread=312, May 19, 2010

[93] Sol Luckman, *Sound, Intention, and Genetic Healing,* http://www.bodymindwisdom.com/article_sound_intention.html. 2006

[94] Ibid.

[95] Ibid.

[96] See D&C 89:10-11 And again, verily I say unto you, all wholesome herbs God hath ordained for the constitution, nature, and use of man— Every herb in the season thereof, and every fruit in the season thereof; all these to be used with prudence and thanksgiving. These food substances are high in alkaline based foods. Other foods to be eaten sparingly are acid based.

[97] Brazyna Fosar and Franz Bludorf, DNA Can be influenced and Reprogrammed by Words and Frequencies, http://www.soulsofdistortion.nl/dna1.html, 2010

[98] DNA can be influenced and reprogrammed by words and frequencies, http://www.soulsofdistortion.nl/dna1.html, 2010.

[99] *ACS' Journal of Physical Chemistry B*, February 06, 2008, http://www.dailygalaxy.com/my_weblog/2008/02/dna-found-to-ha.html.

[100] Ether 2: 3 And they did also carry with them *Deseret*, which, by interpretation, is a honey bee; and thus they did carry with them swarms of bees, and all manner of that which was upon the face of the land, seeds of every kind.

[101] 1 Ne. 18: 6 And it came to pass that on the morrow, after we had prepared all things, much fruits and meat from the wilderness, and honey in abundance, and provisions according to that which the Lord had commanded us, we did go down into the ship, with all our loading and our seeds, and whatsoever thing we had brought with us, every one according to his age; wherefore, we did all go down into the ship, with our wives and our children.

[102] Spencer W. Kimball quoted as saying "My life is like my shoes—to be worn out in service" (as quoted in Gordon B. Hinckley, "He Is at Peace," *Ensign,* Dec. 1985, 41)

[103] Glyconutrients reference, 2 June 2010, http://www.glyconutrientsreference.com/whatareglyconutrients/scientificvalidation.html.

[104] Greg Braden, *The Divine Matrix,* Hay House, Inc., Carlsbad, California, 2007, pgs. 46-50.

[105] Dan Eden, *Is DNA the Next internet?,* http://viewzone2.com/dnax.html, 2010.

[106] Sol Luckman, *Sound, Intention, and Genetic Healing,* http://www.bodymindwisdom.com/article_sound_intention.html. 2006

[107] Moro. 10: 8, And again, I exhort you, my brethren, that ye deny not the gifts of God, for they are many; and they come from the same God. And there are different ways that these gifts are administered; but it is the same God who worketh all in all; and they are given by the manifestations of the Spirit of God unto men, to profit them. ,
D&C 1: 38 What I the Lord have spoken, I have spoken, and I excuse not myself; and though the heavens and the earth pass away, my word shall not pass away, but shall all be fulfilled, whether by mine own voice or by the voice of my servants, it is the same.

[108] Moro. 10: 28 I declare these things unto the fulfilling of the prophecies. And behold, they shall proceed forth out of the mouth of the everlasting God; and his word shall hiss forth from generation to generation

[109] Mormon 8: 27, 40-41, Ether 8: 22, 24

[110] Griffiths, Anthony J. F. (1999). *An Introduction to genetic analysis.* New York: W.H. Freeman. ISBN 071673771X. http://www.ncbi.nlm.nih.gov/books/bv.fcgi?highlight=autosome&rid=iga.section.222, 2010.

[111] President Gordon B. Hinckley, "God Hath Not Given Us the Spirit of Fear," *Ensign,* Oct. 1984.

[112] Seer stones

[113] Weft, woof, transverse threads woven between warp threads

[114] Quincunx: An arrangement of five objects in a square, one at each corner and one in the middle (thus,); especially, an arrangement, as of trees, in such squares continuously. A collection of trees in such squares forms a regular grove or wood, presenting parallel rows or alleys in different directions, according to the spectator's position. See diagram under *quincuncial.*

[115] Sir Thomas Browne, *The Garden of Cyrus*, London, 1736, pg. 34.

[116] http://www.wisegeek.com/what-is-decussation.htm

[117] Joel S. Glaser, *Romancing the Chiasm: Vision, Vocalization, and Virtuosity*, Journal of Neuro-Ophthalmology: June 2008 – Volume 28 – Issue 2 – pp 131-143.

[118] Ibid.

[119] http://www.ncbi.nlm.nih.gov/bookshelf/br.fcgi?book=cell&part=A4895

[120] http://www.ncbi.nlm.nih.gov/bookshelf/br.fcgi?book=cooper&part=A618

[121] Yvonne Bent, Neither is the Man without the Woman in the Lord, El Cerrito, CA. 2005.

[122] Donna Nielsen, *The Beloved Bridegroom*, 1999, Onyx Press, pgs. 157-158

[123] Ibid. pg. 157.

[124] Joseph Smith, *History of The Church of Jesus Christ of Latter-day Saints,* 7 Vols. 5:339.

[125] The power of the heart to entrain is profound and too lengthy to cover in this chapter. It is covered extensively in detail in *Know Ye Not that Ye are the Temple of God,* by the same author.

[126] Alma 30:44.

[127] Margaret Barker, *Creation, A Biblical Vision for the Environment,* Published by T&T Clark International, New York, NY, 2010, pg. 125, *quoting Philo, On Flight.*

[128] Ibid, pgs. 122-123.

[129] Joel S. Glaser, MD, *Romancing the Chiasm: Vision, Vocalization , and Virtuosity,* The Sixth Hoyt Lecture, Journal of Neuro-Ophthalmology: June 2008 – Volume 28 – Issue 2, pp. 131-143.

[130] D&C 121: 36 That the rights of the priesthood are inseparably connected with the powers of heaven, and that the powers of heaven cannot be controlled nor handled only upon the principles of righteousness

[131] D&C 88, 6, 7, 13: He that ascended up on high, as also he descended below all things, in that he comprehended all things, that he might be in all and through all things, the light of truth;..Which truth shineth. This is the light of Christ. As also he is in the sun, and the light of the…The light which is in all things, which giveth life to all things, which is the law by which all things are governed, even the power of God who sitteth upon his throne, who is in the bosom of eternity, who is in the midst of all things.

[132] D Voet, JG Voet, CW Pratt (1999). *Fundamentals of Biochemistry: Biochemical Interactions CD-ROM* – J. Wiley & Sons, 2010. Read more: http://www.brighthub.com/science/genetics/articles/23384.aspx#ixzz0rkKCyFT2.

[133] Abraham 1:2.

[134] Mark Kurlansky, *Salt A World History,* Penguin Group, (USA) Inc. 375 Hudson Street, New York, NY 10014, USA, pg. 29.

[135] H. Clay Trumbull, *The Salt Covenant*, 1899, New York, pg. 12.

[136] Mark Kurlansky, *Salt A World History,* Penguin Book, New York, New York, 2002, pg. 51.

[137] Ibid, pg. 60, *Marco Polo's Travels, Col. Yule's translation*, II., 29, 35, 36, 37, & notes to Chap. 47.

[138] http://fusionanomaly.net/doublehelix.html

[139] Precipitation hardening, called age hardening. A heat treatment technique used to increase the yield strength of malleable materials; relies on changes in solid solubility with temperature to produce fine particles of an impurity phase, which impede the movement of defects in a crystal's lattice. Unlike ordinary tempering, alloys must be kept at elevated temperature for hours to allow precipitation to take place. This time delay is called aging. http://en.wikipedia.org/wiki/Precipitation_strengthening.

[140] Ibid. pg. 44.

[141] Energetics of the protein-DNA-water interaction, 2007, http://www.biomedcentral.com/1472-6807/7/4

[142] Masuru Emoto, *The Hidden Messages in Water,* Sunmark Publishing, Inc., Tokyo, Japan, 2001.

[143] See Harper's *Latin Dictionary*, s vv. "sal," "salio," "saltus."

[144] http://users.rcn.com/jkimball.ma.ultranet/BiologyPages/P/Palindromes.html, 23 May 2010.

[145] http://www.eurogentest.org/aboutus/info/public/unit6/patientsLeafletsEnglish/chromosoneChangesEnglish.xhtml.

[146] Genesis 32:23-29.

[147] In the Standard works there are only a smattering of outright witnesses stating that they saw God face to face: Abraham, Moses, The Brother of Jared, Moroni, Mormon, Nephi, Enos, and Jacob, King Lamoni's entire people, His father, and Joseph Smith.

[148] PSALM 149:1-2, Praise ye the Lord. Sing unto the Lord a new song, and his praise in the congregation of saints. Let Israel rejoice in him that made him; let the children of Zion be joyful in their King.

[149] Sir Thomas Browne, *The Garden of Cyrus,* London, 1736, pg. 34.

[150] Helen Pawlowski, *The Visualization of The Atom*, The Pawlowski Family Trust, Arizona, pgs 21-119.

[151] Sir Thomas Browne, *The Garden of Cyrus,* 1658.

[152] Giovanni Francesco Barbieri, 1591 –1666, Jacob, Ephraim, and Manasseh, http://en.wikipedia.org/wiki/Guercino

[153] Hyatt Carter, *Chiasmus, Chaosmos, Chirality, and Complementarity: Four Intertwining Concepts,* http://www.hyattcarter.com/index.html, 2010.

[154] http://www.meridianinstitute.com/eaem/renulife/book1/contents.html

[155] Isaiah 9:6, 2 Nephi 19:6.

[156] http://www.thebrainlabs.com/brain.shtml

[157] John Bunyan, *Pilgrim's Progress*, London, 1658.

[158] Vitruvius, On Architecture, Vol. 1.2, pps. 3-4.

[159] According to Nibley, the great Egyptian creator God Khnum, at the center of our circular Facsimile 2 of the Book of Abraham is a stylized illustration of God sitting on the ground (His strength comes from contact with the ground, mother earth), throwing a pot – symbolizing creation. Hugh Nibley, One Eternal Round FARMS lecture series (Sept. 5, 1990), Tape four, transcribed by the author, Typescript, pps. 5-6.

[160] Roger Penrose, Fearful Symmetry, Princeton Press.

[161] In Alma chapter 13 there are a number of examples of scriptural chiasmus. The five statements below (verses 2-9) feature a centralized idea within visual symmetry. In some cases the central idea is expressed outside the visual center of the chiasmus. The symmetry is expressed with color. The author is grateful to David Christensen for this example.

This high priesthood being **after the order of his Son**, which order was from the foundation of the world; or in other words, being without beginning of days or end of years,

    being prepared from **eternity to all eternity** according to his foreknowledge of all things—

        Now they were ordained after this manner—being called with a **holy calling**,

            and ordained with a holy ordinance.

        and taking upon them the high priesthood of the **holy order**,

    which calling, and ordinance, and high priesthood, is **without beginning or end**—

Thus they become high priests forever, **after the order of the Son**, the Only Begotten of the Father, who is without beginning of days or end of years.

[162] The 2 intersecting lines were called the *cardo* and the *decumanus*. The raised point of the top of an Egyptian pyramid is the center place of these 2 intersecting lines, for example. Ibid., p. 19. Brigham Young and Wilford Woodruff may have marked the future site of the Salt Lake Temple in this basic manner.

[163] According to Nibley, the Roman God Janus was honored "in the north by the solomn cermonial driving of the nail to hold everything in place." This is the same God featured prominently in our Facsimile 2. He sits at the center there controlling all order - the commos." (Hugh Nibley, One Eternal Round, lecture 9, tape 4, FARMS, p. 7, Sept. 5, 1990.)

[164] See Hugh Nibley, One Eternal Round, Lecture 9, Tape 4, FARMS.

[165] Sir Thomas Browne, The Garden of Cyrus, chapter 1, p. 4.

[166] The figure-8 analemma results from recording the sum of the Earth's elliptical orbit around the Sun, as a result of the tilt of the Earth's axis in relation to the plane of its orbit around the sun. These movements are recorded via photographing its position in the sky (or its light striking the earth) both of which form a figure-8 over one full year. (See illustrations in chapter 7 of Book 2.) Artist Charles Ross has observed this graphic 8 created over time. According to Brenan, "Using a stationary focused magnifying glass, he [Ross] placed wooden planks in a fixed position for 366 consecutive days. The sun's rays burned a pattern in the planks which when graphed showed a precisely executed double spiral...In winter the spiral is counter-clockwise and the coils are wide...after equinox they begin to wind into a clockwise spiral and tighten. They contract until the summer solstice and the right-hand spiral begins to expand after the solstice, straighten again at equinox, and return to a left-handed spiral again in winter to continue the process perpetually" (Martin Brenan, The Stones of Time, Inner Traditions International, p. 190). The author is grateful to Frederick Huchel for added insights on the analemma.

[167] His complete statement reads, "There was a past eternity and there will be a future eternity. The past eternity embraced the sphere of eternal existence which all men had as the spirit offspring of exalted Parents in pre-existence. The future eternity will be that eternal sphere in which the righteous, having gained both immortality and eternal life, will themselves become exalted Parents and have a continuation of the seeds forever and ever." Bruce R. McConkie, Mormon Doctrine, Bookcraft, 2nd ed., p. 240. See also D&C 132:19-25.

[168] W.W. Phelps, Times and Seasons, vol. 5, p. 758. Cited in Joe Sampson, Written by the Finger of God, Wellspring Press, p. 139. Sampson states that the Kabbalah uses the same 2.5 billion year figure in Rosh Hashanah 31a, Sanhedrin 97a, Tamid 7:4.

[169] For a complete discussion of the cross and tau marks see chapters 3 and 6 of the Day Star: Reading Sacred Architecture by the author.

[170] One of the earliest uses of both the pentagram and the *Chi-Rho* symbol in connection with Christianity may have been by Constantine I, the first Christian Roman Emperor in 312-13 AD. As emperor, Constantine implemented new symbols in his government, some on coins. One of these coins featured an inverted pentagram in a circle, its reverse side also featuring the Chi-Rho symbol. In the conclusive battle that made him emperor, Constantine had his soldiers put the Chi-Rho symbol on their shields, a motif featuring the 1st 2 Greek letters of the word "Christ." He reportedly saw a cross of light imposed over the sun, along with the Greek characters. According to Lehner, Constantine ascribed his success in this battle to his conversion to Christianity. (See Ernst Lehner, "Seal and Amulet of Emperor Constantine I," Symbols, Signs, and Signets, World Publishing, p. 582.) In 313 AD Constantine announced the Edict of Milan, proclaiming toleration of Christianity throughout the Western Roman Empire. The letters I.H.S. originally were Latin for In Hoc Signo or "in this sign [thou shalt conquer]." Medieval Christians apparently substituted the words *Iesus Hominum Salvator*, creating a direct link to Christ. Some claim the design was not Christian, but had ancient pagan origins in the sun, as outside influences from the east (including sun worship) were entering the Roman Empire at this time. In 310, before Constantine took control of the empire, he did make use of Mars and Apollo (sun) symbols on the backs of some coins. Mars may have served to symbolically legitimize his rule. According to Bruun, examples of pagan associations (including astrology) continued after Constantine's Christian conversion. (P. Bruun, Studies in Constantinian numismatics: papers from 1954 to 1988.) Hyrum Smith also used these same letters on his cane and sword, potentially to suggest his triumph against evil, sin, etc. (See D. Michael Quinn, Mormonism and the Magic World View, Signature Books, p. 108.)

[171] See Bruce R. McConkie, The Millennial Messiah, Deseret Book, p. 695.

[172] Meir Ben-Dov, In the Shadow of the Temple, Harper and Row, p. 139.

[173] William Clayton Journal, October 20, 1843. The second seal of the new and everlasting covenant, or second anointing, bestows the fullness of the priesthood, allotting the married couple their mansion in heaven as king and priest, queen and preistess, whereas the first seal establishes the family kingdom (Abrahamic—Patriarchal) through marriage. The anointing ordinance anciently was associated with protection and the power to resurrect. It remains so today. (See John F. Hall, The Anointing of the Gods: Sanctification and Authority from Egyptian Pharoahs to Hebrew Priest Kings and Beyond, presentation paper given on October 31, 2009 to the Temple Studies Group, Temple Church, London.) In his dedication prayer for the San Diego California Temple, Pres. Benson stated, "We thank thee for the fullness of the priesthood, exercised therein." Architect Bill Lewis later looked for meaning in this prayer, stating, "The temple itself is a symbol...I just took the dedicatory prayer, and looked through it for symbols, because this is the Prophet speaking, not me...So the symbol, for us as members, is certainly the fullness of the priesthood." (Bill Lewis, Oral History Interview with the author, October 1996, typescript p. 16.)

[174] Pres. Ezra Taft Benson, in his dedication prayer of the San Diego Temple, stated, "We thank thee for the fullness of the priesthood, exercised therein." Bill Lewis as architect of the San Diego California Temple took this statement as justification for the connection between "the Seal" and the fullness of the priesthood. He currently serves as a temple sealer there. Oral History Interview with the author, typescript, p. 16.

[175] This great circle of the sun and the planets, all in the ecliptic, is a central part of the myths of many ancient cultures worldwide, including the Egyptians and Native Americans. The nightly travel below the earth in the darkness of the "underworld" (the duat of the Egyptians) gave rise to the resurrection of the sun each new day. (See Frederick M. Huchel, The Armillary Sphere and the Celestial Sphere, Frithurex Athenaeum, p. 2.)

[176] The 12 signs of the zodiac move through a great circle lasting approx. 25,500 years, so that one "sign" is behind the rising sun, on the vernal equinox sunrise, each lasting about 2200 years on average. This long rotation of the constellations behind the rising sun is part of what is called *the Precession of the Equinoxes*. The precession is caused by the 23.5 degree off-axis tilt of the earth. Some believe the tilt was introduced at the Fall of Adam and Eve.

[177] We are at the tail end of Pisces, transitioning soon to Aquarius, the waterbearer (a good symbol for the return of Christ the King in the Millennium – associated with the symbolism of the Feast of Tabernacles in ancient Israel; a feast featuring the "return of the king" and the pouring of water ceremony [Aquarius]) upon the altar on the 8th day of the feast – the great day. Historically the move from one sign to another every 2000 years or so has marked two important things; 1. The new form of animal sacrifice God directs to be used (from the *bull* [Egypt – Hathor and Adam] - 4500 B.C., to Abraham - *ram* and lamb – 2000 B.C., to Christ – fish, 1 B.C. (He called fishers of men, did miracles utilizing loaves and fishes, ate broiled fish after the resurrection, etc.), and 2. Great world catyclism (the year 2012+?). See chapter 7 for more on the heavens in relation to temple, astronomy, prophecy, etc.

[178] It was Oliver B. Huntington who stated that Joseph Smith said Adam offered "bullocks" as a sacrifice. About the time of the Fall, the vernal equinox sunrise moved from Gemini (the twins – Adam and Eve) into Taurus. Taurus indicates the bull for the sacrifice, lasting from the Fall, through Abraham, to Moses. It was God who provided Abraham a ram (caught by its horns in a thicket) for a substitute sacrifice for Isaac. This was about 2000 B.C. Each of the signs lasts approx. 2000 years on average. (Oliver B. Huntington, quoted by Arnold Auer Reiser, Oct. 4, 1899, cited in John H. Wittord, An Historical Investigation of the Ruined Altars at Adam-ondi-Ahman, Missouri, in Newsletter and Proceedings of the S.E. H.A. [Society for Early Historic Archaeology at BYU], Number 113, [April 15, 1969], p. 6.) For more on ancient beliefs connecting sacrifices to figures in the zodiac, see Giorgio de Santillana and Hertha von Dechend, Hamlet's Mill, David R. Godine Publisher Inc. The author is grateful to Frederick Huchel for introduction to these insights.

[179] Venus is the only known object in the heavens to form a perfect pentagram by its movements (doing so over 8 years). According to Zehren, the 5 points of this pentagram also point, "to five different groups of stars or constellations which were easy to remember; each had a given name…It was only later discovered that the five points moved slowly throughout the vault of heaven as if they were hands of a giant clock…Over a period of four years each point of the pentagram was displaced one day, a 365th part of the zodiac circle…After 1460 solar years the 'hands' stood at their original places. This unit of 1460 years is the Egyptian 'Sothis year' and belongs not only to the god Seth-Sirius but, much more importantly, to the goddess Sothis. And this goddess was not other than…Venus herself…The space of time between the first appearance of the planet Venus and its reappearance at the same place is exactly 1,460 days, i.e. four solar years, which was the calendar used in antiquity by the Greeks to measure the Olympiades, which is also the time interval between the modern Olympic Games. For the Greeks, these 2, 4-year cycles corresponded to Athena, goddess of war, represented by the morning star, and Aphrodite, goddess of love, represented by the evening star. But after 1,460 days Venus becomes the Morning star if it was first the Evening star and vice-versa" (See Erich Zehren, Das Testament der Sterne, in Carl G. Liungman, Dictionary of Symbols, W.W. Norton & Co., p. 334.)

[180] At Parowan Gap in Southern Utah, for example, 2 upright crosses, one above the other appear to represent to the 2, 4-year cycles of Venus, according to Norman. Related variations in Central America are common. On Latter-day Saint temples today, similar 4-part crosses, overlapping one another are found via 8-pointed Venus stars, like those at the Sacramento California Temple. There, 1, 4-pointed star is found in 1 blue, overlaid with another 4-part star in red, both set against a white, circular background. These Venus stars are the primary unifying visual motif of the temple. Christ stated that he was the bright and morning star (Revelation 22:16). See also chapter 8 and the Appendix for much more on Venus motifs. (See V. Garth Norman, The Parowan Gap: Nature's Perfect Observatory, Cedar Fort, pps. 157-83.)

[181] See chapter 8 and the Appendix of The Day Star: Reading Sacred Architecture, book 2, by the author.

[182] The Hopi, for example, currently inhabit the fourth world, having "emerged" into it from a previous world. The Fire Clan was given a 2-sided sacred stone tablet (about four inches square) by Masaw to guide them. Like other clans, they were directed to "migrate" north, south, east and west, before settling on a permanent home. Their combined travel routes formed a great *cross*, the final center place becoming Oraibi on third Mesa in the southwest. Their 4 directional migrations are symbolized, not only the 4 arms of the swastika decorating their pottery, clothing, etc., but in their 4 colors, 4-day purification ceremonies, the 4 pillars holding up kiva roofs, etc. See Frank Waters, Book of the Hopi: The First Revelation of the Hopi's Historical and Religious Worldview, Penguin, pps. 31-36.

[183] See Frank Waters, Book of the Hopi: The First Revelation of the Hopi's Historical and Religious Worldview, Penguin, pps. 31-36.

[184] Joseph Smith Jr., Teachings of the Prophet Joseph Smith, Joseph Fielding Smith, ed., Deseret Book, p. 308.

[32] These tools may have been symbolic of priesthood power. Oliver Cowdery had a special gift from God for using the rod for communication purposes (see the original version of D&C 8:6). Heber C. Kimball used his for revelation (Stanley B. Kimball, ed., On the Potter's Wheel: The Diaries of Heber C. Kimball, Signature, pp. 65, 85, 93). Wilford Woodruff had a special "rod" that he desired "to deposit in the most holy and sacred place in the holy temple of God on the consecrated hill of Zion" (Wilford Woodruff Journal, August 23, 1844). The rod used by Oliver Cowdery and later by Brigham Young in this ancient marking ceremony is apparently now in the First Presidency's private vault at Church headquarters in Salt Lake City. Anciently Aaron's rod was housed in the tabernacle's Holy of Holies (Numbers 17:1-10). See also Journal History, July 28, 1847, LDS Church Archives.

[185] In order, these 8 miraculous water crossings on earth below (connected symbolically to baptism or washing in the temple) include; 1. The rivers turning out of their course for Enoch and his people (Moses 7:13); 2. Moses parting the Red Sea as Israel left Egypt (Exodus 14:22); 3. Joshua crossing over the Jordan river on dry ground (east to west) when the Israelites entered the Promised Land (Joshua 3:15-17); 4. The drying up of the Euphrates when the repentant ten tribes departed Assyria (2 Esdras 13:39-45); 5. The brother of Jared and his people crossing over the great waters westward in their eight barges, each lit by two stones (east to west, Ether 1-3); 6. Lehi and his family crossing the great waters to come to the Promised Land (east to west, 1 Nephi 18); 7. The Saints crossed over the frozen Mississippi River westward when leaving Nauvoo in February of 1846, and 8. The crossing in the future, when those of the north countries shall, "come in remembrance before the Lord…and they shall smite the rocks, and the ice shall flow down at their presence. And an great "highway shall be cast up in the midst of the great deep" (D&C 133:26-27). Most of these crossings are east to west, following the sun's path in the ecliptic crossing the Milky Way, a reflection of being "chosen" rather than cast out. One exception is that of the Israelites leaving Egypt southeast. It was only "the chosen" who entered the Promised Land westward, however, across the Jordan into it, after 40 years of "wandering" in the desert to wipe out the less righteous (one generation). The eight water crossings are found in Denver C. Snuffer Jr., Nephi's Isaiah, Millcreek Press, pps. 245-47. For more on the number eight and rebirth, see chapter 8 of The Day Star: Reading Sacred Architecture by the author.

[186] The author has documented 11 scriptural examples each, of *movement* westward connected to righteousness, as opposed to *movement* eastward in connection with sin. East to west movement is a reflection of the path of light – the sun. This is opposite of temple *orientation* eastward to the rising sun. See endnote 97 hereafter.

[187] Water and light are elements of the perfecting process by way of *purification* (blue watery baptism), *justification* (the baptism of fire and the Holy Ghost [white light]), and *sanctification* in the Lord's red blood Atonement (being redeemed and re-entering the Lord's presence in the Second Comforter experience). All three colors are found in the Nauvoo Temple Daystar windows; an inverted pentagram in a circle surrounded by 12 stones.

[188] See Margaret Barker, The Gate of Heaven, Sheffield Phoenix Press, p. 18. For more on this threshing floor as a reflection of the circling heavens above, see Giorgio de Santillana and Hertha von Dechend, Hamlet's Mill, David R. Godine Publisher Inc.

[189] Ibid, p. 19.

[190] One of these temple rituals was the pouring of water ceremony on the 8th or Great Day of the Feast of Tabernacles. It was accompanied by great light with 10 huge candelabra illuminating the temple precincts of the Jewish temple. Water (female) and light (male) thus had special significance on this, *the 8th day* of the festival, pointing to the Savior as the *light* and the *life* of the world. He is the Tree of Life, with roots extending down into the *watery* underworld and branches reaching up into the *starry* heavens. We are reborn through Him on this 8th day, through cleansing water and the light or fire of the Holy Spirit. In 2 Nephi 31:17 we read, "For the gate by which ye should enter is repentance and baptism by *water*; and then cometh a remission of your sins by *fire* and by the Holy Ghost." Priests used gold pitchers (color of the sun) to bring water from the pool of Siloam to the temple, pouring it out at the base of the altar (along with red wine; both as drink offerings). This also signified Israel's thankfulness for the rain that watered the harvest. More importantly, this special ceremony symbolized the outpouring of the Holy Spirit (John 7:39), and the living water that God freely offered his people anciently; something he will do again freely in person in the Millennium (in the Age of Aquarius—the Water Bearer). Light (knowledge) and blessings will also be poured out upon the church (of the Firstborn), as it was in the age of Pisces, upon the fish (the church in the meridian of time). For more on the light and water connection, see chapter 6 of The Day Star: Reading Sacred Architecture, by the author. For more on other ancient Hebrew Holy Days symbolism see chapter 7.

[191] See Numbers 1:52-2:31.

[192] The fiery pillar resting atop the Tabernacle is thought to be circular. The Holy of the Holies of the Salt Lake Temple is circular with a dome above featuring eight-pointed stars. For more on the concentric zones of the ancient Tabernacle, see Ezekiel 44:23; 1 Chronicles 23:13; 2 Corinthians 6:16-17. See also Lawrence H. Schiffman, "Architecture and Law: The Temple and Its Courtyards in the Temple Scroll," Ed. Jacob Neusner, Ernest S. Frerichs, and Nahum M. Sarna, From Ancient Israel to Modern Judaism, Scholars Press, vol. 1, p. 269, and Matthew B. Brown, The Gate of Heaven, Covenant Communications, p. 62.

[193] As the High Priest progressed westward towards the Holy of Holies inside the ancient Jerusalem temple, he appears to have passed by eight items symbolizing the Savior. These items are, from east to west, the Altar of Sacrifice (lamb), the Laver of Water (living water), the Golden Vine above the door (the True Vine), The temple's east doorway (the Door), The Table of Shewbread (the Bread of Life), the Menorah (the Light of the World), the Altar of Incense (the Mediator), and the Stone of Foundation (the Stone of Israel or the Foundation Stone), replacing the Ark after Solomon. Each of these are titles for the Savior. The number eight symbolizes being reborn – through Christ. See Matthew B. Brown, The Gate of Heaven, Covenant Communications, p. 169.

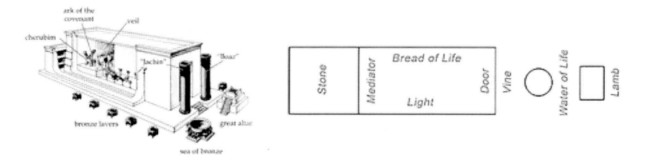

[194] See Appendix B, Christ-Centered Temple Patterns in the Great Pyramid, The Day Star: Reading Sacred Architecture, book 1, by the author.

[195] See chapter six of The Day Star: Reading Sacred Architecture by the author, for a listing of twelve examples in scripture of each direction of movement.

The Way of Life	*The Way of Death*
1. The Law of Obedience (Moses 5:106)	1. Defiance (Moses 5:13-14)
2. The Law of Sacrifice (Moses 5:4-8, 20)	2. Perversion of Sacrifice (Moses 5:18-19, 21)
3. The Law of the Gospel (Moses 5:58-59; 8:19)	3. Works of Darkness (Moses 5:29-31; 47-57; 8:26)
4. The Law of Chastity (Moses 6:5-23; 8:13)	4. Licentiousness (Moses 6:15; 8:14-21)
5. The Law of Consecration (Moses 7:18)	5. Violence and Corruption (Moses 5:31-33; 50; 6:15; 8:28)

[196] The Book of Moses is a temple text. It, along with the Book of Abraham and revelation, were instrumental in helping Joseph Smith restore the temple ordinances. The Book of Moses illustrates well the doctrine of the 2 ways (above); 2 chiastic choices balanced between choosing God at center, resulting in light and life eternal (through His 5 primary covenants), or choosing Satan, resulting in darkness and death. Solomon's Temple featured this chiastic pattern, with 2 sets of 5 pillars balanced on either side of *the way* leading to the Holy of Holies - God. (The chart above is from Jeffrey M. Bradshaw, In God's Image and Likeness, Eborn Books, pps. 338-353.)

[197] Ezra Taft Benson, Teachings 1988, 28 September 1982, p. 121.

[198] See endnote 108 of chapter 3 of The Day Star: Reading Sacred Architecture, by the author for a complete discussion of the cross and tau mark, as well as official statements by Pres. Hinckley regarding our non-usage of the cross.

[199] At Herod's Temple in Jerusalem the temple gates at the border of Temple Mount bordered the camp of Israel. From this space to the Gate of Nicanor represented the camp of Levi. The remainder of the sanctuary itself was considered the camp of God. The sanctity of each of these separate precincts was strictly protected by temple guards, and was marked, walled, signposted, etc. The most sacred area, the Holy of Holies, was accessed only 1 time per year, on the Day of Atonement (on the 10th of Tishri / Nissan, in the 7th or Sabbath month), and only by the High Priest who wore white linen garments (representative of the Savior) on this very special day. All other days he wore blue, the color of priesthood. See Exodus 39:22 and chapter 9.

[200] The towers at the Ogden and Provo Temples were originally yellow in color (like fire—they are now white). The pillar may have centrally rested above a white cloud – the round shape of the temple, reminding us of the fiery pillar rising through the cloud above the ancient Tabernacle. These towers are positioned directly over the centralized celestial room. Feeding into this sacred interior space are surrounding endowment rooms, circling around the outer edge of the building. Before installation of the Moroni statues and the change of the tower's color from yellow or gold to white, some saw the tower instead, as a fountain of living water, reinforced with the woman at the well mural, seen just inside the front entrance of the Provo Temple. This may be a central theme at the Provo Utah Temple. Other motifs at the Provo and Ogden Utah Temples also suggest living waters, such as designs on the exterior pre-fabricated concrete panels surrounding both temples. No implied meaning was given to the author in an interview with their Church architect Emil B. Fetzer.

[201] In scripture the number 1 symbolizes *unity* (that of the Godhead, Zion, man and woman, etc.). This is true of Article of Faith number 1; an expression of the 3 unified Gods making up the Biblical Trinity. Day or period 1 of creation in the books of Genesis, Moses, and Abraham feature the creation of light, and its separation from darkness. The number 1 is a generative number and concept, the center place of origin. At-one-ment is thus associated with the number 1. It is also an independent, indivisible number implying a central or primary focus. The shape of the circle, sphere or point symbolize the number 1 in sacred architecture as seen in overhead domes and below ground level baptismal fonts, as well as spiral staircases. Bread (a symbol for God) was seen in round form in the 12 round loaves on the Table of Shewbread and in the round wafer-like white food called manna in the Old Testament. Those performing temple service anciently wore round hats, similar to crowns. A number of important priesthood ordinances are also connected to the circle, including prayer circles or gathering around a sick person in a priesthood blessing. We are told in scripture that "the course of the Lord is one eternal round" (1 Nephi 10: 19, Alma 7:20). Other scriptures involving the number 1 and the concept of unity include; "And other sheep I have, which are not of this fold: them also I must bring, and they shall hear my voice; and there shall be one fold, and one shepherd" (John 10:16. See also 3 Nephi 15:17.) God has told us, "If ye are not one, ye are not mine" (D&C 42:1). Preaching near the Waters of Mormon Alma taught his people "that there should be no contention one with another, but that they should look forward with one eye, having one faith and one baptism, having their hearts knit together in unity and in love one towards another" (Mosiah 18:21).

[202] Sacred circles occur in scripture (and at the temple) frequently. We see this in the shape of manna from heaven (round white wafers), lavers for washing, and a number of ancient and modern priesthood ordinances, including circumcision (anciently), baptism (in circular fonts), temple cornerstone dedications, movement through temple ordinances (and up and around through ordinance rooms of some temples, such as Salt Lake and Cardston), group priesthood blessings, and prayer circles. Various forms in the temple are circular, including spiral staircases, domed ceilings over square rooms, chandeliers, tables, and other furnishings, and men's hats.

During Joseph Smith's prayer at the dedication of the Kirtland Temple he asked the Lord that the Saints might "mingle their voices with those bright, shining seraphs *around* thy throne with acclamations of praise, singing Hosanna to God and the Lamb" (D&C 109:79, italics added). On June 1, 1978, a great prayer circle surrounded the altar of an upper room in the Salt Lake Temple, where President Spencer W. Kimball at center along with all members of the Council of Twelve Apostles petitioned the Lord. According to Elder David B. Haight, the leadership of the Church had convened to pray about all worthy males receiving and holding the priesthood. It was during this important prayer, conducted in a great circle around the Prophet of the Church, that the revelation came, now Declaration 2 of the Doctrine and Covenants. "President Kimball arose from the altar. We surrounded it according to seniority, I being number twelve. He turned to his right, and I was the first member of the circle he encountered. He put his arms around me, and as I embraced him I felt the beating of his heart and the intense emotion that filled him. He then continued around the circle, embracing each of the brethren. No one spoke. Overcome with emotion, we simply shook hands and quietly went to our dressing rooms" (Elder David B. Haight of the Council of the Twelve Apostles, quoted in Paul B. Skousen, Brother Paul's Mormon Bathroom Reader, Cedar Fort, pp. 74).

Hugh Nibley has documented the Savior surrounded by his Apostles in a number of ancient sources. In the Gospel of Bartholomew, for example, "the Lord takes the Twelve up into the mountain and standing in their midst gives them certain signs and tokens and then departs." In 2 Jeu, a very instructive early Christian text, the Apostles and their wives form a circle around Jesus "so that he can teach them the ordinances of the treasury of light, they being conducted by him through all the ordinances and thereby learning to progress in the hereafter." Then, "all the Apostles, clothed in their garments...placing foot to foot, made a circle facing the four directions of the cosmos" and Jesus standing at the altar proceeded to instruct them in all the signs and ordinances in which the Sons of Light must be perfect" (2 Jeu, 54, [40] and 66-67 [53g] in Schmidt, Gnostische Schriften in Koptischer Sprache, 99; tr., 193. Cited in Hugh Nibley, Mormonism and Early Christianity, FARMS—Deseret Book, p. 64). (See also Hugh Nibley, The Ancient Prayer Circle, Mormonism and Early Christianity, FARMS—Deseret Book.)

[203] In scripture the Savior is often found standing "in the midst" of sacred space, like a sacred altar, or Tree. We read of Christ standing in the middle of the Twelve in sacred prayer, or see Him at the center of innocent children in chapter 17 of 3rd Nephi; the children sitting "upon the ground round about him." When the angels "came down," they "encircled those little ones about." In their appointed place next to the children, the angels "were encircled about with fire." At the outer edge of this sacred circle were their parents and other adults. Finally, beyond them was profane space, fading into the horizon. The Savior positioned the children immediately around him—their proximity closer than the circling angels and the accompanying fire. (See Hugh Nibley, The Ancient Christian Prayer Circle, in, Mormonism and Early Christianity, FARMS / Deseret Book, pps. 45—99. For more on the many Christ-centered connections to the number 13, see chapter 10 of The Day Star: Reading Sacred Architecture, by the author.)

[204] See Laurence Gardner, Lost Secrets of the Sacred Ark, Element, p. 10.

[205] There are 594 chapters on either side of Psalms 118:8 in the Bible. It states; "It is better to trust the LORD than to put confidence in man." The sum of 594 and 594 is 1188. Trusting God is at the chiastic center of scripture.

[206] Many stone circles are geographically close to mound-tombs, yet it is believed the circles were created for the ritual purposes of the living. Research shows that the great stone pillars at Stonehenge, for example, mark important cyclical rhythms in the heavens, like equinoxes and solstices. Yearly festivals and ritual gatherings, possibly celebrating the New Year, renewal, and creation (made possible by careful observation of the sun, the moon, and the stars), may have been practiced here, much like those of other temples worldwide. Ancient cult centers around the world have used standing stones to view the heavens, mark time, and establish calendars. A particularly striking example of 12 stones in the natural environment is Callanish Stone Circle in Scotland (2200 BC), which features 12 tall stones surrounding a taller (15 feet high) and lighter central stone. Single freestanding stones may have been used as markers or memorials of important events and are often called massebas, stela, or menhirs. Uncovered stones, once part of an ancient tomb, are called dolemans. Architectural variations of these ancient single, upright stones may include lingum, obelisks, minarets, towers, and steeples. Stone circles are sometimes called cromlechs. See Molyneaux and Vitebsky, Sacred Earth: Sacred Stones, p. 134.

[207] The Great Pyramid in Egypt is a classic example of documented measure of space pointing to the measure of time in connection with creation itself, a testimony of God. See book 1, Appendix B: Christ-Centered Temple Patterns in the Great Pyramid.

[208] Hugh Nibley and Michael Rhodes, One Eternal Round, FARMS / Deseret Book, pps. 121-25.

209 According to Denver Snuffer, "Equinoxes arrive on the set time appointed by the universe, always at some inconvenience. The inconvenience may be trivial or it may be significant, but it arrives when it arrives at the price to the individual of inconvenience. That allows us to keep the appointed time at the price of sacrifice. Without sacrifice we do not keep the law of heaven. If the equinox is to hold significance and to be kept with ritual observance, then it ought to be done in the appointed way at the appointed time; otherwise there is no sacrifice and no connection with heaven. We get just as sloppy in our own lives…with the organized rituals and then wonder why the powers of heaven withdraw themselves. Now, the important equinox is not the Vernal, but the Autumnal, based upon where we are in history. The Vernal is associated with creation, birth, opening, newness, restoration and holding forth. We are past that now. The Autumnal is associated with closing down, finishing, judgment, and endings. We are there. History has had its play, the work has been offered again, it has been rejected, and now it remains to finish this final scene and get the players off the stage before a new era is to open thereafter." (Denver Snuffer, personal correspondence with the author, 9 March 2010.)

210 Many ancient cultures believed that opening a portal from the underworld to this world, and from this world to the next, occurred at specific important points in time, based on 2 heavenly markers—the equinoxes. We see this in two modern examples in the Restoration. On the fall equinox (September 22-23 of 1823) the portal opened for the angel Moroni to instruct Joseph Smith, doing so five times during a single 24 hour period. He did so over the next four consecutive years (five years total in his heavenly instruction) on this same exact date. (The revelation on the oath and covenant of the priesthood was also given on this date [and September 23rd] of 1832. See D&C 84.) Moroni's instruction was of an ominous fall or harvest season nature, in preparation for the Lord's second coming in *judgment*—upon the wicked when the souls of men are finally harvested (quoting Malichi's prophecies). Whereas Joseph Smith's First Vision appears to have occurred at or near the spring equinox, the time of the Restoration—the time of spring rebirth and hope. This same pattern is evident in the births of John the Baptist in the *fall* (repent and prepare for the first advent of the Lord), versus that of the birth of the Savior and Redeemer of the world in the *spring*. (The west and east towers on the Salt Lake Temple have moon phases marking the October and April birth months of both important figures. They are 6 months apart, dividing the year in half.) Passover and Tabernacles possess similar connections.

On a first visit to the Hopi, Hugh Nibley noted, "These were the only people in the world that still took the trouble to do what the human race had been doing for many millennia—celebrating the great life-cycle of the year, the creation, the dispensations." In comparing the Hopi to the Greeks he stated, "The dancing place was the bare plot which the Greeks called the konistra, the sand path where this world came in contact with the other, at the crucial periods of the year. That was the time when the orcus mundi was open—mundus patet; that is, when the mouth of the other world was open and the spirits of the ancestors attended the rites. By the altar, of course, was the sipapuni, the mouth of the lower world, the orcus mundi, at which the spirits from above and below could meet with their relatives upon the earth. This was the essential year-rite, found throughout the world from the earliest times." (Hugh Nibley, The Roman Games as a Survival of an Archaic Year-Cult, Univ. of California, 1938, in Huchel Canalis Mundorum, p. 309.)

211 Angell had previously assisted Jacob Bump in the interior carpentry of the Kirtland Temple, and William Weeks with various parts of Nauvoo Temple. His work on the Salt Lake Temple, under the leadership of President Brigham Young (who, like Joseph Smith, saw the temple in vision) proved a masterful continuation and expansion of the space-time relationship Joseph first placed on the Nauvoo Temple.

212 This is the year the buttresses where raised high enough for placement of the moon phases. See Richard G. Oman, Exterior Symbolism of the Salt Lake Temple: Reflecting the Faith That Called the Place into Being, BYU Studies, vol. 36, no. 4, (1996-97), p. 46-8. See also John P. Pratt, Passover: Was it Symbolic of His Coming?, *Ensign*, 24 (January 1994), pp. 38-45.

213 For a complete discussion of the ancient Hebrew holy days see chapter 7 of The Day Star: Reading Sacred Architecture by the author.

214 John M. Lundquist, The Temple: Meeting Place of Heaven and Earth, Thames and Hudson, p. 14.

215 Ibid., pp. 83-84. See Leviticus 4:6, 17.

216 See Donna Nielsen, Beloved Bridegroom: Finding Christ in Ancient Jewish Marriage and Family Customs, Onyx Press, p. 56.

217 At present, there are 5 circles of movement in connection with temples (typically within a square). These include; 1. Cornerstone dedication ceremonies (some temples are square, others rectangular); 2. Some of the earliest temple ordinances proceed today (in some temples) through a circle in parts, within a square room; 3. Ascension in temples at Cardston and Salt Lake proceed upwards in one complete circle; 4. Spiral staircases; 5. Temple prayer circles. Ancient prayer circles were described as a "dance." Concourses of angels are also described around god and are moving, "wheels within wheels." Singing, dancing, and prayer may yet again be combined in future prayer circles. Baptism is normally done in a circular font. These are part of 5 separate ordinances (excluding spiral staircases). Some of these may be modern creations, not part of the original temple form.

[218] The word symbolic is italicized, as the *foundation* stones (below ground level) are actually the first stones laid on most buildings. The *cornerstones* (above ground level) are symbolic of them (laid later), and are bathed in light of day. According to Ovason, "The Masonic ritual of the cornerstone was linked with the union of the polarities of light-darkness, of Heaven-Earth". It may have also been associated with the male and female, as the below ground *foundation* stone (in darkness) has connection to the crypt and to "the feminine side", according to Ovason, whereas the above ground *cornerstone* has connection to the sun and man. It should be noted that George Washington laid both of these stones for the U.S. Capital, laying the underground *foundation* stone in the northeast corner (September 18, 1793), and the above ground *cornerstone* at the southeast corner (unknown date) the direction of most light. (See David Ovason, The Secret Architecture of our Nation's Capital, Perennial Books, pps. 77-88.)

[219] The day before twelve Latter-day Saint men symbolically carried a single log to build the first LDS house in Independence, Missouri in preparation for establishing this area as the center place of Zion. This was 12 miles west of Independence. "The log was carried and placed by 12 men, in honor of the 12 tribes of Israel." Sydney Rigdon then dedicated the land for the gathering of the Saints. The next day President Rigdon dedicated the ground for the City of Zion, after which Joseph Smith laid the cornerstone for the temple site at the northeast corner. See Porter, Colesville Branch, pp. 281-311. See also Whitmer, Book of John Whitmer, pp. 86-87.

[220] The Prophet Joseph Smith said: "If the strict order of the priesthood were carried out in the building of Temples, the first stone would be laid at the south-east corner, by the First Presidency of the Church. The south-west corner should be laid next. The third, or north-west corner next; and the fourth, or north-east corner last. The First Presidency should lay the south-east corner stone and dictate who are the proper persons to lay the other corner stones. If a Temple is built at a distance, and the First Presidency are not present, then the Quorum of the Twelve Apostles are the persons to dictate the order for the Temple; and in the absence of the Twelve Apostles, then the Presidency of the stake will lay the south-east corner stone; the Melchizedek priesthood laying the corner stones on the east side of the temple, and the Lesser priesthood those on the west side."

Masons normally dedicate the four cornerstones (above ground) of buildings starting at the northeast corner; the symbolic place where light meets darkness in both the vertical dimension (emerging from the dark ground into the bright sky) and in the horizontal dimension (sunrise on the east versus total shade at the north). Their ceremonies typically also involve the depositing (an offering) of corn (or wheat), wine and oil upon the stone itself. According to Ovason, corn has connection to resurrection and rebirth in antiquity (Egypt). Such a deposit was made during the cornerstone ceremony of the Capital building in Washington D.C. by George Washington and others, after which, "The entire congregation then joined in prayer, followed by Masons chanting honors, and a volley from the artillery". (See David Ovason, The Secret Architecture of our Nation's Capital, Perennial Books, p. 173.)

[221] It was eight years after the Kirtland Temple cornerstones were laid (July 23, 1833) that those at Nauvoo were laid. So few priesthood holders were available in Kirtland on July 23rd of that year that 2 teenagers were hastily ordained to the office of an Elder so that the ceremony could proceed. These 2 young people were; Joseph C. Kingsbury and Don Carlos Smith. Brigham Young said of this occasion, "they had to pick up boys of fifteen or sixteen years of age, and ordain them Elders, to get officers enough to lay the corner stones" (Journal of Discourses, 1:33). Shortages of manpower, tools, materials, and finances were typical in Kirtland at this time. There were only 150 total members of the Church in Kirtland when construction on the temple began. In the Journal of Discourses Brigham Young explained that the southeast cornerstone of the Kirtland Temple was the first part of the foundation of this important temple to be dedicated because this direction receives the most light. Noon was the time chosen to dedicate this foundation area of the temple, again because this is the time of day when the most light is present. The place and time of the dedication both symbolize that the temple is *the* place of light and truth. The southeast cornerstone was laid and dedicated by the first presidency, with other leaders laying the remaining cornerstones in a clockwise rotation. All modern LDS temples continue to be dedicated in this basic pattern.

[222] Gordon B. Hinckley, Conference Report, October 1984, p. 67.

[223] Hugh Nibley, What is a Temple, What is a Temple, BYU Religious Studies Center, pps. 19-23.

[224] Ibid. Procreation was God's first commandment to Adam and Eve.

[225] Brigham Young, Journal of Discourses, 2:29, 33. See Luke 9:58.

[226] Times and Seasons 2 (15 April 1841), Celebration of the Anniversary of the Church, Laying the Corner Stones of the Temple, p. 376.

[227] Archeologists found two stones when excavating the ruins of the original Nauvoo Temple. They are thought to have been used for washing and anointing ceremonies. For more on the green "Stone of Truth," upon which Egyptian coronation ceremonies began (with washing and anointing), see the color green in the chapter 9 of The Day Star: Reading Sacred Architecture.

[228] See Local and Other Matters: The Manti Utah Temple, Deseret News, 1 May, 1877, p. 2.

[229] At the dedication of the Salt Lake Temple cornerstones Brigham Young stated, "So we commence by laying the stone on the southeast corner, because there is the most light." Brigham Young, Millennial Star 15 (1853), p. 488. At St. George, "Precisely at 12 President Young...broke ground at the south-east corner, and, kneeling on that particular spot, he offered the dedicatory prayer." Deseret News, May 2, 1877.

[230] Gordon B. Hinckley, This Great Millennial Year, Ensign, November 2000, p. 67. President Hinckley quotes Ephesians 2:21. The southeast cornerstone of an LDS temple may possess seven potential connections to the Savior. These include:

a. The Foundation of the Church   The chief cornerstone (above ground and in the light) points directly to the Savior, the very foundation of the Church. The apostle Paul told the Ephesians that the Church was built "upon the foundation of the apostles and prophets, Jesus Christ himself being the chief corner stone" (Ephesians 2:20). He is the stone, "which the builders rejected, the same is become the head of the corner" (Luke 20:17).

b. Alpha and Omega   The southeast foundation cornerstone was symbolically the first visual, or above ground stone laid during construction of the Nauvoo and Salt Lake Temples, the last being the capstone. In reality the footing stones at Salt Lake were laid first, 16 feet below ground level. The symbolically important southeast cornerstone and the capstone (the globe underneath the Angel Moroni) are both sacred relic chambers holding items of historical importance. Christ is the First and the Last. He said, "I AM ALPHA AND OMEGA" (Isaiah 44:6; D&C 35:1; 38:1; 39:1).

c. The Light of the World   The southeast foundation cornerstone is the first dedicated because it receives the most light, the premiere symbol for the Savior Jesus Christ who said, "I am the light of the world" (John 8:12). Building construction emerges from the darkness of the foundations below the earth into the glorious light of the heavens above them. The southeast corner of all buildings in the northern hemisphere receives the most sunlight.

d. He Descended below all things and Ascended above all things   The foundation cornerstones are at ground level, whereas the capstone is up high atop the east central tower. Christ descended below all things (death) and ascended above all things (resurrection). "He that ascended up on high, as also he descended below all things. . ." (D&C 88:6).

e. Strong as Stone   Stone is a primary, quality construction material of the temple and of ancient altars because it is durable, strong, and natural (cut out of the mountain without hands, see Dan. 2:45). Christ is the Rock, a tried stone, the stone or rock of Israel. He is sure, solid, consistent, and true (Deut: 32:4, 15; 2 Sam. 23:3; Genesis 49:24, Isa; 28:16; 1 Peter 2:6-8; D&C 50:4).

f. He is the Center   The dedication of temple cornerstones proceeds in clockwise fashion starting at the southeast corner. This circumambulation mirrors the movement of the earth around the sun and draws attention (as all circles do) to the center. The center of our faith is Jesus Christ. All things point to him. "Behold, all things have their likeness, and all things are created and made to bear record of me" (Moses 6:63).

g. The Savior's Birth date   The date of the laying of the stones also points to the Savior. The southeast cornerstone of both the Nauvoo and Salt Lake Temples was laid on April 6th, the organization date of the Church, and more importantly, the revealed birthday of the Savior Jesus Christ (D&C 20:1). President Brigham Young and 3 members of the Twelve laid the southeast cornerstone in an important priesthood ceremony. His counselors were Heber C. Kimball and Willard Richards. This was the 23rd anniversary of the Church. Truman O. Angell, architect, helped in laying the southwest cornerstone. On April 6th, 1892 (39 years later) relics were placed in the capstone of the Salt Lake Temple commemorating the laying of the last stone of the temple, also on the Lord's birthday.

[231] The DNA molecule is the foundation of *life* (genetic information). It features 2 spiraling helics (like a spiraling staircase), which makes 1 complete clockwise turn every 10 rungs (10 is the number of completion or perfection). There are 4 types of 'rungs' each a nucleotide spanning between the two spiraling helics. When looking down in axial view upon the geometry of this double spiral 3 major double *pentagons* appear, each intersecting with the other 2. The spiral and the pentagons are loaded with divine or *phi* proportion inherent throughout all nature (including proportions of the human body) and copied into sacred architecture (see the Appendix). The turning rungs of the DNA molecule are reminiscent of the ascending and descending angels on Jacob's ladder and temple spiral staircases generally. Eternal life is promised and granted in LDS temples. (See Stephen Skinner, Sacred Geometry, Sterling Publishing, pps. 72-73.)

[232] The human DNA protein molecule is shaped like a spiraling staircase, complete with steps in its complementary nucleotides, forming a kind of letter-like code of amino acids using 4 letters; A, C, G, and T. It is a natural "Jacob's Ladder". (In many illustrations of DNA, each step is divided into two chemical parts, left and right (for ascending—descending?). According to Rabbi Jonathan Sacks (Chief Rabbi of Great Britain), "The human genome does seem to me to be one of the rare scientific discoveries that is poetical and even mystical. The Kabbalists actually maintained that everything that exists is the result of *tzerfim*—various permutations of the letters of an alphabet. It now turns out that this is not a metaphor at all. It is actually, literally true...the DNA string of those characters is all a series of letters—A, C, G and T—which, as it were, extend to perform this huge language that is the DNA. All life is exactly as the Bible said, a matter of language, of instructions, of letters, and words. We suddenly realize the deep resonance of the biblical idea: "and God spoke and there was". Professor Jonathan Sacks, Forum, 6 February 2001, quoted in Kleiman, DNA and Tradition, p. 172. For more on the highly symbolic letters of Hebrew alphabet, see Joe Sampson, Written by the Finger of God, Wellspring Press.

[233] Hugh Nibley, Message of the Joseph Smith Papyri, FARMS—Deseret Book, p. 324.

[234] See Plato's Republic, The Myth of Er.

[235] Spiraling motion is also connected the principle of purification. Water is purified naturally, for example, by movement in streambeds, but especially so by natural and man-made purification systems which often use spiraling movement as part of the cleansing process. Sensitive patrons will notice that circles are used in many purifying steps in the temple; in the shape of the baptismal font, movement in early initiatory ordinances, advancement through some ordinance rooms as part of the endowment (at Salt Lake, Cardston, etc.), as well as the most sacred prayer. Purification was symbolized in ancient Israel by the blood of sacrificed animals being sprinkled around the altar in a clockwise fashion, starting with northeast corner (Leviticus 1:11; 4:6, 17). The ancient laver of water used to purify priests was also circular.

[236] Morton Smith, The Case of the Gilded Staircase, Biblical Archaeology Review, September / October 1984, pp. 50-55.

[237] The 112 lunations at the outer edge of the Chartres Cathedral labyrinth may correspond to those of the moon itself; 28 lunations per month (x 4) = 112. The left exterior tower of Chartres features a moon weathervane at top, the right tower a sun–based weathervane. The cathedral is 365.25 feet long (solar year symbolism.) Sun and moon symbolism is extensive there, as on the Nauvoo Temple. (See Stephen Skinner, Sacred Geometry, Sterling Publishing, p. 135.)

[238] Designs for the St. George and Salt Lake Temples originally featured both types of movement. The remodel (for the live endowment) negated this early design. See chapter 6 of The Day Star: Reading Sacred Architecture, by the author.

[239] Keith Stepan Oral History Interview #3 with the author, May 2007, Typescript, p. 1.

[240] According to Huchel, "The ancient sacred dance, whether known as the circle-dance, the ring-dance, or the prayer circle, is well-attested in the early Christian sources. It is found not only in the New Testament, but the Old, and in other cultures, such as ancient Egypt. Dancing had its origin in the temple, and the circle-dance is a simulation of the dance of the angels in heaven, more specifically the orders of the angels which guard the heavenly spheres, as they move in their concentric circles, wheels within wheels." (See Frederick M. Huchel, The Cosmic Ring Dance of the Angels, Frithurex Atheneum Press. p. 149.)

[241] According to Sampson, a distilled version (traditional rabbinical definition combined with ancient Kabbalah) of the Hebrew 6th letter Vav of their 22-letter alphabet may have ties to the "peg or nail that is said to be Polaris and hold the whole universe in place. It is the nail that fixes the stars by forces that cannot be broken or removed. It is the covenants and promises of God to the obedient that cannot be broken by earthly or Satanic forces." Joe Sampson, Written by the Finger of God, Wellspring Publishing, pp. 186-88.

[242] The number two also has symbolic connection to *polar opposition* (rather than complimentary opposition) via things like light and darkness exhibited in the mark of the beast as a *seal* in the forehead or hand versus the *seal* of the Holy Spirit of Promise (see the Book of Revelation). The number two also has reference to *the law of witnesses* (two priesthood holders witnessing a baptism, two at the Sacrament Table, two serving side by side on missions, two pillars at the entryway to Solomon's Temple, etc.)

[243] The vesica pisces is also connected to fertility, creation, the vulva, and the female principle, and hence to Venus and the number 5 (the number associated with life through Christ's grace).

[244] See endnote 21.

[245] The sign or constellation symbolizing Christ (Pisces) is established visually by the sun rising in (in front of or against) the constellation of Pisces behind it, seen at early dawn (when the stars are still visible), and specifically at the spring equinox. Most *signs* last about 2200 years on average, as part of the 25,500 year cycle of the precession of the equinox (the time it takes all 12 signs to complete one revolution, positioned in front of the rising sun at the spring equinox). We are at the tail end of Pisces, transitioning soon to Aquarius, the water-bearer (a good symbol for the return of Christ the King in the Millennium – associated with the symbolism of the Feast of Tabernacles in ancient Israel; a feast featuring the "return of the king" and the pouring of water ceremony upon the altar [Aquarius]). Historically the move from one sign to another every 2000 years or so has marked two important things; 1. The new form of animal sacrifice God directs to be used (from the *bull* [Egypt – Hathor and Adam] - 4500 B.C., to Abraham - *ram* and lamb – 2000 B.C., to Christ – fish, 1 B.C. (He called fishers of men, did miracles utilizing loaves and fishes, ate broiled fish after the resurrection, etc.), and 2. Great world catyclism (the year 2012+?). See Giorgio de Santillana and Hertha von Dechend, Hamlet's Mill, David R. Godine Publisher In. The author is grateful for additional insights supplied by Frederick Huchel.

[246] Positioned at the sacred threshold to the Holy Place of Solomon's Temple, Jachin and Boaz may have represented a barrier that only a sanctified and properly dressed high priest could pass, entering thereafter into the divine presence one day per year—the Day of Atonement (Leviticus 16:30). According to Lundquist, these pillars symbolized "the legitimizing role of the temple and the dynasty of David in the minds of the people." The right (south) pillar was named Jachin, meaning "He will establish the throne of David, and His kingdom to His seed forever," carrying the message that Yahweh had established both the dynasty and the temple. The left (north) pillar was named Boaz, meaning "In the strength of Yahweh shall the king rejoice," suggesting that the power emanating from the sanctuary is that of Yahweh. (See John M. Lundquist, "The Legitimizing Role of the Temple," Temples of the Ancient World, FARMS, Deseret Book, pps. 137; 218. See also 1 Kings 7:15-22; 2 Chronicles 3:15-17.)

In addition, the symmetry of the two pillars appear to have represented strong governance via the rule of *king* and *priest*. The Boaz pillar appears to have represented judgment (*mishpat*) centered in *kingly* rule in connection with the tribe of *Judah* (Boaz was the great-grandfather of David, King of Israel). Jachin (the first high priest of the temple) is the right pillar (when facing east) and appears to have symbolized *priestly* power or righteousness (*tsedeq*) in connection with the tribe of *Ephraim*. Historically the tribe of Joseph (Ephraim) held the birthright to the priesthood, whereas Judah held the scepter of kingly rule. "Ephraim also is the strength of mine head; Judah is my lawgiver" (Psalm 60:7). After Christ's ministry and the destruction of the temple, the scepter of rule passed to Ephraim (the Gentiles). In the very last days this rule will return eastward, joined with Ephraim—the first becoming the last, once again ruling and reigning as part of the established union of the Kingdom of God on the earth (see 1 Nephi 13:42 and D&C 90:9). These two strong lineages (pillars) remain the primary channels of salvation for the world and may be further tied to our two great pillars of wisdom—the sticks of Joseph and Judah (the Book of Mormon and Bible). Together they mark *the way* of salvation (Ezekiel 37:15). From a political perspective the two named pillars may have symbolized that Israelite kings were established by Jehovah Himself, and that they reigned by His kingly power and priestly authority through the priesthood. While the priest administers *covenants* in his priesthood *robes*, the king administers the *law* and wears a *crown*. Therefore, the pillars may have reminded viewers that in the Millennium these two heavenly and worldly governments will come together. Latter-day Saint Melchizedek priesthood holders who receive and honor all the covenants of the temple are promised to one day reign as *kings* and *priests* with their wives (queens and priestesses). This is part of the Patriarchal Priesthood.

The 18 cubit high pillars (12 cubits around) were freestanding with no lintel joining them, potentially suggestive of the ancient rift between Judah and Ephraim (Israel). This rift may have been healed in the marriage of Christ. A strong case for the reconciliation of Judah and Ephraim may be *in* the marriage of Christ (Judah bloodline – patriarchal) to Mary Magdalene (Ephraim bloodline – matriarchal). This case is made by Dr. Vern Swanson (among others) in his book *Dynasty of the Holy Grail: Mormonism's Sacred Bloodline*, Cedar Fort Publishing. He provides evidence for the Savior's marriage to 3 potential wives: Mary Magdalene and Mary and Martha, the Bethany Sisters (all of the Tribe of Ephraim). Numerous early Church leaders claim Christ was married, including Brigham Young, Heber C. Kimball, Orson Pratt, Orson Hyde, Lorenzo Snow, Jedediah M. Grant, and Joseph F. Smith. According to Swanson, the sacred bloodline of Christ (with the patriarchal priesthood's right to rule and reign on earth) was carefully hidden for centuries, primarily for protection, then finally surfacing in the blood of the Prophet Joseph Smith and many other Church leaders who may be literal descendants of Christ through a sacred blood lineage descending through families in Britain (to where so many of the early Church leaders trace their ancestry). This nation utilizes 2 coat of arms symbols connected to Judah and Ephraim—the *unicorn* (wild ox or bull, symbol of the tribe of Ephraim – priestly rule) along with the *lion* (symbol of the tribe of Judah – kingly reign). With this sacred blood in his veins, Joseph Smith would have the birthright to rule in Israel through both the *Patriarchal* priesthood and the Melchizedek priesthood via *ordination* to the same (with *keys* through John the Baptist; Peter, James, and John; and Moses (gathering), Elias (patriarchal priesthood), and Elijah (Melchizedek priesthood – sealing power). The Savior may have been married to more than one wife for the following reasons: 1. To insure the sacred or royal *patriarchal bloodline* of Church leadership down and to Joseph Smith. Prior to Abraham receiving the Melchizedek priesthood, priesthood was given through 'the fathers' and was patriarchal (Abraham 1:3). Bishops who are literal blood descendants of Aaron have right to this office today (D&C 107:76). Patriarchs *to the Church* were all blood relatives through Joseph Smith's father and Hyrum Smith until this official position was done away with; 2. To *fulfill the law* of the new and everlasting covenant of marriage and set an example for living it, as given to many prophets, leaders, and others in the Church (Christ set the example in being baptized, though he was sinless "to fulfill all righteousness"). Other reasons for the plurality of wives may include: 3. It was a test for some early Church leaders, like Heber C. Kimball and his wife Vilate, who were both tested with this law (D&C 132) before receiving the fullness of the priesthood (see the Life of Heber C. Kimball, p. 323); & 4. The highest degree of the Celestial kingdom appears to be made up of more women than men due to their greater capacity for spirituality. Mercy would dictate that those worthy of this kingdom and the right to bear and raise children into the eternities would need to fulfill this law. In Isaiah 4:1, "seven women take hold of one man" in marriage "to take away our reproach" due to the lack of men after the many wars on earth.

Parley P. Pratt, in addressing Christ and the birthright lineage of the modern *Apostles,* who apparently also have this blood, stated, "In the lineage of Abraham, Isaac, and Jacob, according to *the flesh,* was held the right of heirship to the keys of priesthood for the blessings and for the salvation of all nations. From this lineage sprang the Prophets, John the Baptist, Jesus, and the Apostles; and from this lineage sprang the great Prophet and restorer in modern times Joseph Smith, and the Apostles who hold the keys under his hand...it has been through the ministry of that lineage, and the keys of [that] priesthood held by the lawful heirs according to the flesh...But no man can hold the keys of priesthood or the Apostleship...unless he is a literal descendant of Abraham, Isaac, and Jacob. Jesus Christ and his ancient Apostles of both hemispheres were of that lineage... The world has from that day to this been manufacturing priests, without any particular regard to lineage." (See Parley P. Pratt, Journal of Discourses 1:261, 10 April 1853. See also Vern Grosvenor Swanson, Dynasty

[247] *Temple Guards*   Two symmetrical pillars at important thresholds, like those of Solomon's Temple and later Christian structures, including LDS temples today, may also serve as symbolic guardians. Over 150 references to guards are found in the Bible, most serving to "protect rulers, their possessions, and their edicts. They were employed throughout the ancient Near East by Egyptian pharaohs (Genesis 37:36), Babylonian kings (Daniel 2:14), and Israelite rulers (2 Kings 11:4-6)." (See Ryken, Wilhoit, and Longman, eds., The Dictionary of Biblical Imagery, Intervarsity Press, p. 353.)

Two angels guarded the entrance to the Garden of Eden, the earth's first temple space (Genesis 3:24). Levites served as sentinels or doorkeepers for the temple in ancient Israel (1 Chronicles 9:17-24). Angelic sentinels guard the presence of God in heaven (D&C 132:18-19). According to Truman Angell, at Kirtland both he and Brigham Young saw "two Personages before each window, leaving and approaching each other like guards would do"—protecting the Lord's house. (See Truman O. Angell, Autobiography, p. 10, LDS Church Archives. Cited in Matthew B. Brown and Paul Thomas Smith, Symbols in Stone, Covenant Communications, p. 52.)

Guards and witnesses are combined in one for those receiving the key of knowledge necessary to pass into the divine presence symbolically in today's temples. Brigham Young taught that we must learn the "laws and ordinances by which we can be prepared to pass from one gate to another, and from one sentinel to another, until we go into the presence of our Father and God." (See Brigham Young, Journal of Discourses vol. 12, p. 163.)

[248] *Witnesses*   Two witnesses are used in most functions within the Church, to witness truth, confirming priesthood covenants, and guard their correct administration. Anciently, God placed the Israelites under covenant to obey His law using the two stone tablets of the ten Commandments. Today, the stick of Judah (the Bible) and the stick of Joseph (the Book of Mormon) serve as two witnesses for the gospel in its fullness. The appearance of these ancient "sticks" was also pillar-like. Two great books will be used in judging the dead: One on earth—"the book of their works" (kept by a temple recorder) and 1 in heaven—"the book of life" (kept by angels). The number two in scripture is consistently associated with the qualitative concepts of either the law of witnesses establishing truth, or the principle of opposition; complementary opposition (as in man and woman), or antagonistic opposition, as in light and darkness. (See 2 Nephi 2:11). Good examples of two witnesses include the following: God the Father served as a 2nd witness to the Savior's baptism (Matthew 3:17), at His Transfiguration (2 Peter 1:17), in His visit to the Nephites (3 Nephi 11:7), and in the First Vision (JS-H 1:17). In priesthood blessings, One brother anoints and the other seals then blesses. 2 prophets are to be raised up to the Jewish nation in the last days (Revelation 11 and D&C 77:15). Two great world capitals will exist under the government of God—the city of New Jerusalem in a cleansed America and the Jerusalem of a cleansed Palestine. Two sets of 12 will govern with Him—the 12 Apostles of the old world, and the 12 disciples of the new (1 Nephi 12:8-10). Two lambs were sacrificed in ancient Israel—one in the morning and one in the evening (Leviticus 1:9). Anciently two guardians or witnesses were seen in the two cherubim sewn on the ancient temple veil and in the two gold cherubim with wings on the mercy seat of the ark (Exodus 25:18, 22; 1 Kings 6:23-28). The laying-on of hands involves two hands by priesthood bearers. Men and women receiving eternal life are kings and queens, priests and priestesses. Two types of symbolic trees were in the Garden of Eden—the Tree of Knowledge and the Tree of Life. Two stones were part of the Urim and Thummim. These and many more all serve as complimentary witnesses.

[249] *Joseph and Hyrum Statues*   Both statues were moved in 1911 and placed in the open space between the temple and the south visitor's center. Some evidence exists for their burial in this area, their bodies potentially secretly removed by Brigham Young and taken to the valley as "precious cargo" in the first group of Saints entering the valley in 1847 (see chapter 10 of The Day Star: Reading Sacred Architecture, by the author). Brigham Young taught that any person seeking the celestial kingdom must first be approved by Joseph Smith: "No man or woman in this dispensation will ever enter into the celestial kingdom of God without the consent of Joseph Smith. From the day that the priesthood was taken from the earth to the winding-up scene of all things, every man and woman must have the certificate of Joseph Smith, Junior, as a passport to their entrance into the mansion where God and Christ are... I cannot go there without his consent. He holds the keys of that kingdom for the last dispensation—the keys to rule in the spirit-world; and he rules there triumphantly, for he gained full power and a glorious victory over the power of Satan while he was yet in the flesh, and was a martyr to his religion and to the name of Christ, which gives him a most perfect victory in the spirit-world. He reigns there as supreme a being in his sphere, capacity, and calling, as God does in heaven" (Brigham Young, Journal of Discourses 7:289, 9 October 1859). The Prophet Joseph stated, "I myself hold the keys of this last dispensation, and I forever will hold them in time and in eternity" (Quoted by Lucy Mack Smith, reporting a discourse given by Joseph Smith in early 1832 in Kirtland, Ohio. Lucy Mack Smith, "The History of Lucy Smith, Mother of the Prophet," 1844-45 manuscript, book 13, p. 5, Church Archives. Cited in the Teachings of the Presidents of the Church, Melchizedek Priesthood Personal Study Guide, The Church of Jesus Christ of Latter-day Saints, p. 512).

[250] *Pillars as Memorials*   The two great free-standing pillars at Solomon's Temple—Jachin and Boaz—may have not only been guardians and witnesses, they may have also been *memorials* of the Lord's presence during much of the 40 year sojourn in the wilderness. We read in Exodus, "And the LORD went before them by day in a *pillar* of a cloud, to lead them the way; and by night in a *pillar* of fire, to give them light; to go by day and night" (Exodus 13:21, italics added). The word for "pillar" in Hebrew is *amwd*, having the root meaning "to establish," "to stand," "stand still, unmoving, stable, steadfast," "stand upright, arise," "support," and "stability." These same meanings are attached to the Egyptian *Djed* pillar. In addition, the word for the ancient Hebrew god *El* comes from the root word *ail* meaning "pillar." The author is grateful to Frederick Huchel for the Hebrew insights on the pillar.

²⁵¹ *Two Trees – Male and Female*   The elemental creation nature of the temple often points us to complimentary opposition in male and female. The two pillars may thus also represent male and female, the right tree—the Tree of Life (male – ever fertile), associated with the evergreen or conifer; and the left with the female — the Tree of Knowledge of Good and Evil. It was Eve who was seduced by the serpent with a promise of additional knowledge (Genesis 3:5). Two trees are found in the Garden room of the Salt Lake Temple. The author is grateful to Frederick Huchel for insights connecting tree types and the male or female.

²⁵² According to Nibley, "the name of Heliopolis, the On of the Bible, appears no less than three times on the rim of the Joseph Smith hypocephalus, making it unique among hypocephali. The symbol of the Holy Place is twice drawn in a special way, as a spear between two columns. The same ideogram is found on a few other hypocephali, e.g., Br. Mus. No. 8445a, where it occurs only once. It is the spear of Horus of Heliopolis with which he overcame the Adversary, the Serpent, when he took the rule. Mrs. Reymond suggests that it represents 'the magical power which was created by the Earth-god at the beginning of the world...As to the two columns flanking the spear, the Jews, according to W. Kornfeld, were quite aware that the two famous pillars, Boaz and Jachin...strength and capital righteousness, that stood at the entrance to the Temple of Solomon (2 Chronicles 3:17), 'belonged to the solar cult of On." (Hugh Nibley, The Three Facsimiles from the Book of Abraham, pps. 25-26).

²⁵³ The Ben-ben stone was iron-based, thought to have became magnetically oriented to the north celestial pole in its fall to earth, thus orienting it naturally to Polaris and the imperishable stars of the north from whence it came (the ancients thought the gods dwellt there). The Kabba at Mecca also features a magnetically charged meteorite set in the northeast corner of its black cube-shaped shrine. The ancient name for this sacred Egyptian city was *Iwnw*. The root iwn meaning 'column' or 'pillar.' On was the 'city of the pillar,' the place of Creation. According to Nibley, the ancient Pyramid Texts associate the primeval hill rising from the waters of creation with Atum, the oldest creator sun-god in Egypt." The *Iwnw* (Heliopolis) hieroglyph represents a pillar or Egyptian obelisk (the benben stone atop it). Two Egyptian hieroglyphs appear to represent *iwnw*. One utilizes a spear or benben-like stone at its top, the other a motif utilizing three pillars, the one at center taller than the other two. This triangle form appears to represent the Egyptian word "benben." Some believe the spear of *iwnw* is the Spear of Osirus, positioned between two pillars, potentially used to open "the way" back to God. (See R. T. Rundle Clark, Myth and Symbol in Ancient Egypt, Thames and Hudson, p. 39. See also Nibley and Rhodes, One Eternal Round, FARMS / Deseret Book, pps. 171-72.)

The erect pillar at On appears to have had phallic connotations in connection with creation. Clark adds, "The temple which enclosed the Ben-ben stone was the centre of calendrical rites as well as the scene of the rising of the High God. It was the place where the mysteries of creation were ceremonially repeated." (R. T. Rundle Clark, Myth and Symbol in Ancient Egypt, Thames and Hudson, p. 39. Nibley adds, "The names of the greatest sacred centers in Egypt are all designated as places of standing stones." See Hugh Nibley and Michael Rhodes, One Eternal Round, FARMS / Deseret Book, p. 172.)

²⁵⁴ The potential wives of a married Christ may have included Mary Magdalene and the Bethany Sisters—Mary and Martha. Numerous early Church leaders claim He was married, including Brigham Young, Heber C. Kimball, Orson Pratt, Orson Hyde, Lorenzo Snow, Jedediah M. Grant, and Joseph F. Smith. According to Swanson, the sacred bloodline of Christ (with right to rule and reign on earth) was carefully hidden for centuries, primarily for protection, finally surfacing in the blood of the Prophet Joseph Smith and many other Church leaders who may be literal descendants of Christ through a sacred blood lineage descending through families in Britain. (See Vern Grosvenor Swanson, Dynasty of the Holy Grail, Cedar Fort,. See also Ogden Kraut, Jesus Was Married, Utah Pioneer Publishing.)

²⁵⁵ Israel clearly understood that sun = father, moon = mother, and stars = children. He stated: "What is this dream that thou has dreamed? Shall I and thy mother and thy brethren indeed come to bow down ourselves to thee to the earth?" (Genesis 37:10).

²⁵⁶ See chapter 10 in The Day Star: Reading Sacred Architecture, by the author, for more on translation, the 144,000, Zion, etc. See also John M. Pontius, The Triumph of Zion, CFI.

²⁵⁷ The Nauvoo Temple features the clearest visual illustration of endless posterity of any LDS temple, not only because of its unique moonstones and sunstones, but also because of its explosion of numerous and diverse types of stars. No other temple features as many stars on its exterior (432 total), in as much variety (5 types; 4 outside and 1 more inside), or with their unique juxtapositioning to one another. This provides important clarity of doctrine. Joseph Smith's placement of the regular 5-pointed upright stars only on the upper portions of the octagonal tower, as well as their presence there in great numbers, appears to signal *eternal lives*—endless posterity in this case. Some believe other scriptural references to "lives" has association with coming to this or other worlds in different times to continue our growth, work out our salvation, support God in His mission, or assist and support family or others. Eternity is a very long time, providing some merit for this interpretation. For more on the iconography of the Nauvoo Temple, see The Day Star: Reading Sacred Architecture, by the author.

[258] "The plains of Olaha Shinehah, or the place where Adam dwelt, must be a part of, or in the vicinity of Adam-ondi-Ahman. This name Olaha Shinehah, may be, and in all probability is, from the language of Adam. We may without great controversy believe that this is the name which Adam gave to this place, at least we may venture this as a probable guess. Shinehah, according to the Book of Abraham, is the name given to the sun. (Abraham 3:13). It is the name applied to Kirtland when the Lord desired in a revelation to hide its identity. (Sec. 82). Elder Janne M. Sjodahl, commenting on the name Olaha Shinehah, has said: 'Shinehah means sun, and Olaha is possibly a variant of the word Olea, which is 'the moon' (Abraham 3:13). If so the plains of Olaha Shinehah would be the Plains of the Moon and the Sun, so called, perhaps because of astronomical observations there made'...it may be reasonable that here in this valley important information was made known anciently in relation to the stars of our universe." (Joseph Fielding Smith, *Church History and Modern Revelation*, 2:97-98, quoted in Church Educational System, Doctrine & Covenants Student Manual, The Church of Jesus Christ of Latter-day Saints, 289-90). It was there that Adam made sacrifice on the ancient altars Joseph Smith later identified (and which the pulpit-altars inside the historic temples are patterned after). Heber C. Kimball was with Joseph Smith when he identified the stones as the ancient altar of Adam. He stated that they resembled the pulpits of the Kirtland Temple. (See Orson F. Whitney, Life of Heber C. Kimball, 2nd ed., Stevens and Wallis, pp. 208-9).

[259] In the Adam-God theory, attributed to Brigham Young, God and his companion descended to earth to plant man on earth. Michael is thus God in this scenario, Eve our Mother in Heaven. This doctrine was later refuted by many others, including Pres. Kimball.

[260] Basic building measurements for Chartres also appear to be associated with the sun and moon. According to John James, the length of Chartres is 365 1/4 feet, potentially pointing to a solar calendar year. "I believe this is countered by the labyrinth and its lunar calendar for symbolic reasons." John James, The Master Masons of Chartres, West Grinstead Publications.

[261] The 112 lunations at the outer edge of the Chartres Cathedral labyrinth may correspond to those of the moon itself; 28 lunations per month (x 4) = 112. In addition, there are 28, 180-degree turns in the labyrinth. See Stephen Skinner, Sacred Geometry, Sterling Publishing, p. 135.

[262] The Garden Room of the Salt Lake Temple is an especially good example. At its front are 3 arched doorways, along with 1 at back, and another 1 to the right (entrance to the next room). Each features a half-circle arch above the rectangular door. Above the central front doorway is a sun symbol in yellow, clasped hands above it, and an all-seeing eye farther up on the wall. One connection to the half circle above the rectangle so prominently displayed at Nauvoo and Salt Lake is particularly enlightening. According to Joseph Smith's *Egyptian Alphabet and Grammar* (translation decoding notes for the Book of Abraham), the phonetic name of the graphic denoting the earth is *J ah O eh*, the unspoken name of God, which Christians render as *Jehovah*. The last or 5th line of Joseph's notes in his Egyptian Alphabet and Grammar relating to the symbol for planet earth (a circle with a simple perpendicular x or cross inside it) reads: "The earth under the governing power of oliblish, Enish go on dosh, and Kai e van rash, which are grand ~~governing~~ key or in other words, the governing power, which governs the fifteen fixed stars that ~~belong~~ governs the earth, sun and moon, (which have their power in one) with the other twelve moving planets of this system. Oliblish—Enish go on dosh, and Kail ven rash, are the three grand central ~~stars which~~ powers that govern all the other creations, which have been sought out by the most ages of all the fathers, since the beginning of the creation, by means of the Urim and Thummim:" (Cited in Joe Sampson, Written by the Finger of God, Wellspring Press, p. 140). Sampson suggests that the earth is named after the God who created and controls it. In whole, the squared circle appears to signify the earth (named after its creator) and its 4 quarters, 4 angels, etc. Dissecting its parts we also have 2 halves, the lower half circle symbolizing the earth below (*toan*) and the one above representing heaven (*oan*). The rising nature of the upper half circle appears to symbolize the return of the bridegroom to join with His Church during the Millennium.

Some Egyptian alphabet and grammar ideograms, left to right: 1. Oan – upper regions, heaven or rainbow; 2. Toan – lower region, moon or earth; 3. Zi Oan – Zion; 4. J ah O eh – Jehovah or earth (first cross symbol); 5. To An or untu – horizon, valley or lower region; and 6. Hep – 2/3rds (1/3 of hosts cast down?). Courtesy of Joe Sampson and Wellspring Press.

²⁶³ See Donna B. Nielsen, Beloved Bridegroom: Finding Christ in Ancient Jewish Marriage and Family Customs, Onyx Press, p. 55. Nielson states that this ancient bridal canopy symbolized 1. the house of the bridegroom to which he welcomes the bride; 2. the tabernacle in the wilderness where God and Israel began their life together; 3. the divine light that surround all creation; 4. the covering of God over the couple to be married; 5. the bridal chamber where the consummation of the wedding took place; and 6. a portal or gateway symbolizing the couple's entrance into the covenant of marriage and accompanying emotional, physical, and spiritual transitions.

Half-circles over rectangles, similar to a bridal canopy, left to right: Salt Lake Temple east door; St. Louis Missouri Temple Jacob's Ladder motif with Star of David; Nauvoo Temple rising sun window; & Vernal Utah Temple rising sun window.

²⁶⁴ See J.E. Cirlot, A Dictionary of Symbols, Barnes and Noble Books, p. 323.

²⁶⁵ Swastikas (common in many ancient cultures worldwide) have been found embedded in the stonework of the Jerusalem temple mount and are thought to have been present at the time of Christ (see Joan Comay, The Temple of Jerusalem, Weidenfeld and Nicolson, p. 160). For a discussion of the swastika's transition from a symbol of good to a symbol of evil, see chapter 2. Opposing volutes have also been identified with the waters of life in antiquity. Matthew Brown cites Moscati in stating that the opposing volutes on the arches above the first 1ˢᵗ floor Melchizedek priesthood pulpit-altars may represent the Waters of Life (the 4 rivers of paradise) that originate at the tree of life. He states, "In Mesopotamian art, whorls symbolize water." Sabatino Moscati, The Face of the Ancient Orient: A Panorama of Near Eastern Civilization in Pre-Classic Times, Doubleday, pp. 97-98, cited in Matthew B. Brown and Paul Thomas Smith, Symbols in Stone, Covenant Communications, p. 87. See also John M. Lundquist, The Temple: Meeting Place of Heaven and Earth, Thames and Hudson, p. 91.

²⁶⁶ Martin Brenan, The Stones of Time, Inner Traditions International, p. 195.

²⁶⁷ This large 8-foot entrance stone lies horizontally in front of the main entrance, admitting light into the mound on the winter solstice sunrise. A line at the center of the stone splits the spirals, turning right on the left, and left on the right. It features 3 spirals in a triangle relationship at left (the 3ʳᵈ one potentially illustrating Venus, according to Brenan, the brightest heavenly body next to the sun and moon), and 2 spirals side by side in opposing form at the right, along with other geometric forms. Stone L19, struck by light in the mound's central interior space, also features opposing spirals: 3 at top (similar to the 3 on the entrance curbstone) and 2 sets of 2 opposing spirals below it. Huge curbstones around the perimeter of the mound contain extensive rock art with moons, suns, and stars apparently expressing time, season, etc. Differing moon phases are represented via oscillating wavy lines. (See Martin Brennan, The Stones of Time, Inner Traditions International, pps. 72-81).

²⁶⁸ The Chinese yin–yang symbol also makes use of two opposing spirals, representative of polarity or the unity of complementary opposites—the primal forces in the universe, including that of male and female. The *yin* is a receptive, passive, cool, dark, female force associated with the moon and water. The *yang* is a warm, masculine force associated with movement, heat, light, and the sun. (See Carl G. Liungman, Dictionary of Symbols, W.W. Norton and Company, p. 357.)

[269] *Spirals and Swastikas at Kirtland* The Kirtland Temple features extensive use of opposing spirals (and interlaced circles) throughout the temple, along with some swastikas. Opposing spirals are found at the roofline, on exterior windows, and on the temple's octagonal tower. Of special note is their appearance atop *pillars* associated with the sacred pulpit-altars inside. Those of the second floor, for example, feature opposing spirals carved at the top of each of their 12 smaller pillars.

Two opposing swastikas are found on the outer edges of the 1st floor west window above the Melchizedek priesthood pulpit-altars. These hold up the arch of the rising sun motif of the top half of the window. Two opposing swastikas are also found centrally located just below the rising sun of the 1st floor east window, above the Aaronic priesthood pulpit-altars. This window was created by Truman O. Angell and features a long vine and a tree of life motif on its central keystone (both symbols of the Savior). At total of 4 sets of opposing squarish spirals are found on the 2nd floor west window just below the rising sun motif of the window. The 2nd floor east window features 2 sets of squarish spirals inside its thick arch. All pulpit-altars on both floors feature 12 total pillars (dividing the pulpits) with a squarish spiral atop each. Both Truman Angell (future architect of the Salt Lake Temple) and Jacob Bump had a hand in this woodwork. Spirals are also found atop the corners of the doors leading in the second floor assembly area (from the inside). Flattened opposing spirals are found below the rising sun symbols above both the east main floor entrance doors to the temple (viewed from the inside). According to Hall, these flattened spirals are *Meander* symbols, representing clouds and rolling thunder. (See Halls' Illustrated Dictionary of Symbols in Eastern and Western Art, p. 4; Leland H. Gentry, "Adam-ondi-Ahman: A Brief Historical Survey," BYU Studies, vol. 13, no. 4 [Summer 1973] p. 561. All spirals and swastikas were observed by the author during visits to the Kirtland Temple.)

The placement of opposing spirals or swastikas atop the interior pillars is similar to vertical usage of the sun and the moon on the later Nauvoo Temple pillars of heaven, where the doctrine connected to them was finally revealed to the general body of the Saints. The pillars of the first floor pulpit-altars feature interlaced circles—potential chain-like symbols, suggestive of eternal (sealed) family relationships. Significantly, like those at Nauvoo, the moon symbols at Kirtland rest only *below* a chiastic central sun symbol, in this case the important sunburst windows on the 1st and 2nd floors (the *aht* motif of Egypt). Joseph Smith had acquired the Egyptian mummies and papyri at Kirtland and had begun their translation there. The placement of these moon and sun symbols on *pillars* is important, as pillars appear to be strongly connected to sacred covenant making throughout scripture and specifically in Revelation 12:1. And though the new and everlasting covenant of marriage was not written down or introduced to the Saints until the Nauvoo period (1843), Joseph Smith understood its principles well, as early as 1831 (the year it was revealed to him), 5 years before the dedication of the Kirtland Temple. According the heading of D&C 132, "Although the revelation was recorded in 1843, it is evident from the historical records that the doctrines and principles involved in this revelation had been known by the Prophet since 1831."

Some claim the simple geometric motifs of the Kirtland Temple are uninspired, derived only from historic carpentry pattern books. As the first temple of the Restoration, this temple is far too important to feature uninspired motifs at important points in its interior. The use of ancient male and female marriage symbols in consistent fashion at the top of the covenant oriented pillars at both Kirtland, Nauvoo and Salt Lake dispel this conclusion. Even though a more limited portion of our current endowment was presented to single and married men at Kirtland, the use of these symbols there prefigures the New and Everlasting Covenant of Marriage later presented to married couples inside the Nauvoo and succeeding temples. Truman Angell as carpenter at Kirtland constructed perhaps the clearest visual representation of this doctrine through his use of these symbols on the second floor east interior window. These were made under the direction of the Prophet Joseph Smith. Angell would later go on to design the Salt Lake Temple under the direction of Brigham Young, along with others.

[270] *Nauvoo Temple Spirals and Swastikas* Opposing spirals (positioned vertically) are found on the small Doric pilasters found on the west exterior of the Nauvoo Temple near the upper Holiness to the Lord plaque. Corinthian pillars appeared in the attic story of the historic Nauvoo Temple, where patrons progressed through various ordinance rooms until reaching the celestial room in the east end. (See Glen M. Leonard, Nauvoo: A Place of Peace, A People of Promise, Deseret Book – BYU Press, p. 262.) In the southeast corner of this floor, just off the celestial room, was Brigham Young's office where marriage sealings were performed. The joining of sun and moon (man and woman) in opposing spiral symbols is especially appropriate in and on the Nauvoo Temple, where the New and Everlasting Covenant of Marriage was first presented worthy Saints.

President Gordon B. Hinckley appears to have replaced the original opposing spirals (or swastikas) first seen on the pulpit-altar pillars at Kirtland with sun, moon, and earth motifs now present on them. Clear sun motifs are found on the highest tier of the pulpit-altar pillars, each with rays extending outward. Moon and earth motifs may be represented on the two lower tiers of pulpits, although no markings confirm this. All motifs atop the pulpit pillars at Nauvoo are round, circle-in-square symbols. Only the top tier orb features "rays." These orbs appear to reflect the same hierarchy of the Nauvoo Temple's exterior pilasters, as addressed in Revelation 12:1. The probability that suns and moons are both utilized upon the 12 pulpit-altar pillars at Nauvoo, much like the opposing swastikas or spirals atop those in the Kirtland Temple, creates a strong connection between both sets of motifs, again potentially symbolizing man and woman in a *covenant* relationship with God. It is this covenant where creation may proceed endlessly in the peopling of worlds.

[271] *Salt Lake Opposing Spirals*   Each of the Salt Lake Temple's successive endowment rooms features opposing spirals (many atop covenant-oriented pillars), again possibly illustrating the New and Everlasting Covenant of Marriage. All Endowment Room doorways, for example, feature rising sun-themed circles in a half-circle dome above the doorway, reminiscent of the Nauvoo Temple exterior windows, but with the addition of the round sun-like disc. Inside these circles are eight spirals: four sets of opposing spirals, two at each of the four points of the compass. (The Salt Lake Temple also features 8 spiral staircases, each with 8 flights.) Even the large lighted arch over the veil features opposing spirals. In addition, opposing spirals are found on the walls of some of the ordinance rooms. In the Terrestrial Room, for example, eight sets of spirals are found on each of the primary pillars surrounding the room. Below these opposing spirals are large chain-like designs, suggestive of eternal family relationships. Three appropriate, related concepts thus come together on the Salt Lake Temple's Terrestrial Room pillars: 1. sacred covenant-making (symbolized by the *pillars*); 2. the eternal union of man and woman (symbolized in the *opposing spirals* at their top); and 3. the "sealed" nature of this covenant, made between man and woman, and between them and God. Their resulting children (numerous pomegranates on the ancient tabernacle pillars Jachin and Boaz) are forever bound to them, as symbolized in the chain-like, horizontal *figure-8 motifs*. Like the 30 exterior pilasters of the Nauvoo Temple, and the interior windows of the Kirtland Temple, the 50 exterior pilasters of the Salt Lake Temple also feature sunstones over the top of moonstones (Revelation 12:1), but with added earthstones below. This provides additional symbolism beyond marriage, connected to graded intelligences, advancing kingdoms, and the space-time relationship.

[272] The preferred arrangement in megalithic art is for the sun to be on the right and the moon on the left (as the rock faces east). See Martin Brenan, The Stones of Time, Inner Traditions International, pps. 171, 193.

[273] There are also 13 windows on the south side of the Draper Temple, direction of most light. The number 13 is closely tied to Christ (see chapter 10 of The Day Star: Reading Sacred Architecture, by the author). The number 24 is thought to have connection to the Twelve in the Old World and New World. It is also thought to represent the Twelve with their wives in a prayer circle surrounding the Savior in antiquity.

[274] Eugene Seaich, A Great Mystery: The Sacred Marriage and Bridal Chamber in Early Christianity and Judaism, unpublished manuscript, Salt Lake City, 1979.

[275] *King and Queen of Heaven*   As discussed earlier, the five pillars at the entrance to the ancient tabernacle and the five pillar-like lamp-stands on both sides of the long axis path to the oracle in Solomon's Temple appear to have association to "the way" of scripture, and the archetypal *axis mundi* to God—the fiery pillar of light connecting the worlds (Jacob's Ladder). The lamp-stands of Solomon's Temple also have connection to *Asherah*—the wooden pillar associated with the Queen of Heaven, consort of God (associated with the altar). Fertility and creation are also implied. (For more on the ancient Asherah, see Daniel Peterson, Daniel C. Peterson, Nephi and His Asherah, Journal of Book of Mormon Studies, vol. 9, pps. 16-25.) The number five has widespread use in Egypt, scripture and sacred architecture, in connection wtih life and eternal life through Christ's grace – His love and Atonement. See endnote 26 of chapter 8 of The Day Star: Reading Sacred Architecture, by the author, for extensive examples of the symbolism of the number 5.

[276] *Wedjat Eyes*   According to Budge, the opposing orientation of two ancient Egyptian *utchats* (wedjat) eyes may have also pointed to sun and moon symbolism, the right eye representing the sun and the left eye representing the moon. Budge explains that in addition to sun and moon symbolism the 2 opposing eye motifs (the right eye of Ra—the sun—and the left eye of Ra—the moon) may represent the separate halves of the daily course of the sun, and the place where the living are under the protection of He who controls all power. (See E. A. Wallis Budge, The Mummy: A Handbook of Egyptian Funerary Archaeology, Cambridge UP, p. 316.)

Note that this Egyptian symbol features a spiral form at its bottom corner. Two opposing eye *utchats* are found in Facsimile Two (figure three). Joseph Smith described figure three stating that it, "is made to represent God sitting upon his throne, clothed with power and authority, with a crown of eternal light upon his head; representing also the grand keywords of the Holy Priesthood, as revealed to Adam in the Garden of Eden, as also to Seth, Noah, Melchizedek, Abraham, and all to whom the Priesthood was revealed." (See Joseph Smith, Explanation, Facsimile 2 [figure 3] of the Book of Abraham.)

[277] *Creation and Fertility*   Sacred marriage is a first step in creation. The first commandment given Adam and Eve in the Garden was to multiply and replenish the earth. The sin of homosexuality lies in part with the negation of this principle. Consistent with the sun and moon and other motifs as marriage or creation symbols (many atop temple pillars) are the decorated capitals atop Jachin and Boaz. These two tall brass pillars at Solomon's Temple had large capitals, each featuring 200 pomegranates surrounding them. Pomegranates were an ancient symbol of fertility (1 Kings 7:20). According to Frankel and Teustch, the sweet tasting purple-colored pomegranate had red flowers, a potential sign of love and passion. According to the Midrash, pomegranates were thought to produce 613 seeds. Many of the 613 requirements of Judaism are connected to the sanctity of marriage. Such fruitfulness is tied to its many seeds and, in a temple context, to the endless eternal offspring promised those in the New and Everlasting Covenant. Pomegranates were also found on the hem of the ancient High Priest's robe and on the Mercy Seat of the Ark of the Covenant. This unique purple fruit was additionally associated with Rosh Hashanah (civil New Year's Day), as its brown calyx at top resembles a crown. Kings were coronated on this ancient Hebrew holy day. Brigham Young grew pomegranate trees at his summer home in St. George, Utah. Other motifs express fertility, creation, and male and female on temples throughout the ancient world, including alphabetical characters.

Generative Power in Facsimile 2   The words around the circumference of Facsimile two and other symbols inside it express the generative, creative power of God. Quoting President Joseph F. Smith, Skinner has stated, "The union of both Adam and Eve 'was required to complete man in the image of God.' We have both a Heavenly Father and a Heavenly Mother, a truth borne out by scripture: And God said, 'Let us make man in our image, after our likeness...So God created man in his own image, in the image of God created he him; male and female created he them' (Genesis 1:26-27). The Gods are of both genders, male and female." [277] This is evident in Abraham 5:7-20 where the use of the plural "Gods" is seen in those creating man and woman. President Smith added, "All men and women are in the similitude of the universal Father and Mother and are literally the sons and daughters of deity." (Joseph F. Smith and the First Presidency, "The Origin of Man," reprinted in Ensign, February 2002, p.29. Cited in Andrew Skinner, Temple Worship, Deseret Book, pp. 17-18.)

Symmetry in Facsimile 2 figures from the Book of Abraham, left to right: Close up of a typical Wedjat eye with spiral – figure 3; Horus (Christ) with dual Wedjat eye motifs left and right, and light over head – figure 3; Central deity figure with opposing heads – figure 1; Upper deity form with horns – figure 2; and Two baboons – figure 1 (one higher)

Two Becoming One   The symmetry of opposing heads on god figures in Facsimile Two (rather than the traditional four heads), and opposing wedjat eyes and baboons suggest male and female duality, typical of the circle and square and marriage. Most hypocephali feature a four-headed god in this position, symbolizing the four cardinal directions of space. Skinner suggests that the Bible "uses the singular construction when referring to Deity because of the complete unity that exists between eternal marriage partners, specifically the Gods. Adam's response to receiving a companion perfectly suited to him reflects this oneness: 'This [woman] is now bone of my bones, and flesh of my flesh' (Genesis 2:23)". (See Andrew Skinner, Temple Worship, Deseret Book, p. 103.) Here in the dual-headed figure, two come together and become one in God through temple covenants. Their promise is exaltation and eternal life—to be like God. They are the image of God—*Elohim*—exalted parental gods (*Elohim* is a Hebrew word expressing plurality of gods).

Mother in Heaven   Although Latter-day Saints rarely speak of a Mother in Heaven, the concept is neither foreign nor should it be uncomfortable. References to a Mother in Heaven can be found in many ancient sources. In the Gospel of Truth, for example (found as part of the papyri at Nag Hammadi in Egypt), we read, "The word of the Father clothes everyone from top to bottom, purifies, and makes them fit to come back into the presence of their Father and their heavenly mother." (See Hugh Nibley, Temple and Cosmos, FARMS, Deseret Book, p. 122. Nibley cites The Gospel of Truth 23:33; 24:7). The concept of a male god and his female consort appears typical of early first dynasty Egyptian Gods such as Ra and his consort Unas, or Amen and his consort Ament. In consoling Zina D. Huntington upon the death of her mother on July 8, 1839, the Prophet Joseph Smith stated that not only would she come to know her mother once again on the other side, but "more than that, you will meet and become acquainted with your eternal Mother, the wife of your Father in Heaven." Surprised, Zina then asked "And have I then a Mother in Heaven?" The Prophet Joseph then replied, "You assuredly have. How could a Father claim His title unless there were also a Mother to share that parenthood?" This same concept was taught his plural wife Eliza R. Snow. She addressed this principle in her song, "Oh My Father," hymn #292. (See Susa Young Gates, Eliza R. Snow Smith, History of the Young Ladies Mutual Improvement Association, LDS Church, November 1869 to June 1910, Deseret News, 1911, pps. 15-16). Elohim is frequently used in association with "the council of the Gods" in the pre-existence. In Facsimile 2, Book of Abraham it may signal our God and His eternal companion—a representation of our possible exaltation in the same covenant relationship. See Genesis 1:26-27.

278 "The Gap" is an ancient Native American temple site near Parowan Utah, featuring two mountains, the north and south peaks, in which the sun rises and sets due and east and west between them at the equinoxes - mirroring the duat valley of the Egyptians. The site features some 1500 pieces of Native American rock art connecting it directly to the heavens in sophisticated fashion. (See V. Garth Norman, The Parowan Gap: Nature's Perfect Observatory, Cedarfort. See also endnote 123 below for more on The Gap.)

279 See BD 17, Faulkner, Ancient Egyptian Book of the Dead, p. 44, in Hugh Nibley and Michael D. Rhodes, One Eternal Round, Deseret Book, pps. 41, 108-10.

280 Parowan Gap is a break in a small mountain range. The break runs east to west, with rock art filling much of the small valley. The rock art has intimate connections to the heavens, marking Polaris, Venus, the moon and sun, and some of their conjunctions and cycles. Shadow marking rock art, rock cairns pointing to solstices and equinoxes, and conjunctive rock art all mark time there. According to Budge, the Egyptians believed that close to mountains was the region of the Tuat or Duat - a valley in which the sun rose and set in a circular path. This underworld (the pathway of the sun at night) was the place in which the souls of the dead, upon departing this world, made their way into and through the Tuat. This was the kingdom of the dead; the place where Osiris attained his supreme power over all the dead. Budge felt that the Tuat lied far away in the north. (Polaris rests directly over the north peak of the Gap.) A safe journey through the Duat or Tuat was possible, as seen in Ra successfully making the journey each night, then rising each morning as the sun on the horizon eastward - the Egyptian *aht* motif – the rising sun on the horizon hieroglyph. (See E.A.Wallace Budge, the Book of the Dead: The Papyri of Ani, Scribe and Treasurer of the Temples of Egypt, about B.C. 1450. 3 vols. New York: Putnams's Sons, 1913, in The Message of the Joseph Smith Papyri, FARMS / Deseret Book, 2nd ed.) The author is grateful to Frederick Huchel for initial insights into the importance of the Gap as an important Native American temple site. Huchel and the author both recognized connections to the Egyptian Duat (often addressed by Nibley) in the two caves at Parowan Gap (at the east and west ends) on a trip in 2009.

281 Margaret Barker, The Gate of Heaven, Sheffield Phoenix Press, p. 149.

282 Many LDS temples face east, perhaps signaling conversion of the Gentile nations (primarily from Europe), including the Kirtland and Salt Lake City Temples. Whereas the Nauvoo Temple is reversed, perhaps pointing to the future conversion of the Remnant (the descendants of Lehi of Jewish blood in the west). The Book of Mormon informs us of the eventual rejection of the fullness of the gospel by the gentiles (3 Ne. 16:10), the fullness then taken back to Jews of the far east. The Lord's sacred bloodline will then once again have the fullness in the last days, signaled by important temples at two world capitals; New Jerusalem, built by mostly by the Remnant in North American, and the temple at Jerusalem of the Old World, built by the Jews.

283 For a complete discussion of the relationship of pillars to covenant-making, first established in scripture at Beth El by Jacob and his vision of the ladder, see chapter 4 of the Day Star: Reading Sacred Architecture, by the author.

284 Archeologist V. Garth Norman confirmed this annual event using a transit during construction of the temple. He also informed the temple architect (Keith Stepan) of a direct alignment of the rising sun above Mount Timpanogos through the roundel of the east Jacob's Ladder window at about 7am on April 6, which formed a light pattern directly opposite on the west wall of the Celestial Room. The builders latter created a circle in square motif (mirroring the design of the Jacob's Ladder window in the west wall) to mark this point (just above the west exit doors). Author's interview with Norman, 4 March, 2010. For more on the covenant connection to pillars, see chapter 4 of The Day Star: Reading Sacred Architecture, by the author.

285 Like inspired sacred temples and settings the world over, the Mount Timpanogos Temple features symbolic and literal connections to the heavens above, and to living water (or the underworld – the past) below. Like the Salt Lake, Manti, St. George and Nauvoo Temples, it has living water below it. The temple is also aligned perfectly with Mount Timpanogos to the east and Mount Nebo to the south; the two tallest mountains in the county. Mountain alignment is a pattern found in Central and South America. (Personal correspondence by the author with V. Garth Norman, archeologist and consultant with Keith Stepan, designer of the Mount Timpanogos, Utah Temple. Stepan later became the managing director of temple construction for the Church under Pres. Hinckley.)

[286] This particular alignment was not intentional. Architect Keith Stepan stated, "Later on, after it was built, the surveyor from BYU came and said, "Did you know that the highest point west is Timpanogos and the highest point south is Nebo and the angel's right there [centered and aligned with both]. The celestial room window faces that way [east] and on the winter solstice, and the summer solstice, exactly on the face, the sun comes right through the window [celestial room], and there's a wall over on the other side of the room and you can see the circular pattern." Archeologist V. Garth Norman states that it is on April 6th that the rising sun over Timpanogos is perfectly aligned with the temple, striking the roundel of the east Jacob's Ladder window and then traveling the length of the celestial room, striking the circle in square motif of the room's west wall opposite. The gold chandelier blocks this path to some degree (Interview with the author, 2/4/2010). According to Stepan these kinds of results typically appear in temple construction and appear to be mostly unplanned occurrences. They are nevertheless representative of inspiration. (Keith Stepan, Oral History Interview #2 by the Author, November 2006, p. 6.)

[287] See the research of Izapa by V. Garth Norman in publications such as V. Garth Norman, Izapa Sculpture, Part 1 (album) and 2 (text), New World Archeological Foundation, Brigham Young University, and V. Garth Norman, Book of Mormon—Mesoamerican Geography: History Study Map, Arcon Inc.

[288] Vertical alignment over living water is part of the true "Temple" pattern, rather than that of an Endowment House. Archeologist V. Garth Norman confirmed the alignments using a transit during construction of the temple. He also informed the temple architect of a direct alignment of the rising sun above Mount Timpanogos through the roundel of the east Jacob's Ladder window on April 6, about 7am, forming a light pattern directly opposite on the west wall of the celestial room. The architects latter created a circle in square motif (mirroring the design of the Jacob's Ladder window in the west wall to mark this point, just above the west exit doors). Author's interview with V. Garth Norman, archeologist, 4 March, 2010.

[289] For a complete discussion of alignment to water and light as part of true temple patterns, see chapter 6 of the Day Star: Reading Sacred Architecture, by the author.

[290] Important events occur at important points in time; time marked by the heavens. Many ancient cultures believed portals opened at the two symmetrical equinoxes, dividing the year in half; to heaven above at the spring equinox, and to the underworld below at the fall equinox. These portal points may be represented by the temple veil (heaven - light) and font (underworld - water). Both are connected to important events in antiquity, and to the Prophet Joseph Smith and the Restoration, including the First Vision (at or near the spring equinox), and Moroni's repeated visitations to the young Prophet as part of the Coming forth of the Book of Mormon (all on the fall equinox). This ancient book addresses our future judgment. Moroni brought it forth from the dust (the past or the dead) on the fall equinox (September 22-23 of 1823). The portal was opened for the angel Moroni to instruct Joseph Smith, doing so five times during a single 24 hour period. He did so over the next four consecutive years (five years total in his heavenly instruction) on this same exact date. (The revelation on the oath and covenant of the priesthood was also given on this date [and September 23rd] of 1832. See D&C 84.) Moroni's instruction was of an ominous fall or harvest season nature, in preparation for the Lord's second coming in *judgment*—upon the wicked when the souls of men are finally harvested (quoting Malichi's prophecies). Whereas Joseph Smith's First Vision appears to have occurred at or near the spring equinox, the time of the Restoration—the time of spring rebirth and hope. This same pattern is evident in the births of John the Baptist in the *fall* (repent and prepare for the first advent of the Lord), versus that of the birth of the Savior and Redeemer of the world in the *spring*. (The west and east towers on the Salt Lake Temple have moon phases marking the October and April birth months of both important figures. They are six months apart, dividing the year in half.) Passover and Tabernacles possess similar connections.

On a first visit to the Hopi, Hugh Nibley noted, "These were the only people in the world that still took the trouble to do what the human race had been doing for many millennia—celebrating the great life-cycle of the year, the creation, the dispensations." In comparing the Hopi to the Greeks he stated, "The dancing place was the bare plot which the Greeks called the konistra, the sand path where this world came in contact with the other, at the crucial periods of the year. That was the time when the orcus mundi was open—mundus patet; that is, when the mouth of the other world was open and the spirits of the ancestors attended the rites. By the altar, of course, was the sipapuni, the mouth of the lower world, the orcus mundi, at which the spirits from above and below could meet with their relatives upon the earth. This was the essential year-rite, found throughout the world from the earliest times." (Hugh Nibley, The Roman Games as a Survival of an Archaic Year-Cult, Univ. of California, 1938.)

[291] According to Sampson, *Alph* (our English A) is represented in the number 1 and is associated with the First Being, he who exercises supreme power. It is a male letter representing the bull, the great sire, God in his strength and power. *Beth*, the second letter of the Hebrew alphabet (the English B) is a female letter, representing the number 2. It has associations with house, garden and womb, along with creation and wisdom. See Joe Sampson, Written by the Finger of God, Wellspring Press, pps. 163-70.

[292] According to Nibley, the outer circle of hieroglyphs on Facsimile 2 reads, "I am DJebb't(Y) in the temple of the Benben in Heliopolis, most exalted, most glorious, the copulating bull, who has no equal." He adds, "In the Egyptian rites and the Old Testament, as also on our Hypocephalus, we find the strange conjunction of Nut and Ra, both of which are the supreme symbol of reproductive power. On Facsimile 2 the Bull in the rim is specifically designated as the "Great Procreating Bull without equal" (k3 nk nn shny.f), and is matched with the great mother Cow (figure 5) ...Is it not a coincidence that Abraham was promised that he would be the father of great nation, that his seed should be as the stars of the heaven, that all the nations of the earth should be blessed in it exactly on the day that he became 100 years old" (Genesis 17:1-8).

Facsimile 2 is associated with many concepts assisting us on our journey home to God. One of these is the concept of creation, the generative power of God, often expressed through "fertility" motifs within some contexts. According to Hugh Nibley, "The standard Hypocephalus, Speleers finds, is divided into two equal parts; the theme of all of them is "Creationism," indeed the only known examples of creationism, i.e., of a spiritual creation preceding the physical one, is found on a Hypocephalus [E6319]. He finds this strange, since the doctrine of creationism is very ancient, while the Hypocephali are of late idea."

The Leyden Egyptian Hypocephalus (1 of some 125 known hypocephali) provides a point of comparison for Facsimile 2 of the Book of Abraham for Anti-Mormons. They use this particular Hypocephalus to denigrate the work of Joseph Smith, making it look overly sexual, ignoring legitimate creation or fertility motifs and related concepts in the ancient world. Such persons do not understand the sacred promises inherent in the New and Everlasting Covenant (of Marriage) relative to child bearing in the eternities, and to "creation" generally; a central theme of the Temple Endowment.

We know that *Min* (the God replacing the "holy ghost" figure [#7 of Fac. 2]) in the Leyden Hypocephalus is a "ithyphallic god," that is, a sexually aroused male deity sometimes seen in Egyptian hieroglyphics. According to Michael Rhodes, "Joseph Smith mentions here [Fac. 2] the Holy Ghost in the form of a dove and God 'revealing through the heavens the grand key-words of the priesthood.' [It was the Holy Ghost who "overshadowed" Mary in the New Testament before the Christ child was conceived.] The procreative forces, receiving unusual accentuation throughout the representation, may stand for many divine generative powers, not least of which might be conjoined with blessing of the priesthood in one's posterity eternally" (Michael Rhodes, BYU *Studies*, Spring 1977, p. 273).

Anti-Mormons use Nibley's comments on *Min* against Joseph Smith's work. Nibley stated, "As the supreme sex symbol of gods and men, *Min* behaves with shocking promiscuity, which is hardly relieved by its ritual nature...His sacred plants were aphrodisiacal...and he is everywhere represented as indulging in incestuous relationships with those of his immediate family; he had the most numerous and varied religious entourage of all the gods, consisting mostly of his huge harem...The hymns, or rather chanting of his worshippers were accompanied with lewd dancing and carousing...to the exciting stimulus of a band of sistrum-shaking damsels" (Hugh Nibley, Abraham in Egypt, FARMS, Deseret Book, p. 210).

We utilize the inspired Joseph Smith Facsimile 2 in our scriptures (the only known hypocephali featuring divine proportion [see chapter 10 of The Day Star: Reading Sacred Architecture, by the author]), not the Leyden Hypocephalus. Though initially disturbing, figure 7 of the Leyden Hypocephalus may simply illustrate the procreative powers of the Gods in such settings. Procreation is expressed in Facsimile 2 via the wording around the outer portion of circle and in the Hathor cow figure, which features a female figure standing at the loins of the animal holding a lotus flower (both symbols of fertility), etc. As creator of the heavens and earth, and the begetter of the race, God shares these blessings with those who covenant with Him in the temple. These powers assist us in receiving exaltation and eternal life; to become like Him and our Heavenly Mother. Nibley concludes, stating, "Thus...Fac. No. 2 takes us to the one center on earth in which the pattern of the cosmos was studied and modeled, the heavenly scheme of things for men and gods alike being faithfully reflected on earth. It was likewise the one place held in reverence by both Israel and Egypt, where the patriarchal rulers of both nations assumed their sacred trust by marriage. (See Hugh Nibley, All about the Hypocephalus, Part I, A Golden Fleece?" p. 277. See also Hugh Nibley, The 3 Facsimiles from the Book of Abraham, The Maxwell Institute, BYU).

In the Adam-God theory, attributed to Brigham Young, God and his companion descended to earth to plant man on earth. Michael is thus God in this scenario, Eve our Mother in Heaven. This doctrine was later refuted by many others, including Pres. Kimball.

Reading Between the Lines: Finding & Diagramming Chiasmus Across the Entire Book of Mormon

Greg Carlston

Reading Between the Lines: Finding and Diagramming Chiasmus Across the Entire Book of Mormon by Greg Carlston

INTRODUCTION

Because chiasmus, the style of repetitive writing used by prophets for millennia is highly impressive for its deep complexity, the following interpretation is just one of the many ways that the chiasmus in the Book of Mormon can be displayed.

This diagram was produced by copying all of the text of the Book of Mormon, into a Word document, then deleting the text for the chapters, but retaining the chapter headings from each of the book's 238 chapters. The text of the Preface precedes the main part of the diagram. The chapter headings for each chapter were treated like individual verses and the related chiastic pairs were identified and labeled. In this diagram, no words are left out or rearranged. Due to the large number of chiastic pairs, numerical labels (1-2-3...3-2-1) are used instead of the traditional alphabetical labels (a-b-c...c-b-a). The parallelisms are "tabbed" into place in the typical chiastic format to make it easier to find the matching pairs. The numbers in blue are the chapters in the respective books. The book titles are in blue italic.

Chiasmus in the Book of Mormon varies as small to long phrases within individual chapters. It can also be seen in across entire chapters, across complete books in the Book of Mormon, and across the Book of Mormon in its entirety. When I realized this, I attempted to diagram the entire Book of Mormon as one chiasm. This diagram is the result of many hours of work. In my opinion, the complexity of the chiastic writing in the Book of Mormon is so great that no human effort could have produced it. Joseph Smith, with his rural nineteenth century education, could not have done it. Not even the prophets of the Book of Mormon could have produced the book's complex structure. This diagram is additional affirmation that the Book of Mormon is what it purports to be: A collection of ancient writings containing holy doctrines of salvation written and translated by the gift and power of our God and delivered to a young prophet by an angel. The Book of Mormon truly is another testament of the divinity of Jesus Christ. The Book of Mormon is a gift from God that we that might be sanctified from sin, and enjoy the words of eternal life in this world, and eternal life in the world to come. (Moses 6:59)

I usually post my work as PDF's which open on just about any kind of an operating system, but the PDF format for the size needed to display my chiastic interpretations doesn't print out very well. This document is being posted as an MS Word document. If you download the document, you can use the underlined number labels of the parallelisms as hyper-links to navigate quickly between the first and second phrases of each parallelism. By pressing the control key on a PC or the command key on the MAC and then clicking on an underlined number, you can switch between phrases without having to scroll through the entire document to see if the phrases match. This system works well on Windows OS - I hope it works well for you. I haven't finished linking every pair yet, but I think you'll find that enough are linked so that you will be able to navigate forward and back through the document quite quickly.

Regarding the "matchability" of parallelisms: This work is my own interpretation. Some scholars may not agree with me that there is a strong correlation between all of the phrases that I have identified in order for the entire selection to be considered one large selection of chiastic writing. However, based on my experience of having identified over five thousand chiastic parallelisms within hundreds of chiasms, I think the parallelisms are reasonably well correlated. One very consistent aspect of long passages of chiasmus is that during the process of indentifying parallelisms, at strategic points, perfectly matching parallelisms appear like markers on a trail. Those markers are in bold. Some of the parallelisms are close matches and some are identified because the "rhythm" of the chiastic pattern dictates that just one word or a long phrase should match another. Other parallelisms are comparisons, contrasts, similar wording, prophecy/fulfillment, cause/outcome, outcome/cause, or grammatical matches (such as questions or exclamations). Some matches are topical, some are based on an actions taken by a person or persons, some parallelisms are simply words that match. Even though my view of what constitutes a chiastic parallelism may seen to be relaxed, I believe a definite chiastic pattern exists in the Book of Mormon in its entirety.

The objective of this work is to present the book of Mormon as a work so deeply complex that it must command the respect of all who read it - regardless of whether they accept it's precepts. And for those who are sincerely seeking to know the truth of all things, I hope my work will help to affirm for you that the Book of Mormon is truly of divine origin.

If you have any comments or corrections, feel free to contact me at gregcarlston@gmail.com.

The Book of Mormon Formatted to show the Entire Book as a Chiastic Passage

Preface
1 AN ACCOUNT
2 WRITTEN BY THE HAND OF MORMON UPON PLATES TAKEN FROM
3 THE PLATES OF NEPHI
4 Wherefore,
5 it is an abridgment of the record of
6 the people of Nephi, and also of the Lamanites—
7 Written to the Lamanites, who are a remnant of the house of Israel; and also
8 to Jew and Gentile—Written by way of
9 commandment, and also by the spirit of prophecy and of revelation— Written and
10 sealed up, and hid up unto the Lord, that they might not be destroyed—
11 To come forth by the gift and power of God unto the
12 interpretation thereof—Sealed by the hand of Moroni, and hid up unto the Lord,
13 to come forth in due time
14 by way of the Gentile—
15 The interpretation thereof by
16 the gift
16 of God.
15 An abridgment
14 taken from the Book of Ether also, which is a record of the people of Jared, who were
13 scattered at the time the Lord
12 confounded the language of the people, when they were building a tower
11 to get to heaven— Which is
10 to show unto the remnant of the House of Israel what great things the Lord hath done for their fathers; and that they may know
9 the covenants of the Lord, that they are not cast off forever—And also
8 to the convincing of the Jew and Gentile that JESUS is the CHRIST, the ETERNAL GOD,
7 manifesting himself unto
6 all nations—And now,
5 if there are faults they are the mistakes of men:
4 wherefore, condemn not
3 the things of God, that ye may be found spotless at the judgment-seat of Christ.
2 TRANSLATED BY JOSEPH SMITH, JUN. Published by The Church of Jesus Christ of Latter-day Saints Salt Lake City, Utah, USA 1988
1 First English edition published in 1830

The First Book of Nephi
1 Nephi begins   END
2 the record of his people—
3 Lehi sees in vision
4 a pillar of fire and reads from a book of prophecy—
5 He praises God, foretells the coming of the Messiah, and prophesies
6 the destruction of Jerusalem— He is persecuted by the Jews. About 600 B.C. CH2
7 Lehi takes his family into the wilderness by the Red Sea— They leave their property—
8 Lehi offers a sacrifice to the Lord and teaches his sons to keep the commandments—(The beginning of obedience)—Laman and Lemuel murmur against their father—(The beginning of rebellion)
9 Nephi is obedient and prays in faith: the Lord speaks to him, and he is chosen to rule over his brethren. CH3 Lehi's sons return to Jerusalem to obtain the plates of brass—Laban refuses to give them up— Nephi exhorts and encourages his brethren—Laban steals their property and
10 attempts to slay them—Laman and Lemuel smite Nephi and are reproved by an angel. CH4
11 Nephi slays Laban at the Lord's command and then secures the plates of brass by stratagem—
12 Nephi persuades Zoram to join Lehi's family in the wilderness. CH5 Sariah complains against Lehi (*About* the loss of her sons)— Both rejoice over the return of their sons—
13 They offer sacrifices—
14 The plates of brass contain writings of Moses and the prophets—They identify Lehi as a descendant of Joseph—Lehi prophesies concerning his seed and the
15 preservation of the plates. CH6 Nephi writes of the things of God— His purpose is to persuade men to
16 come unto the God of Abraham and be saved 7 Lehi's sons return to Jerusalem and enlist Ishmael and his household in their cause—
17 Laman and others rebel — Nephi exhorts his brethren to have faith in the Lord — They bind him with cords and plan his
18 destruction — (microcosm of brother against brother see last #8) - He is freed by the power of faith
19 His brethren ask forgiveness—Lehi and his company offer sacrifice and burnt offerings. CH8
20 Lehi sees a vision of the tree of life—He partakes of its fruit and

1st Nephi

220

21 his family to do likewise—He sees a rod of iron, a straight and narrow path, and the mists of darkness that enshroud men—Sariah, Nephi, and Sam partake, but Laman and Lemuel refuse. CH9

22 **Lehi predicts the Babylonian captivity**—He tells of the coming among the Jews of

23 **a Messiah, a Savior, a Redeemer**—He tells also of the coming of the one who should baptize

24 **the Lamb of God**—Lehi tells of the death and resurrection of.

25 **the Messiah**—He compares

26 the scattering and

27 gathering of Israel to an olive tree—Nephi speaks of the Son of God, of the gift of the Holy Ghost, and of

28 the need for righteousness. CH11 Nephi sees the Spirit of the Lord and is shown in vision

29 the tree of life—He sees the mother of

30 the Son of God and learns of the condescension of God—

31 He (Nephi) sees the baptism, ministry, and

32 the **crucifixion** of the Lamb of God—He sees also

33 the call and ministry of the twelve apostles of the Lamb 12 Nephi sees in vision.

34 **the land of promise;** the righteousness,

35 **iniquity,** and

36 **downfall of its inhabitants;** the coming of the Lamb of God among them; how the twelve disciples and the twelve apostles shall judge Israel; the loathsome and filthy...

37 **the church of the devil** set up among the Gentiles; the discovery and colonizing of America; the loss of many plain and precious parts of the Bible; the resultant state   of gentile

38 apostasy;

39 the restoration of the gospel, the coming forth of Latter-day scripture, and the building up of Zion. CH 14

40 An angel tells Nephi of the blessings and cursings to fall upon the Gentiles—

41 **There are only two churches: the Church of the Lamb of God and the church of the devil**—The saints of God in all nations are persecuted by the great and abominable church

42 the end of the world. CH 15 Lehi's seed are to receive the gospel from the Gentiles in the latter days—**The gathering of Israel** is likened unto an olive tree whose natural branches shall be grafted in again—

43 Nephi interprets the vision of the tree of life and speaks of the justice of God in dividing the wicked from the righteous. CH 16 The wicked take the truth to be hard—Lehi's sons marry the daughters of Ishmael—The Liahona guides their course in the wilderness—Messages from the Lord are written on the Liahona from time to time—Ishmael dies; his family murmur because of afflictions. *About 600-592 B.C.* CH 17 **Nephi is commanded to build a ship**—His brethren oppose him—He exhorts them by recounting the history of God's dealings with Israel—He is filled with the power of God—His brethren are forbidden to touch him, lest they wither as a dried reed. CH 18

44 **The ship is finished**—The births of Jacob and Joseph are mentioned—The company embarks for the promised land—The sons of Ishmael and their wives join in revelry and rebellion—Nephi is bound, and

45 **the ship is driven back by a terrible tempest**—

46 Nephi is freed, and by his prayer the storm ceases—They arrive in the promised land. CH 19

47 **Nephi makes plates of ore and records the history of his people**—

48 The God of Israel shall come six hundred years from the time Lehi left Jerusalem—Nephi tells of His sufferings and crucifixion—The Jews shall be despised and scattered until the latter days, when they shall return unto the Lord. *ABOUT* CH 20

49 The Lord reveals his purposes to Israel—They have been chosen in the furnace of affliction and are to go forth from Babylon—Compare Isaiah 48.

50 Messiah shall be a **light** to the Gentiles and shall free the prisoners—Israel shall be gathered with power in the last days—Kings shall be their nursing fathers—Compare Isaiah 49. CH 22 Israel shall be scattered upon

51 all the face of the earth—The gentiles shall nurse and nourish Israel with the gospel in the last days—

52 **Israel shall be gathered** and

53 saved, and

54 the wicked shall burn as stubble—

55 **The kingdom of the devil shall be destroyed, and Satan shall be bound.** *Between 588 and 570 B.C.* *The Second Book of Nephi*

56 Lehi prophesies of a land of liberty—His *(Lehi's)* seed shall be scattered and smitten if

57 they reject the Holy One of Israel—

58 He exhorts his sons to put on the armor of

59 righteousness. CH 2

60 **Redemption cometh through the Holy Messiah**—Freedom of choice (agency) is essential to existence and progression—Adam fell that men might be—

61 **Men are free to choose liberty and eternal life.** CH 3 **Joseph in Egypt saw the Nephites in vision**—**He prophesied of Joseph Smith, the Latter-day seer; of Moses, who would deliver Israel;** and of

62 the coming forth of

63 the Book of Mormon. CH 4

64 Lehi counsels and blesses his posterity—He dies and is buried—

65 **Nephi glories in the goodness of God to him**—Nephi puts his trust in the Lord forever. CH 5

66 Nephites separate themselves from the Lamanites *(this is the beginning of the Nephite nation),* keep the law of Moses, and build a temple

67 **Because of their unbelief, the Lamanites are cursed, receive a skin of blackness,** and

68 become a scourge unto

69 the Nephites. CH 6

70 Jacob recounts

71 Jewish history: Their Babylonian captivity and return; the ministry and crucifixion of

2nd Nephi

221

222

125 Many
126 false churches shall be built up in the last days—They shall teach false and vain and foolish doctrines—
127 Apostasy shall abound because of
128 false teachers—
129 The devil shall rage in the hearts of men— He shall teach all manner of false doctrines. CH 29
130 Many gentiles shall reject the Book of Mormon—They shall say: We need no more Bible—
131 The Lord speaks to
132 **many nations**— He will judge
133 the world out of the books thus written. CH 30 Converted gentiles shall be numbered with the covenant people—
134 Many Lamanites and Jews shall believe the word and become a delightsome people—Israel shall be restored and the wicked destroyed. CH 31 Nephi tells why Christ would be baptized— Men must follow Christ, be baptized, receive the Holy Ghost, and endure to the end to be saved—Repentance and baptism are the gate to the strait and narrow path— Eternal life comes to those who keep the commandments after baptism. CH 32
135 Angels speak by the power of the Holy Ghost—Men must pray and gain knowledge for themselves from the Holy Ghost . CH 33
136 Nephi's words are true—
137 **They testify of Christ**
138 Those who believe in Christ will believe Nephi's words—They shall stand as a witness before the judgment bar. *Between 559 and 545 B.C.* ***The Book of Jacob***

Jacob
139 The words of his preaching unto his brethren. He confoundeth
140 **a man who seeketh to overthrow the doctrine of Christ.** A few words concerning
141 **the history of the people of Nephi.**
142 Jacob and Joseph seek to persuade men to believe in Christ and **keep his commandments**—Nephi dies—
143 Wickedness prevails among the Nephites. *About 544-421 B.C. CH 2*
144 Jacob denounces the love of riches, pride, and unchastity—Men should seek riches to help their fellow men—
145 Jacob condemns the unauthorized practice of plural marriage— The Lord delights in the chastity of women. *About 544-421 B.C. CH 3* The pure in heart receive the pleasing word of God—
146 Lamanite righteousness exceeds that of Nephites— Jacob warns against fornication, lasciviousness, and every sin. *About 544-421 B.C. CH 4* All the prophets worshipped the Father in the name of Christ—Abraham's offering of Isaac was in similitude of God and his Only Begotten—Men should reconcile themselves to God through the atonement—The Jews shall reject the foundation stone. *About 544-421 B.C. CH 5* Jacob quotes Zenos relative to the allegory of the tame and wild olive trees—They are a likeness of Israel and the gentiles—The scattering and gathering of Israel are prefigured. Allusions are made to the Nephites and Lamanites and all the house of Israel— Gentiles shall be grafted into Israel—
147 Eventually the vineyard shall be burned. *About 544-421 B.C. CH 6* The Lord shall recover Israel in the last days— Then the world shall be burned with fire—
148 Men must follow Christ to avoid the lake of fire and brimstone. *About 544-421 B.C. CH 7* Sherem denies Christ, contends with Jacob, demands a sign, and is smitten of God—
149 All of the prophets have spoken of Christ and his atonement— The Nephites lived out their days as wanderers, born in tribulation, and hated by the Lamanites. *ca544-421 B.C*

The Book of Enos
150 **Enos prays mightily and gains a remission of his sins** — The voice of the Lord comes into his mind promising salvation for the Lamanites in **a future day**—
151 Nephites sought to reclaim the Lamanites in their day—Enos rejoices in his Redeemer. *ABOUT 420 B.C.*

Jarom
152 **The Book of Jarom**
153 The Nephites keep the law of Moses, **look forward to the coming of Christ, and prosper in the land**— *About 399-361 B.C.* **The Book of Omni**

Omni
154 Many prophets labor to keep them in the way of truth. *About 399-361 B.C.* **The Book of Omni**
155 Omni, Amaron, Chemish, Abinadom, and Amaleki, each in turn, keep the records—Mosiah discovers
156 the people of Zarahemla who came from Jerusalem in the days of Zedekiah —He is made king over them—The Mulekites had discovered Coriantumr, the last of the Jaredites. King Benjamin succeeds Mosiah—

The Words of Mormon
157 Men should offer their souls as an offering to Christ. **The Words of Mormon** Mormon abridges their history onto the plates of Mormon—He inserts the plates of Nephi into the abridgement—
158 King Benjamin establishes peace in *(Note: The following passage is placed here to indicate that in addition to the topical matches shown in this diagram, on a deeper level in the verses, matches also exist. In other words this diagram is like a framework on which all of the verses of the Book of Mormon can be displayed.) v18* Wherefore, with the help of these, king Benjamin, by laboring with all the might of his body and the faculty of his whole soul, and also the prophets, did once more establish **peace in the land.** *(Note how this text matches and precedes both beginning and ending texts of #159.)*
159 **the land.** *About A.D. 385*

Mosiah
160 King
161 King
162 Benjamin teaches his sons the language and prophecies of their fathers—
163 Their religion and civilization have been preserved because of the records kept on the various plates—
164 **Mosiah is chosen as king and is given custody of the records and other things. CH2**
165 King Benjamin addresses his people— He recounts the equity, fairness, and spirituality of his reign—He counsels them to serve their heavenly King—
166 Those who rebel against God shall suffer anguish like unquenchable fire. CH3 King Benjamin continues his address—The Lord Omnipotent shall minister among men in a tabernacle of clay—Blood shall come from every pore as he atones for the sins of the world—His is the only name whereby
167 **salvation** comes—Men can put off the natural man and become saints through the atonement—The torment of
168 the wicked shall be as a lake of fire and brimstone. CH4 King Benjamin continues his address—

223

Mosiah

Alma

225

Alma

INTRO
BEGINNING
CENTER
END

Alma

Nephi

236 Ammonihah—Zoram leads the Nephites to victory over the Lamanites—**Alma and Amulek and**
many others preach the word—
237 **They teach that after his resurrection Christ will appear to the Nephites**. *ABOUT 81–77 B.C.*
An account of
238 the sons of Mosiah, who rejected their rights to the kingdom for
239 the word of God, and
240 went up to the land of Nephi to preach to the Lamanites; their
241 **sufferings** and **deliverance** — according to the record of
242 Alma *(the son of Alma the Elder)*. CH17
242 The sons of Mosiah have
241 the spirit of **prophecy** and of **revelation. They**
240 go their several ways to declare
239 the word to the Lamanites—Ammon goes to the land of Ishmael and becomes the servant of King
Lamoni— Ammon saves the king's flocks and slays his enemies at the waters of Sebus. *About* 77
B.C.; verse 4, *About* 91–77 B.C.; and verses 5–39, *About 91 B.C.*CH18
238 King Lamoni supposes that Ammon is the Great Spirit
237 **Ammon teaches the king of the creation, of God's dealings with men, and of the redemption that**
comes through Christ—Lamoni believes and falls to the earth as if dead. *About90 B.C.*CH19
Lamoni receives the light of everlasting life and sees the Redeemer—His household fall into a
trance, and some see angels
236 Ammon is
235 preserved miraculously—
234 **He baptizes many and establishes a church** among them. *About 90 B.C.*CH20
233 The Lord sends Ammon to Middoni to deliver his imprisoned brethren—Ammon and Lamoni meet
Lamoni's father, who is king over all the land—Ammon compels the old king to approve
232 the release of his brethren. *About 90 B.C.* An account of the preaching of Aaron, and Muloki, and
their brethren, to the Lamanites. Comprising chapters 21 to 26 inclusive. CH21
231 **Aaron teaches the Amalekites About Christ and his atonement**—Aaron and his brethren are
imprisoned in Middoni—After their deliverance
230 they teach in the synagogues and make many converts—Lamoni grants religious freedom to the people in the
land of Ishmael. *ABOUT 90–77 B.C.* CH22 Aaron teaches Lamoni's father about the creation, the fall of Adam,
229 **the plan of redemption through Christ**—The king and all his household are converted—How the land was
divided between the Nephites and the Lamanites. *About 90–77 B.C.* CH23 Religious
228 freedom is proclaimed—The Lamanites in seven lands and cities are converted—They call themselves Anti-
Lehies and are
227 freed from the curse—
226 The Amalekites and the Amulonites reject the truth. *About 90–77 B.C.* CH24 The Lamanites come against
225 the people of God—
224 The Anti-Nephi-Lehies rejoice in Christ and are visited by angels—They choose to suffer death rather than to
defend themselves— More Lamanites are converted. *About 90–77 B.C.* CH25 Lamanite aggressions spread—The
seed of the priests of Noah perish as Abinadi prophesied—
223 Many Lamanites are converted and join the people of Anti-Nephi-Lehi—They believe in Christ and keep the law
of Moses. CH26
222 Ammon glories in the Lord—
221 **The faithful** are strengthened by the Lord and are given knowledge—
220 **By faith** men may bring thousands of souls unto repentance—God has all power and comprehendeth all things.
ABOUT 90–77 B.C. CH27
219 The Lord commands Ammon to lead the people of Anti-Nephi-Lehi to safety—Upon meeting Alma,
218 Ammon's joy exhausts his strength—The Nephites give them the land of Jershon—They are called
217 **the people of Ammon**. *ABOUT 90–77 B.C.* CH28
216 The Lamanites are defeated in a tremendous battle—Tens of thousands are slain—
215 **The wicked are consigned to a state of endless woe;**
214 **the righteous** attain a
213 **never-ending happiness**. *ABOUT 77–76 B.C.* CH29
212 Alma desires to cry repentance with angelic zeal—The Lord grants teachers for all nations—
211 Alma glories in the Lord's work and in the success of Ammon and his brethren. *ABOUT 76 B.C.*CH30
210 Korihor, the antichrist, ridicules Christ, the atonement, and the spirit of prophecy—He teaches that there is no God, no
fall of man, no penalty for sin, and no Christ.
209 Alma testifies that Christ shall come and that all things denote there is a God—

208 Korihor demands a sign and is struck dumb—The devil had appeared to Korihor as an angel and taught him what to say—He is trodden down and dies. *ABOUT 76-74 B.C.* CH31

207 Alma heads a mission to reclaim the apostate Zoramites—The Zoramites deny Christ, believe in a false concept of election, and worship with set prayers—The missionaries are filled with the Holy Spirit—

206 Their afflictions are swallowed up in the joy of Christ. *ABOUT 74 B.C.* CH32

205 **Alma teaches the poor** whose afflictions had humbled them—Faith is a hope in that which is not seen which is true—Alma testifies that angels minister to men, women, and children—Alma compares the word unto a seed—It must be planted and nourished—Then it grows into a tree from which the fruit of eternal life is picked. *ABOUT 74 B.C.* CH33 Zenos taught that men should pray and worship in all places, and that judgments are turned away because of the Son—Zenock taught that mercy is bestowed because of the Son—Moses had lifted up in the wilderness a type of the Son of God. *ABOUT 74 B.C.* CH34 Amulek testifies that the word is in Christ unto salvation—Unless an atonement is made, all mankind must perish—The whole law of Moses points toward the sacrifice of the Son of God—The eternal plan of redemption is based on faith and repentance. Pray for temporal and spiritual blessings—This life is the time for men to prepare to meet God—Work out your salvation with fear and trembling. *ABOUT 74 B.C.* CH35

203 The preaching of the word
204 destroys the (priest-)craft of the Zoramites—They expel
202 the converts, who then join the people of Ammon in Jershon—
201 Alma sorrows because of the wickedness of the people. *ABOUT 74 B.C.*

200 **The commandments of Alma to his son Helaman.** CH36 Alma testifies to Helaman of his conversion by an angel—He suffered the pains of a dammed soul; he called upon the name of Jesus, and was then born of God—Sweet joy filled his soul. *ABOUT 74 B.C.* CH37

199 He saw concourses of angels praising God—His converts have tasted and seen as he did. *ABOUT 74 B.C.* CH37

198 **The plates of brass and other scriptures** are preserved to bring souls to salvation—The Jaredites were destroyed because of their wickedness—Their secret oaths and covenants must be kept from the people—Counsel with the Lord in all thy doings **As the Liahona guided the Nephites, so the word of Christ leads men to eternal life.**

197 The commandments of Alma to his son Shiblon. CH38 Shiblon was persecuted for righteousness' sake—

196 **Salvation is in Christ,** who is the life and the light of the world—Bridle all your passions. *About 74 B.C.* The commandments of Alma to his son Corianton. CH39

195 Sexual sin is an abomination—Corianton's sins kept the Zoramites from receiving the word—Christ's redemption is retroactive in saving the faithful who preceded it. *About 74 B.C.* CH40 Christ bringeth to pass the resurrection of all men—The righteous dead go to paradise and the wicked to outer darkness to await the day of their resurrection—All things shall be restored to their proper and perfect frame in the resurrection. CH41 In the resurrection men come forth to a state of endless happiness or endless misery—

194 Wickedness never was happiness—Carnal men are without God in the world—Every person receives again in the restoration the characteristics and attributes acquired in mortality. *About 74 B.C.* CH42 Mortality is a probationary time to enable man to repent and serve God—The fall brought

193 **temporal and spiritual death** upon all mankind—**Redemption comes through repentance**—God himself atoneth for the sins of the world **Mercy is for those who repent**—All others are subject to God's justice—Mercy cometh because of the atonement. **Only the truly penitent are saved.** *About 74 B.C.* CH43 Alma and his sons preach the word—

192 The Zoramites and other Nephite dissenters become Lamanites—The Lamanites come against the Nephites in war—Moroni arms the Nephites with defensive armor—The Lord reveals to Alma the strategy of the Lamanites—The Nephites defend their homes, liberties, families, and religion—The armies of Moroni and Lehi surround the Lamanites. CH44 Moroni commands the Lamanites to make a covenant of peace or be destroyed—Zerahemnah rejects the offer, and the battle resumes—

191 Moroni's armies defeat the Lamanites. *About 74-73 B.C.* The account of the people of Nephi, and their

190 wars and dissensions, in the days of Helaman, according to

189 the record of Helaman, which he kept in his days. CH45 Helaman believes the words of Alma—Alma prophesies the destruction of the Nephites—He blesses and curses the land—Alma is taken up by the Spirit, even as Moses—Dissension grows in the Church. *About 73 B.C.* CH46 Amalickiah conspires to be king—Moroni raises the title of liberty—He rallies the people to defend their religion—

188 True believers are called Christians—

187 A remnant of Joseph shall be preserved—

186 **Amalickiah and the dissenters flee to the land of Nephi**—Those who will not support the cause of freedom are put to death. CH47 Amalickiah uses treachery, murder, and intrigue to become king of the Lamanites—The Nephite dissenters are more wicked and ferocious than the Lamanites. *About 72 B.C.* CH48 Amalickiah incites the Lamanites against the Nephites—Moroni prepares his people to defend the cause of the Christians—He rejoiced in liberty and freedom and was a mighty man of God. *About 72 B.C.* CH49 The invading Lamanites are unable to take the fortified cities of Ammonihah and Noah—Amalickiah curses God and swears to drink the blood of Moroni—

185 Helaman and his brethren **continue to strengthen the Church.** *About 72 B.C.* CH50 Moroni fortifies the lands of the Nephites—They build many new cities—

184 Wars and destructions befell the Nephites in

183 the days of their wickedness and abominations—

182 Morianton and his dissenters are defeated by Teancum—Nephihah dies and his son Pahoran fills the judgment-seat. *About 72-67 B.C.* CH51

181 The king-men seek **to change the law** and set up a king—Pahoran and the freemen are supported by the voice of the people—Moroni compels the king-men to defend their liberty or be put to death. Amalickiah and the Lamanites

Alma

Alma

Helaman

145 Samuel the Lamanite prophesies the destruction of the Nephites unless they repent—They reject and stone the prophets, and are encircled about by demons, and seek for happiness in doing iniquity. *ABOUT 6 B.C.*

144 Samuel predicts light during the night and a new star at Christ's birth—Christ redeems men from temporal and spiritual death—The signs of his death include

143 three days of darkness, the rending of the rocks, and great upheavals of nature. *ABOUT 6 B.C.* CH15 The Lord chastened the Nephites because he loved them—

142 Converted Lamanites are **firm and steadfast in the faith**—The Lord will be merciful unto

141 the Lamanites in the latter days. *ABOUT 6 B.C.* CH16 The Nephites who believe Samuel are baptized by Nephi. Samuel cannot be slain with their arrows and stones—Some harden their hearts, and others see angels—

3rd Nephi

140 **The unbelievers say it is not reasonable to believe in Christ** and his coming in Jerusalem. *ABOUT 6–1 B.C.* ***Third Nephi, The Book of Nephi, The Son of Nephi who was the Son of Helaman***

And Helaman was the son of Alma, who was the son of Alma, being a descendant of Nephi, the king of Zedekiah, the king of Judah. CH1 Nephi the son of Helaman departs out of the land, and

139 his son Nephi keeps the records—Though **signs and wonders abound**, the wicked plan to slay the righteous— The night of Christ's birth arrives— The sign is given and a new star arises—Lyings and deceivings increase, and the Gadianton robbers slaughter many. CH2 Wickedness and abominations increase among the people—The Nephites and Lamanites unite to defend themselves against the Gadianton robbers—Converted Lamanites become white and are called Nephites. CH3 Giddianhi, the Gadianton leader, demands that Lachoneus and the Nephites surrender themselves and their lands—Lachoneus appoints Gidgiddoni as chief captain of the armies—The Nephites assemble in Zarahemla and Bountiful to defend themselves. CH4 The Nephite armies defeat the Gadianton robbers—Giddianhi is slain, and his successor, Zemnarihah, is hanged— **The Nephites praise the Lord** for their victories. CH5 The Nephites repent and forsake their sins—

138 Mormon writes the history of his people and declares the everlasting word to them—Israel shall be gathered in from her long dispersion. CH6 The Nephites prosper. Pride, wealth, and class distinctions arise—The Church is rent with dissensions—Satan leads the people in open rebellion—Many prophets cry repentance and are slain—Their murderers conspire to take over the government. CH7 The chief judge is murdered, the government is overthrown, and the people divide into tribes—

137 **Jacob, an antichrist**, becomes king of a league of tribes—

136 Nephi preaches repentance and faith in Christ—

135 **Angels minister** to him daily, and he raises his brother from the dead—

134 **Many repent and are baptized**. CH8 Tempests, earthquakes, fires, whirlwinds, and

133 physical upheavals attest the crucifixion of Christ—

132 **Many people** are destroyed—Darkness covers the land for three days—Those who remain bemoan their fate. CH9 In the darkness

131 the voice of Christ proclaims the destruction of

130 **many people** and cities for their wickedness—He also proclaims his divinity, announces that the law of Moses is fulfilled, and invites men to come unto him and be saved. CH10

129 There is silence in the land for many hours—

128 The voice of Christ promises to

127 gather his people as a hen gathereth her chickens—

126 The more righteous

125 part of the people had been preserved. –35

124 **Jesus Christ did show himself unto the people of Nephi**, as the multitude were gathered together in the land Bountiful, and did minister unto them: and on this wise did he show himself unto them. Comprising chapters

11 to 26 inclusive. CH11 The Father testifies of his Beloved Son—

123 Christ appears and proclaims his atonement—The people feel the wound marks in his hands and feet and side—They cry Hosanna—He sets forth the mode and manner of baptism—

122 The spirit of contention is of the devil—Christ's doctrine is that men should believe and be baptized and receive the Holy Ghost. CH12 Jesus calls and commissions the Twelve—He delivers to the Nephites a discourse similar to the Sermon on the Mount—He speaks the Beatitudes—His teachings transcend and take precedence over the law of Moses—Men are commanded to be perfect even as he and his Father are perfect—Compare Matthew 5. CH13 Jesus teaches the Nephites the Lord's Prayer—They are to lay up treasures in heaven—

121 The Twelve in their ministry are commanded to take no thought for temporal things—Compare Matthew 6. CH14 Jesus commands: Judge not; ask of God; beware of

120 **false prophets**—

119 He promises salvation to

118 those who do the will of the Father—Compare Matthew 7. CH15 Jesus announces that the law of Moses is fulfilled in him—The Nephites are the other sheep of whom

117 he spake in **Jerusalem**—Because of iniquity

116 the Lord's people in

115 **Jerusalem**…

114 the scattered sheep of Israel. CH16 Jesus will visit others of the lost sheep of Israel—

113 In the latter days the gospel will go to the Gentiles and then to the house of Israel—

112 The Lord's people shall see eye to eye when he brings again Zion. CH17 Jesus directs the people to ponder his words and pray for understanding—

111 He heals their sick—He prays for the people, using language that cannot be written—Angels minister to and fire encircles their little ones. CH18 Jesus institutes the sacrament among the Nephites—They are commanded to pray always in his name—

110 Those who eat his flesh and drink his blood unworthily are damned—The disciples are given power to confer the Holy Ghost. CH19 The Twelve Disciples minister unto the people and pray for the Holy Ghost—They are baptized and receive the Holy Ghost and the ministering of angels—

145 Samuel the Lamanite prophesies the destruction of the Nephites unless they repent—They and their riches are cursed—They reject and stone the prophets, are encircled about by demons, and seek for happiness in doing iniquity. ABOUT 6 B.C. CH14

144 Samuel predicts light during the night and a new star at Christ's birth—The signs of his death include

143 three days of darkness, the rending of the rocks, and great upheavals of nature. ABOUT 6 B.C. CH15 The Lord chastened the Nephites because he loved them—

142 Converted Lamanites are **firm and steadfast in the faith**—The Lord will be merciful unto

141 the Lamanites in the latter days. ABOUT 6 B.C. CH16 The Nephites who believe Samuel are baptized by Nephi. Samuel cannot be slain with their arrows and stones—Some harden their hearts, and others see angels—

3rd Nephi

140 **The unbelievers say it is not reasonable to believe in Christ** and his coming in Jerusalem. *ABOUT 6–1 B.C.* **Third Nephi, The Book of Nephi, The Son of Nephi who was the Son of Helaman** And Helaman was the son of Helaman, who was the son of Alma, who was the son of Alma, being a descendant of Nephi, who was the son of Lehi, who came out of Jerusalem in the first year of the reign of Zedekiah, the king of Judah. CH1 Nephi the son of Helaman departs out of the land, and

139 his son Nephi keeps the records.—Though **signs and wonders abound**, the wicked plan to slay the righteous— The sign is given and a new star arises—Lyings and deceivings increase, and the Gadianton robbers slaughter many. CH2 Wickedness and abominations increase among the people—The Nephites and Lamanites unite to defend themselves against the Gadianton robbers—Converted Lamanites become white and are called Nephites. CH3 Giddianhi, the Gadianton leader, demands that Lachoneus and the Nephites surrender themselves and their lands—Lachoneus appoints Gidgiddoni as chief captain of the armies—The Nephites assemble in Zarahemla and Bountiful to defend themselves. CH4 The Nephite armies defeat the Gadianton robbers—Giddianhi is slain, and his successor, Zemnarihah, is hanged— The Nephites repent and forsake their sins—

138 **The Nephites praise the Lord** for their victories. CH5 The Nephites repent and forsake their sins— Mormon writes the history of his people and declares the everlasting word to them—Israel shall be gathered in from her long dispersion. CH6 The Nephites prosper. Pride, wealth, and class distinctions arise—The Church is rent with dissensions—Satan leads the people in open rebellion—Many prophets cry repentance and are slain—Their murderers conspire to take over the government. CH7 The chief judge is murdered, the government is overthrown, and the people divide into tribes—

137 **Jacob, an antichrist**, becomes king of a league of tribes—

136 Nephi preaches repentance and faith in Christ—

135 **Angels minister** to him daily, and he raises his brother from the dead—

134 **Many repent and are baptized.** CH8 Tempests, earthquakes, fires, whirlwinds, and

133 physical upheavals attest the crucifixion of Christ—

132 **Many people** are destroyed—Darkness covers the land for three days—Those who remain bemoan their fate. CH9 In the darkness

131 the voice of Christ proclaims the destruction of

130 **many people** and cities for their wickedness—He also proclaims his divinity, announces that the law of Moses is fulfilled, and invites men to come unto him and be saved. CH10

129 There is silence in the land for many hours—

128 The voice of Christ promises to

127 gather his people as a hen gathereth her chickens—

126 The more righteous

125 part of the people had been preserved. –35

124 **Jesus Christ did show himself unto the people of Nephi**, as the multitude were gathered together in the land Bountiful, and did minister unto them: and on this wise did he show himself unto them. Comprising chapters 11 to

26 inclusive. CH11 The Father testifies of his Beloved Son—

123 Christ appears and proclaims his atonement—The people feel the wound marks in his hands and feet and side—They cry Hosanna—He sets forth the mode and manner of baptism—

122 The spirit of contention is of the devil—Christ's doctrine is that men should believe and be baptized and receive the Holy Ghost. CH12 Jesus calls and commissions the Twelve—He delivers to the Nephites a discourse similar to the Sermon on the Mount—He speaks the Beatitudes—His teachings transcend and take precedence over the law of Moses—Men are commanded to be perfect even as he and his Father are perfect—Compare Matthew 5. CH13 Jesus teaches the Nephites the Lord's Prayer—They are to lay up treasures in heaven—

121 The Twelve in their ministry are commanded to take no thought for temporal things—Compare Matthew 6. CH14 Jesus commands: Judge not; ask of God; beware of

120 **false prophets**—

119 He promises salvation to

118 those who do the will of the Father—Compare Matthew 7. CH15 Jesus announces that the **law of Moses is fulfilled** in him—The Nephites are the other sheep of whom

117 he spake in **Jerusalem**—Because of iniquity

116 the Lord's people in

115 **Jerusalem**…

114 the scattered sheep of Israel. CH16 Jesus will visit others of the lost sheep of Israel—

113 In the latter days the gospel will go to the Gentiles and then to the house of Israel—

112 The Lord's people shall see eye to eye when he brings again Zion. CH17 Jesus directs the people to ponder his words and pray for understanding—

111 He heals their sick—He prays for the people, using language that cannot be written—Angels minister to and fire encircles their little ones. CH18 Jesus institutes the sacrament among the Nephites—They are commanded to pray always in his name—

110 Those who eat his flesh and drink his blood unworthily are damned—The disciples are given power to confer the Holy Ghost. CH19 The Twelve Disciples minister unto the people and pray for the Holy Ghost—They are baptized and receive the Holy Ghost and the ministering of angels—

62 shall come forth by the

61 power of God—Woes pronounced upon those who breathe out wrath and strife against

60 the work of the Lord—The Nephite record shall come forth in a day of

59 wickedness, degeneracy, and apostasy. CH9

58 Moroni calls upon those who do not believe in Christ to repent—He proclaims a God of miracles, who...pours out gifts and signs upon the faithful—

57 Miracles cease because of unbelief—Signs follow those who believe—

56 Men are exhorted to be wise and keep the commandments. *A.D. 400-421* **The Book of Ether** CH1 Moroni abridges the writings of Ether. Ether's genealogy set forth—

55 **The language of the Jaredites is not confounded** at the Tower of Babel—

54 The Lord promises to lead them to a choice land and

53 make them a great nation. CH2

52 The Jaredites prepare for their **journey to a promised land**—It is

51 a choice land whereon men must serve Christ or be swept off— The Lord talks to the brother of Jared for three hours— **They build barges**. The

50 Lord asks the brother of Jared to propose how the barges shall be **lighted**. CH3

49 The brother of Jared sees the finger of the Lord as he touches the sixteen stones—

48 Christ shows his spirit body to the brother of Jared —Those who have a perfect knowledge cannot be kept from within the veil—

47 Interpreters are provided to bring **the Jaredite record** to light. CH4 Moroni iscommanded to seal up **the writings** of the brother of Jared—They shall not be revealed until...

46 **men have faith even as the brother of Jared** —Christ commands men to believe his words and those of his disciples. Men are commanded to repent **and believe the**

gospel and be saved CH5

44 Three witnesses and the work itself shall stand as a testimony of the truthfulness of the Book of Mormon. *(The finished ship itself was a witness of God's hand in lives of Lehi's family.)* CH6

45 **The Jaredite barges are driven by the winds to the promised land**—

43 The people praise the Lord for his goodness—Orihah is appointed king over them—

42 Jared and his brother pass away in death. CH7 Orihah reigns in righteousness— Amid usurpation and strife

41 **the rival kingdoms of Shule and Cohor are set up** — *(two kingdoms: Shule - righteous, Cohor - wicked)*

40 Prophets condemn the wickedness and idolatry of the people, who then repent. CH8 There is strife and contention over the kingdom.

39 Akish forms an oath-bound secret combination to slay the king —

38 Secret combinations are of

37 **the devil** and result in

36 **the destruction of nations**—

35 Modern Gentiles are warned against the **secret combination** which shall seek to overthrow the freedom of

34 **all lands, nations, and countries**. CH9

33 The kingdom passes from one to another by descent and

32 **intrigue and murder**—

31 Emer saw

30 the Son of Righteousness—Many prophets cry repentance—

29 A famine and poisonous serpents plague the people. CH10 One king succeeds another—

28 Some of the kings are righteous; others are wicked—When righteousness prevails,

27 the people are blessed and prospered by the Lord. CH11 Wars, dissensions, and wickedness dominate Jaredite life— Their prophets predict

26 the utter destruction of the Jaredites unless they repent— The people reject the words of the prophets. CH12 The prophet Ether exhorts the people to believe in God—Moroni recounts the wonders and marvels done by faith— Faith enabled the brother of Jared to see

25 **Christ**

24 **The Lord gives men weaknesses** that they may be humble— The brother of Jared moved Mount Zerin by faith—Faith, hope, and charity are essential to salvation—

23 **Moroni saw Jesus face to face**. CH13

22 **Ether speaks of a New Jerusalem to be built in America** by

21 the seed of Joseph—

20 He (Ether) prophesies, is cast out, writes the Jaredite history, and foretells the destruction of the Jaredites—War rages over all the land.

19 The iniquity of the people brings a curse upon the land—Coriantumr engages in warfare against Gilead, then Lib, and then Shiz—Blood and carnage cover the land. CH15

18 **Millions of the Jaredites are slain in battle**— Shiz and Coriantumr assemble all the people to mortal combat—

17 **The Spirit of the Lord ceases to strive with them**—

16 The Jaredite nation is utterly destroyed—

15 Only Coriantumr remains. *The Book of Moroni* CH1

14 **Moroni writes for the benefit of the Lamanites**—

13 **Pray with real intent—The Spirit of Christ enables men to know good from evil**—

12 **Satan persuades** men to deny Christ and do evil—The prophets manifest the coming of Christ—By faith miracles are wrought and angels minister—Men should hope for

11 **eternal life** and cleave unto charity. CH8 Infant baptism is an evil abomination—Little children are

10 **alive in Christ** because of the atonement—

9 **Faith**, repentance, meekness and lowliness of heart, receiving the Holy Ghost, and

8 **enduring to the end**

7 lead to salvation. CH9

Ether

Moroni

6 Both the Nephites and the Lamanites are depraved and degenerate—They torture and murder each other—

5 **Mormon prays that grace and goodness** may rest upon Moroni forever. CH10 A testimony of the Book of Mormon comes by

4 the power of the Holy Ghost—The

3 gifts of the Spirit are dispensed to the faithful—Spiritual gifts always accompany faith—

2 **Moroni's words speak** from the dust—Come unto Christ, be perfected in him, and sanctify your souls. *About A.D. 421*

1 THE END

INTRODUCTION   PREFACE   BEGINNING   CENTER   END

233

DISCOVERIES IN CHIASMUS

A PATTERN IN ALL THINGS

DISCOVERIES IN CHIASMUS

—◆—

A PATTERN IN ALL THINGS

Compiled by

Yvonne Bent

DIGITAL
LEGEND

New York

Send inquiries to:

Digital Legend Press and Publishing
1994 Forest Bend Dr.
Salt Lake City, UT
84121

To see the complete Digital Legend library, visit www.digitalegend.com
For info write to: info@digitalegend.com or call toll free: 877-222-1960

ISBN: 978-1-937735-10-4

Printed in the United States of America First Printing: November 2011 (V1)

Book interior layout by Alisha Bishop